Defending Eastern Europe

Defending Eastern Europe

The defense policies of new NATO and EU member states

Edited by

Jacek Lubecki and James W. Peterson

MANCHESTER UNIVERSITY PRESS

Copyright © Manchester University Press 2021

While copyright in the volume as a whole is vested in Manchester University Press, copyright in individual chapters belongs to their respective authors, and no chapter may be reproduced wholly or in part without the express permission in writing of both author and publisher.

Published by Manchester University Press
Oxford Road, Manchester M13 9PL
www.manchesteruniversitypress.co.uk

British Library Cataloguing-in-Publication Data is available

ISBN 978 1 5261 4756 1 hardback
ISBN 978 1 5261 7187 0 paperback

First published by Manchester University Press in hardback 2021

This edition first published 2023

The publisher has no responsibility for the persistence or accuracy of URLs for any external or third-party internet websites referred to in this book, and does not guarantee that any content on such websites is, or will remain, accurate or appropriate.

Typeset by Newgen Publishing UK

Martin Marcin, Kamil Beneš, Patrik Štěpánek
These are the names of three Czech soldiers who died fighting in Afghanistan. Our volume is dedicated to them. They are representative of those who served in the military from the new NATO members and who gave their lives in NATO- and US-led military operations in Afghanistan and Iraq.

Contents

List of tables	viii
List of contributors	ix

1 Introduction: membership anniversaries and theoretical
   security models – James W. Peterson and Jacek Lubecki   1

2 Cold War security experiences of Eastern European states
   – Jacek Lubecki   20

3 Anti-communist revolutions and the emergence of states
   responsible for their own defense – Jacek Lubecki   34

4 NATO: Partnership for Peace (PfP) and a staggered admission
   process – James W. Peterson   52

5 The EU as a security provider in Eastern Europe – Michael Baun   65

6 Secure East-Central European NATO members: the Czech
   Republic, Hungary, and Slovakia – James W. Peterson and
   Jacek Lubecki   83

7 Stable Balkan NATO/EU members: Albania and Bulgaria
   – Ivan P. Nikolov and James W. Peterson   106

8 Vulnerability of former Yugoslav NATO (Slovenia, Croatia,
   Montenegro, and North Macedonia) and non-NATO
   (Bosnia-Herzegovina, Kosovo, and Serbia) states
   – James W. Peterson   131

9 States with significant security issues: Poland, Romania, and
   Moldova – Jacek Lubecki and James W. Peterson   145

10 Challenged Baltic states: Estonia, Latvia, and Lithuania
   – Olavi Arens   165

11 Conclusion: moving beyond the 15–20–year anniversaries to
   stable policies in a time of constant political turmoil
   – James W. Peterson and Jacek Lubecki   184

Bibliography	192
Index	217

Tables

4.1	Military capabilities of new NATO states in 2019	63
5.1	Share of Russia in national extra-EU imports, first semester 2019	72
9.1	Contribution of the former Soviet bloc/East-Central European and Balkan countries to the "War on Terror"	161

Contributors

Olavi Arens is Professor of History at Georgia Southern University. He is a native of Estonia and received his undergraduate degree from Harvard and his Ph.D. from Columbia University. He is currently the Academic Executive Director of the Association for the Advancement of Baltic Studies. He has published numerous articles on Estonian and Baltic History in academic journals and as book chapters on topics such as American relations with the Baltic states, the Brest-Litovsk Treaty, the Russian Revolution in Estonia and the state of Baltic Studies in exile. His special area of interest is early twentieth-century Baltic history. He is currently researching US foreign policy toward the Baltic states from 1918 to 1922.

Michael Baun received his Ph.D. in Foreign Affairs from the University of Virginia in 1988. He is currently Professor and Marguerite Langdale Pizer Chair of International Relations at Valdosta State University, where he teaches in the Department of Political Science. His primary field of research interest is European politics and the European Union. He is the author of *An Imperfect Union: The Maastricht Treaty and the New Politics of European Integration* (Westview Press, 1996) and *A Wider Europe: The Process and Politics of European Union Enlargement* (Rowman & Littlefield, 2000). He is co-author of *The Czech Republic and the European Union* (Routledge, 2011) and *Cohesion Policy in the European Union* (Palgrave Macmillan, 2014). He is co-editor of several other books, including *Governing Europe's Neighborhood: Partners or Periphery* (Manchester University Press, 2007), *EU Cohesion Policy after Enlargement* (Palgrave Macmillan, 2008), and *The New Member States and the European Union: Foreign Policy and Europeanization* (Routledge, 2013). His other publications include numerous book chapters and articles on European and EU politics in such journals as *Political Science Quarterly, Journal of Common Market Studies, Journal of European Integration, Publius, German Politics and Society,*

German Studies Review, *Regional and Federal Studies*, and *Europe-Asia Studies*. He is currently working on a book on US–Europe relations.

Jacek Lubecki is Associate Professor of Political Science and International Studies at Georgia Southern University. His publications include "Echoes of Latifundism" (*Eastern European Politics and Societies*, winter 2004), "Poland in Iraq" (*The Polish Review*, summer 2005), "Reconstructing Galicia" (*Europe-Asia Studies*, 2010), and "Józef Piłsudski's Influence on Polish Armed Forces of the Interwar Period" (*The Polish Review*, 2011). His book entitled *Defense Policies of East-Central European Countries after 1989: Creating Stability in a Time of Uncertainty* (co-written with James Peterson) was published by Manchester University Press in 2019.

Ivan P. Nikolov currently is the Director of the Center for International Programs at Valdosta State University and Professor in International Studies. A native of Bulgaria, Ivan studied in several countries, including Poland, Russia, and the United States, and holds doctoral degrees in Economics and in Higher Education/International Education. His interests are in international political economy, politics, and global education.

James W. Peterson is Professor Emeritus in Political Science at Valdosta State University. His book publications include *NATO and Terrorism: Organizational Expansion and Mission Transformation* (Continuum, 2011), *Building a Framework of Security for Southeast Europe and the Black Sea Region: A Challenge Facing NATO* (The Edwin Mellen Press, 2013), *American Foreign Policy: Alliance Politics in a Century of War* (Bloomsbury, 2014), *Russian-American Relations in the Post-Cold War World* (Manchester University Press, 2017), and *Defense Policies of East-Central European Countries after 1989: Creating Stability in a Time of Uncertainty*, with Jacek Lubecki (Manchester University Press, 2019).

1

Introduction: membership anniversaries and theoretical security models

James W. Peterson and Jacek Lubecki

Controversy has swirled, again, around questions connected with membership in the North Atlantic Treaty Organization (NATO) in recent years, and financial contributions to the various defense budgets of members have been in the center of it. President Trump in particular has been threatening toward alliance partners that do not contribute at least 2% of GDP to defense expenditures. From a long-term perspective, however, there is nothing new in US calls on NATO allies to increase their defense burdens. On the other hand, the refugee issue, unprecedented in its scale and severity since World War II, has undone the solidarity of EU members, as strong nationalist political figures have resisted the openness of borders to the refugees as well as pressures to locate them in partner countries. The UK left the EU as the result of these and other pressures. Thus, the European security system, centered around NATO and the EU, is buffeted by new and old crises as forces of convergence and divergence are affecting the region.

Who are the three people to whom this book is dedicated? They are members of the Czech military who lost their lives in a suicide attack in Afghanistan on August 5, 2018, participating in a mission established under American leadership after the 9/11 attacks. Their deaths remind us of the value of the alliances and the varied contributions made by the new member states admitted 15–20 years ago. These contributions are important; some countries of "new Europe" contributed to NATO and US military operations and deployments at dramatically high levels. Poland, the biggest contributor, suffered 66 dead and 611 wounded soldiers in Iraq and Afghanistan and rotated some 50,000 troops through these countries in the state's largest combat/stability operations since World War II.[1] Poland was closely followed by Romania, Croatia, and Estonia in terms of their proportional military effort (if not the size, these being fairly small countries) of their contributions to the "war on terror." Few people know that the nation of Georgia, not covered in this book, was, proportionally to its economy and population, the most generous military ally of the US/NATO in Iraq and Afghanistan.

2   *Defending Eastern Europe*

It is time for an assessment of the foreign and defense policy experiences of Eastern European states in both NATO and the EU, at the time of the anniversaries of their several decades in both organizations. In light of the Balkan wars of the 1990s as well as of the post-9/11 Afghan and Iraqi Wars, the new alliance partners felt both pressure and the opportunity to take part in foreign conflicts as well as in the follow-up peacekeeping and peacemaking deployments. Then, crises and fissures intervened, most importantly, the Russo-Ukrainian conflict, the EU's multiple crises, and the election of President Trump. What have the new members gained from participation in these allied commitments, and what have been the costs and benefits to them as a result? How should we assess the balance of these countries' memberships in the Western security community and the prospects for their future roles? What conceptual and theoretical perspectives can help us in our inquiry?

Theoretical perspectives

In light of the fifteenth and twentieth anniversaries of the NATO and EU memberships of many East European states in 2019, it is important to examine their actual security and military defense conditions from theoretical perspectives that can inform future policy considerations.

First, we will use alliance theory as descriptive of the roots of the interactions of the states in alliance relationships. Alliances can offer a method for overcoming the geographic distance between and among the states in the region. They can also offer a conversational format for addressing sharp political systemic differences within that geographic space. Profound cultural and ethnic differences exist also within the area designated as Eastern Europe, and well-designed alliance frameworks can offer ways of establishing working agreements in spite of those sharp cultural contrasts. In other words, by "alliance theory" we refer to a set of theoretical perspectives, focusing on institutional factors which allow for cooperation regardless of potential geographical, cultural, ideological, and topological differences and distances (Hendrickson 2002). Especially, constructivism offers to us a more specific perspective on how different countries in question interact with the established institutional frameworks of NATO and the EU. In particular, "role theory," as formulated by Aggestam (2004), offers a framework to understand how and why countries in question perceive what they "should" do or affect what they do within these institutions (Aggestam 2004).[2]

Second, convergence and divergence theories, derived from realism, liberalism, and constructivism, can reinforce the building picture of changing and evolving alliance patterns. These theories are particularly useful

Introduction 3

in portraying methods through which the alliance partners can cope with powerful variables that exist outside the alliances but affect their internal perspectives. One strong convergent force was communism and membership in the Warsaw Pact during communist times, and those patterns still provide "legacies" to states within the region. The pressure of Western practices and values has been the dominant theme during the past 30 years, and it is important to examine how they also have brought the various states together. Liberalism, especially, offers a powerful perspective that explains how the countries of Eastern/East-Central Europe were pulled toward the Western security community, found their place in it, and, today, coexist largely in peace as contrary to their previous pattern of inter-state war, suspicion, and hostility (Doyle 1986). Liberalism, also, expects countries' foreign policy to be driven by economic imperatives of prosperity. In this respect, paradoxically, economic interests are driving many of the states in question to reach out to illiberal Russia and Asian states, especially China, for trade links and benefits. Of course, China has intruded with its economic interests into the area as well.

Divergent pressures are equally strong on the region and its alliance partnerships. For example, the states have been differently impacted by the Russian annexation of Crimea in 2014 and its implications for their own security. These differentials are obviously dictated by forces of geopolitics, and realism is the theoretical framework that best informs our understanding here. Briefly, there is a fundamental distinction to be made between "secure" countries which do not border Russia (the Czech Republic, Slovakia, Hungary) and "frontier" countries that do (Poland, the Baltic countries, and, indirectly, Romania – the latter through its connection to Moldova and its relationship with Transnistria). The former countries do not fear Russia and behave accordingly; the latter do and express their fear in massive efforts at military spending, while they also attempt to gain reassurance against Russia from NATO and the US by diplomatically and, disproportionally, materially supporting the US and NATO in Iraq and Afghanistan. In addition to this fundamental "realist" and geopolitical factor of divergence, the Balkans represents its own system of geopolitical insecurities determined by pro-Russian (Greece, Serbia, partially Bulgaria) and anti-Russian (Croatia, North Macedonia, Kosovo, and Albania) countries. Neighboring Turkey is a traditional NATO partner but has moved in an authoritarian and pro-Russian direction, and tugs on the Balkan defense policies in particular.

The flow of refugees into the region in 2015 and after has also had a differential impact, for the Balkan nations have felt those pressures in the most intense ways. This newly opened "Middle Eastern frontier" issue of the relationship of Europe to the flow of immigrants opened yet different dimensions of divergence and convergence in the region. Most East European countries, regardless of the actual impact that refugees had on them, reacted with hostility to the potential influx of "aliens," thus reflecting not only the still fairly raw nationalisms of the region, but also, clearly, an attempt to counter-balance German attempts to dictate the EU's refugee policies: a form of "soft realism." Crucially, though, East-Central European countries across the board showed that they have a set of "strategic cultures" – yet another useful concept – resentful and hostile to any perceived infringement on their sovereignty. The constructivist concept of "strategic culture" as defined by Gray (1999) thus permits us to illuminate and explain both divergence and convergence in the respective countries' policies on any number of issues, including the relationship with Russia, Germany, and the refugee issue.[3]

Third, and broadly, it is important to look at the domestic politics of the countries in question and how they dictate the respective countries' defense and security policies. What we can broadly call "defense policy theory" is based on insights provided by the field of comparative politics and provides an insightful way of examining factors that play a role within the individual states and affect their respective alliance behavior. For instance, in some states, due to complex internal politics, there has been a significant growth of domestic illiberalism within their political party systems, with effects on defense policies.

There are many domestic factors that influence national security policy choices. The general environment in which policy choices are made is vital. How do public attitudes and elite perspectives inform conclusions about which states are adversaries and which are allies (Peters 2016, 397–9). Findings about this question can guide an understanding of why the Baltic states center their defense strategies on Russian ambitions while Hungary and the Czech Republic are less concerned. For the former countries' public opinion, Russia is an adversary but for the latter it is less so. Technological capabilities are also significant, and the role of NATO senior partner America is critical in this environmental variable (Peters 2016, 404). Clearly, the technology of NATO/EU member Poland exceeds that of non-partner Serbia in the Balkans. Public opinion can also factor into defense policy decisions, and this has been important in US decisions about the continued military presence in Iraq and Afghanistan (Peters 2016, 404–5). It also conditions Czech apprehension about extended outside military commitments as well as Romanian willingness to take on broader regional obligations.

Terrorism and possibilities of ethnic or religious insurgencies have preoccupied partners in both alliances for a large part of the twenty-first century. All of the states in the region have concerns about these threats, and some have had actual experiences with them. Should anti-insurgency policies rest

Introduction 5

on liberal assumptions about the need to confront it with increased attention to the poverty and inequity that lies beneath the attacks? Conversely, should realist perspectives prevail, for they would establish firm costs that terrorists or insurgents must pay in efforts to cut off any possibility that they could realize their agendas (Cochran et al. 2003, 417–19)? Liberalism may be more likely in Bosnian calculations, given their tragic civil war in the 1992–5 period. However, realism may be the preferred Albanian strategy in light of the huge refugee flow of 2015–16. Further, there is no doubt but that civil liberties considerations factor into defense policy calculations as well. The United States experienced sharp legal and political challenges on that fundamental value after the 9/11 attacks (Kraft and Furlong 2013, 482–7). The Serbian record in the 1990s suggest that its reputation needs restoration on this vital factor, as it attempts to thread its national security policy between Russian and Western demands. With its attention to relationships among Bosniaks, Serbs, and Croats, Bosnia-Herzegovina and its leaders have built up structures and forms that attempt to balance defense policy moves with attention to the rights and liberties of each ethnic group.

Policy thus depends on a range of domestic calculations. The broad environment sets the stage in defining who is an adversary and who an ally, but available technology and public attitudes are conditioning variables as well. With the continuing threat from terrorism and insurgencies, liberal and realistic views often clash in the region in determining what steps to take to combat or eliminate the enormous dangers. Civil liberties are always an underlying policy concern, and protection of them in the face of tremendous threats to life and limb is a continuing challenge.

Therefore, in an anniversary year, it is possible to describe how all three sets of theoretical frameworks can work together to enlighten future needs of both the individual states and the two overlapping alliances that are available to them.

Historical background

Admission to NATO has been staggered over the 1999–2019 period. In 1999, the Czech Republic, Hungary, and Poland became formal members of NATO after several years' participation in the Partnership for Peace (PfP) program. In 2004, the list of seven new NATO members included Bulgaria, Estonia, Latvia, Lithuania, Romania, Slovakia, and Slovenia. Then, in 2009, Albania and Croatia became formal members, with admission to Montenegro postponed to 2017. (North Macedonia received a promise of membership in the near future in 2018 and formal admission in 2020.) EU membership occurred in 2004 for eight of the states that joined

6 *Defending Eastern Europe*

NATO between 1999 and 2004, and plans were finalized with Romania and Bulgaria in 2007, while Croatia entered in 2013. The EU has also granted candidate membership to Albania, North Macedonia (formerly the Yugoslav Republic of Macedonia), Montenegro, and Serbia. Bosnia-Herzegovina and Kosovo have received promises of consideration for candidate status in the future, while Moldova remains neutral. Thus, 2019 is an important 15- or 20-year anniversary for most of these members, the ones that had joined the alliances in either 1999 or 2004.

Communist period

This section will center on the experience of the Eastern European states in the period preceding the fall of communist rule in their neighborhood. During the last two decades of the Cold War (1968–89), the security of the northern tier of the region under consideration was tied to the Soviet Union via the Warsaw Treaty Organization (WTO). However, the Balkans were different: here "independent" communist states of Yugoslavia and Albania coexisted with the bizarre phenomenon of a WTO member with a theatrically independent foreign and security policy: Romania, and only Bulgaria was a reliable Soviet ally. Here also two NATO member states, Greece and Turkey, seemed always to be on the brink of war against each other. Clearly, the Balkans looked like a nightmare for both NATO and WTO/Soviet strategists, and both sides of the Cold War de-emphasized the Balkans' strategic importance, while focusing their main axis of confrontation on the German–Central European front.

In 1968, Moscow reacted to reforms in Czechoslovakia by mobilizing WTO partners in an invasion that quashed the Dubček reform movement. The four invading militaries included the Soviet Union, Poland, Hungary, and Bulgaria (Kramer 2010, 48–52). When the Polish Solidarity movement rallied much of the population of that nation to stand up for its rights in 1980, an expected WTO or Soviet invasion did not take place. Instead, Moscow was able to obtain the willingness of the Polish military to crack down on Solidarity and impose communist controls again. These hardline Soviet responses to cries for meaningful change ended with the 1985 advent of Mikhail Gorbachev to power in the Soviet Union and his unwillingness to use Soviet military force to suppress change.

Overall, the legacies of the communist period are multiple, often hidden but sometimes in "plain sight." Strategic cultures of the countries in question were dramatically affected by the communist and late communist period: for instance, post-communist Hungary continued its tradition of demilitarization and security "opportunism" largely started under

Introduction   7

communism. Legacies of communism also matter, for the very desire to distance themselves from communism explains much about the eagerness with which the countries of the region embraced liberalism and liberal institutions in the 1989–2010 period (Barany 1995, 112–13). Forgetting the communist experience, in turn, explains a lot about the sudden eruption of illiberalism in the region, roughly after 2010.

The three theoretical perspectives that anchor this discussion of the late communist period are pertinent in linking it all to a range of broader dynamics in the international arena. Alliance theory calls attention to the basic relationship between Moscow and its Warsaw Pact partners. For instance, the Warsaw Pact invasion of Czechoslovakia as well as the crackdown on the Polish Solidarity movement may seem to have closed the distances that had been developing within the alliance. However, the harshness of Brezhnev's reaction to reform pressures for democratization backfired, strengthening hopes in both for future enhanced freedom from their Soviet overlord. Convergence/divergence and defense policy formation theories can underline the sharp cultural, economic, and political differences between the northern and southern geographic sectors of the bloc. The Balkans under communism, with the exception of Yugoslavia, tended as a whole to have experienced more severe economic challenges, brutal authoritarian leaders, and an almost continuous effort (except for Bulgaria) to move away from Soviet supervision. However, the more established economies and political systems further north possessed strength, limited independence, and economic contributions that fed Soviet appetites in a range of areas. Finally, legacies from this period of communist and Soviet controls percolated into the defense policy-making process after the end of communism in many ways. The imperfectness and variety of democratic patterns after 1991 reflected the difficulty of departing from decades of communist controls.

In Chapter 2, the late communist experiences of the East European states and their whole region will be at the center of the discussion.

Early post-communist period

Most of the states in the region were unprepared to take responsibility for their own defense in the years after the 1989 anti-communist revolutions throughout the bloc. Therefore, it is important to present a picture of their struggles to provide successor state defense policies to those of the WTO. Their dependence on control by Moscow had turned over all decision-making power in the security area to that senior ally, and so their relatively large military forces were simply surprised by the flow of control into their hands and those of the new reform-minded political leaders. There

8 *Defending Eastern Europe*

were differences in the pace of post-1989 change, for the Balkan nations maintained central controls far longer than did their neighbors further north. However, even these patterns were not consistent, for multiparty rule emerged in Bulgaria by the end of 1990. Further, Yugoslavia's central rule atrophied very quickly with the pressure for a series of independent states and the ensuing wars.

Briefly, the countries in question found themselves partially "unwillingly" in the position of strategic self-reliance, and they had to do the best with their newly found autonomy. This was a period of experimentation and incertitude. On the one hand, liberal idealists like Czech President Václav Havel or Hungarian intellectual György Konrád talked about a world in which both NATO and the Warsaw Pact would be abolished, to be perhaps replaced by collective security mechanisms provided by the Organization on Security and Cooperation in Europe (Hyde-Price 1996, 242–3; Leff 1997, 221–2). On the other hand, more realistically minded leaders, like Poland's Lech Wałęsa, talked about NATO-bis, which was to be an alliance of all former WTO countries minus Russia, and a Central-European alternative to both NATO and Russia, thus reviving Poland's 1918–38 "Intermarium" dreams. In the meantime, all countries looked with horror at the self-destructive savagery of the wars of Yugoslavian succession.

In addition, significant border changes disrupted foreign policy calculations and equations. Yugoslavia broke up into five and eventually seven different states, while Czechoslovakia ended its 75-year tradition and divided up into the Czech Republic and Slovakia. While the new, shrunken Yugoslavia and the Czech Republic inherited the defense machinery of their former wider states, the breakaway segments of their federations had to start nearly from scratch. In addition, the former East German state merged into the broader German nation and simply became part of the strategies that the former West German entity had devised. The three Baltic states experienced the radical transformation from being republics in the Soviet Union to the status of independent states, with essentially no militaries to speak of.

Given the end of the Cold War, considerable shrinkage of the defense sector occurred in most of these emergent states, provoked by the countries' economic collapse, but balanced by needs of strategic self-sufficiency. While predictions of an ensuing "democratic peace" partially materialized, the general fear of instability exemplified by wars of Yugoslavian and Soviet succession (Nagorno-Karabakh, Abkhazia, the Georgian civil war, Transnistria) was propelling the countries toward a search for stable security and defense frameworks. In this respect, the gravitational pull of not just Western-style liberal models of capitalism and democracy but also Western defense institutions were irresistible. It was helped by the Western European (especially

Introduction 9

German) desire to secure a neighborhood of peace and stability, and the US desire to keep NATO, the anchor of US influence in Europe and Eurasia, as a vibrant, viable, and expanding institution. Thus, the interests of both "East" and "West" converged.

From the vantage point of theory, there was a kind of vacuum that developed in the region after the fall of communism. The states lacked autonomous defense strategies, had not yet set up new governmental patterns, and looked around with interest at several possible collective security models. It is not surprising that pressures for divergence dominated the region in the early years after 1989, and any sense of direction was unclear or nonexistent. The eruption of the Balkan civil wars in the mid-1990s did make a difference in their perceptions about defense preparedness, and discussions among them and with senior Western partners became more colored by convergence. It is also true that alliance theory can be useful in comprehending the impact of the geographic changes that occurred with the break-up of several important federative states. Internal geographic distance now characterized both the former Yugoslav and Czechoslovak states, and the political systems as well as ethnic groups that emerged from both were diverse. Any alliance-type tugs that existed as part of their previous federation structures had disappeared, and the need intensified for some kind of substitute. Defense policy questions also emerged and intensified, and thus both realism and focus on domestic politics can assist in understanding particular choices that individual states made. Why did states like the Czech Republic, Hungary, and Poland hook their national interests to a PfP plan that led to early NATO entry? What led Serbian leaders to use such force against new neighbors in an effort to hang on to the ideal of Serbianism in the Balkans?

The struggles and opportunities of this immediate post-communist era will receive careful analysis in Chapter 3.

NATO and EU outreach to post-communist states

The next emphasis will be on the effort of the West to integrate the newly non-communist states into the framework of the existing NATO. Invitations by NATO to its PfP programme as well as the possibility of actual membership in that Western alliance took place in the early 1990s. Each interested Eastern European nation needed to demonstrate how and why it was ready for such a process, and the criteria for membership included democracy and human rights as well as defense and security capabilities. The NATO approach to these newly emancipated states had serious repercussions further east, for the new Russian leadership after 1991 expressed concern about the Western alliance marching to their border and even including eventually

10 *Defending Eastern Europe*

three former Soviet republics. It reminded them of the old Cold War fears of a capitalist encirclement, and in fact during the Cold War Western military forces were located in West Germany, Turkey, Iran, and even the northwestern islands of Alaska. However, the tragic wars on the territory of the former Yugoslavia strengthened Western resolve to bring into NATO countries in the Eastern European region that might have noted particular concerns about the spread of the violence into their own territories. Conversely, NATO leaders understood the advantage of having leaders and militaries in the neighborhood of civil wars play a strategic role in containing the violence for their own and the region's benefit.

Outreach by the EU was also part of the security process in the Eastern European region, and the interactions between that organization and the new democracies were also of significance. While the pull of domestic liberal-democratic and economic benefits to potential new members in that organization was probably paramount, there also was a foreign policy component of EU membership under the initial heading of the Common Foreign and Security Policy (CFSP). EU leaders understood that incorporation of former communist nations into their midst would provide a heightened sense of security as well as another prod to democratic developments within those nations and republics. Whereas NATO admitted three such nations in 1999, seven in 2004, two in 2009, one in 2017, and one in 2020, the EU chose to admit eight in 2004, two in 2007, and one in 2013. Preparedness for EU membership had figured importantly in the admission in prior decades of the Mediterranean nations, and it played a delaying role for Eastern Europe as well. Admission to the EU of these nations paid off on December 2, 2004, a date on which NATO passed over management of the peacemaking process in Bosnia-Herzegovina to the EU. Neighborhood Eastern European states were thus able to provide considerable assistance through deployments of military forces that possessed "niche" capabilities of a specialized nature.

Of course, alliance theory is vital in comprehending the admission process to both of these organizations. In a sense, alliance preconditions and requirements became a substitute for Soviet controls and a critical element for overcoming distances within the region. Additionally, both alliances would need to struggle to integrate states with such a diversity of ethnic differences as well as political histories. Expectations about the stability of the post-Yugoslav states gave way to powerful currents of divergence in the 1990s, for the bitter wars displayed the sharp differences between the Serbian-dominated smaller Yugoslavia and the other new states such as Bosnia-Herzegovina. The NATO alliance responded with air attacks at times on the Serbian military and was, thereby, drawn into the divergence-spawned violence in Bosnia and later in Kosovo. EU leaders also wrestled

Introduction 11

with divergent factors such as the wide economic disparity between Estonia and Slovenia, on the one hand, and, on the other, Albania and North Macedonia. Designing meaningful defense policies toward the new Russia became a major challenge for NATO leaders, especially given the shifts and uncertainties of the steps taken toward the region by President Boris Yeltsin. Further, public opinion within the traditional EU members became a factor in the process of admitting new states that lacked experience with managing Western-style militaries, a largely capitalist economy, or establishing more pluralistic political institutions. Devising fair and balanced defense policies toward the entire East European region required a sensible blend of realism and liberal policy considerations.

NATO will constitute the essence of Chapter 4 and the EU of Chapter 5.

Case studies

Secure East-Central European alliance partners

The four East-Central European states, also known as the Visegrád Four, all possessed levels of development that appealed to both the EU and NATO, and it is important to assess their rather lengthy experience with NATO and somewhat shorter history in the EU. It is no surprise that three of them joined the military organization at the earliest point in 1999 (Peterson 2011b, 20–31). Both their proximity to the troubled Balkan states and their ability to contribute peacekeeping troops to locations in their own neighborhood made their early membership an important step in NATO's widening sphere of activities and contributions. All four became members of the EU at the earliest possible point in 2004, and Slovakia joined the military alliance in the same year (Mahncke 2004, 62). The Slovak case was an anomaly, for it did not gain entry with its former partner state the Czech Republic in 1999. Partly it was a question of economic development but mainly a consequence of its authoritarian political leadership under the Mečiar regime (Kirschbaum 1995, 282–8; Leff 1997, 226–7). Thus, all four East-Central European nations were well positioned and prepared for the commitments that they could make to the transatlantic and European organizations. For example, the Poles managed a large sweep of territory south of Baghdad after the beginning of the Iraq War, and contributed significantly to NATO operations in Afghanistan. In 2002, the Czechs acquired from the Prague NATO conference responsibility for "niche" contributions such as medical equipment, helicopter units, and field hospital units. Thereby, the new members could be part of both organizations' operations that accorded with their population size and military capabilities. Poland's security has been

12   *Defending Eastern Europe*

reduced after the Russian take-over of Crimea in 2014, and more discussion of it will take place below under the heading of "States with significant security issues."

Convergence of systems was characteristic of the incorporation into the alliances of the Czech Republic, Hungary, and Slovakia. In terms of economic preparedness, both the earlier Czechoslovakia and Hungary had been the most developed within the region. Therefore, they alternated in the top position on that criterion, for full membership in both organizations. Each also moved to adoption of early elections after 1991, and a fully active multi-party system developed in short order in both states. Another common feature was their proximity to the troubled Balkans, and alliance planners envisioned this as a strength that could make them strong contributors to a sense of their region as a meaningful home. In terms of alliance theory, both broad organizations admitted the Czech Republic and Hungary at the earliest possible moment. However, defense policy formation theory would suggest that the five-year delay in NATO membership for Slovakia was based on its political differences from the others in the late 1990s. Its authoritarian political patterns, largely a result of a presence of a large Hungarian minority in Slovakia, made it less prepared for military contributions to either alliance. At the same time, significantly, potential and real ethno-political animosities between Hungary and its Slavic neighbors to the north were not barriers to alliance activities, contrary to similar factors in the Balkans.

Policy commitments of the four northern tier states quickly followed in terms of their military engagements in both Afghanistan and Iraq. While Hungary, the Czech Republic, and Slovakia mostly offered niche contributions such as special operations forces, airport protection, and provision of field hospitals, Poland contributed combat troops with full-spectrum military capabilities including assault helicopters and armored infantry. The convergence and divergence factors between Poland and the other countries will be further analyzed, but more than different capabilities were at stake. As we will show, Poland's defense policies differed from Czech, Slovak, and Hungarian policies from the beginning of the post-communist transformation, with Poland's systematically higher military budgets, more militaristic political culture, and a high threat perception of Russia. This last factor, while muted prior to 2014, made Poland's defense policies qualitatively different from its Visegrád neighbors.

However the security situation of Poland became quite jeopardized after the Russian take-over of Crimea in 2014. In light of that radically new development, Chapter 6 on the most secure East European partners will include only the Czech Republic, Hungary, and Slovakia. Attention to the complicated Polish situation will be postponed until Chapter 9.

Introduction   13

Balkan NATO and EU members

It is also important to explore and clarify the manifold developments in the varied and diverse Balkan states in the southern section of the region. The Balkans were quite different in their preparedness for membership in both NATO and the EU. Unlike the Baltic or Visegrád states, the Western Balkans were torn by unrest and bitter wars in the mid-1990s. While the Eastern Balkans largely avoided wars (the war in Transnistria in 1991 was one exception), the EU had not been prepared to admit either Romania or Bulgaria with the enlargement in 2004, for their economic development was lower than that of the other admitted former communist states. However, the war in Afghanistan made major demands on all NATO members for contributions, and the broader threat of al Qaeda and the war in Iraq necessitated the entry of strategically positioned Eastern Balkan states into NATO in 2004.

With the break-up of Yugoslavia into five and eventually seven states, a series of wars, and the subsequent uneven patterns of democratic development in the Balkans, there were tough decisions that both NATO and EU needed to make about their institutional expansions in the former Yugoslavia. The most developed Slovenia became a full NATO member as early as 2004. Eventually, the EU admitted Romania and Bulgaria in 2007, three years after their entry into NATO. Croatia became a NATO member in 2009 and part of the EU in 2013. Finally, Montenegro most recently entered the Western military alliance in 2017, while economically poor Albania joined NATO in 2009. Finally, in 2020 North Macedonia became the most recent member of the alliance. These admission decisions gave both organizations an enlarged landscape into the Balkans with the promise of greater political stability and economic development for the new members. Of course, most of them already, prior to membership, had been deploying both troops in NATO and EU missions, so in effect the dual membership processes formalized what had already been existing practice. Romania has acquired special security responsibilities in the past few years, and thus more discussion of it will take place below in the section entitled "States with significant security issues."

There were interesting patterns of divergence between the two alliance admissions patterns. For example, NATO brought in all seven of its Balkan members states between 2004 and 2020, for they all contributed to several significant strategic projects. Romania, Bulgaria, and Slovenia were relatively close to the Balkan states most afflicted by wars in the 1990s, and they constituted a kind of barrier against the turmoil that emanated from the post-9/11 wars in Iraq and Afghanistan. Subsequent admission of Albania, Montenegro, and North Macedonia helped strengthen Western resolve

14   *Defending Eastern Europe*

after the Russian take-over of Crimea, also to the east. In contrast, the EU admitted only the first three, as their principal determinant of admission was economic preparedness and ensuing democratic political development. Croatia entered the EU nearly a full decade after Slovenia and Bulgaria, for the authoritarian Tudjman regime in the 1990s raised doubts about the political path that the state was likely to take. Alliance and defense policy theories also help to clarify these NATO/EU differences, for both organizations took very seriously both ethnic and political differences in the area of Southeast Europe. Finally, all the states contributed to Western defense policy requests, as they dispatched troops to Iraq and Afghanistan even when they were PfP partners in NATO rather than full members. Certainly, such military contributions and sacrifices made NATO leaders willing to consider upgrade to full status, but other admission criteria acted as brakes or warning signs on those decisions.

Balkan non-NATO/non-EU states: Bosnia-Herzegovina, Kosovo, and Serbia

In contrast, three successor states to Yugoslavia did not gain official entry into either multinational organization. The wars in the Balkans in the 1990s were the principal reasons for their inability to join either organization. Bosnia-Herzegovina had the most lengthy and costly war, but Kosovo Albanians also experienced a tough battle with the Serbs at the end of the decade. Kosovo's tiny size and relative poverty also made it difficult to envision that it could contribute at the same level as Croatia or Slovenia. Serbia had been the aggressive force in the 1990s with invasions of three other former republics, and its challenge was to rebuild stability, with entry into the larger organizations postponed to a later date. However, all these states still had gained PfP status with NATO and played a role in the missions of that alliance as well as the EU. With Serbia, its foreign policy alignment with Russia is a factor, even though similar patterns did not prevent Greece or Cyprus from being members of either NATO (Greece) or the EU (Cyprus).

Initially after 1991, there was considerable idealism about policy prospects for the independent states that emerged or broke out from former Yugoslav space. There had been sharp disagreement about the nature of the federation created after the close of World War I. Was it to be a Serb-dominated entity or a co-equal federation of all the nationalities? Pre-communist and communist Yugoslavia offered different answers to this dilemma: in the former, attempts to create an equitable confederative solution failed and were replaced with Serbian domination, while in the latter, ethnic politics were balanced through repression of all nationalisms and attempts to dissolve them by careful balances of power and decentralization.

Introduction 15

With the fall of communist Yugoslavia, there was a faint hope that a liberal confederation of equal nations might be created after all failed just like it did after 1918. As militant nationalist forces took over, Serbian nationalist leaders sought to carve out a "Greater Serbia" which meant wars with Croats, Bosniaks, and Kosovo Albanians who all sought their own nationalistic solutions (Peterson 2013, 8–9). Eventually, NATO interventions in the conflict contributed to Serbian defeats by the end of the century. NATO and, later, the EU offered its own "imperial" solution to the problem of nationalist conflicts through coercively supervised series of forced compromises between the warring forces, covered by a façade of liberal institutions. In alliance theory terms, the outreach into the region by both Western alliances offered a kind of substitute or new method for closing the distances between the successor states of former Yugoslavia. In terms of convergence/divergence theories, the wars that afflicted all four eventual states revealed and reinforced profound divergences among the cultures and ethnic groups that had traditionally lived in the Western Balkans. The Bosniaks constituted the largest ethnic group in Bosnia-Herzegovina, and yet they did not achieve any semblance of political control in that republic or state until establishment in 1995 of the trilateral presidency, after its imposition in the Dayton Accord that closed out the official war. Similarly, the substantial Albanian minority in Macedonia put much pressure on the Slavic majority for a more prominent role in the state, eventually leading to an insurgency in 2001. The sharp difference between Serbia and its 90% Albanian majority in Kosovo generated first a civil war in 1999 and then the new but vulnerable state of Kosovo in 2008. Within the entire East European region, there was no stronger illustration of the power of divergent forces that were multi-dimensioned, but included a combination of poverty, ethno-religious nationalism, and authoritarian leadership at their causal core.

For the purposes of this discussion, Albania and Bulgaria will receive coverage in Chapter 7 as the most stable of the Balkan states, for they each developed considerable autonomy and force on defense questions within the framework of NATO. The seven post-Yugoslav states include Bosnia-Herzegovina, Croatia, Kosovo, Montenegro, North Macedonia, Serbia, and Slovenia. The study will classify them in Chapter 8 as vulnerable states due to their small size, geographic location, and/or failure to join either NATO or the EU.

NATO/EU states with significant security issues: Poland, Romania, and Moldova

Poland and Romania moved into a changed security situation due to very different circumstances. Poland's defense situation was more jeopardized in the face of the Russian threat to Northeastern Europe after 2014, while Romania carried the legacy of its ambiguous relationship with Moldova and its Transnistrian crisis, and its acquired NATO responsibilities in terms of missile defense which caught the attention of potential enemies further east. Poland and Romania share their substantial security concerns about Russia, which is a traditional enemy of both countries. Significantly, Poland and Romania were anti-Soviet allies in the 1920s and 1930s, were both attacked by the Soviet Union in the 1939–40 period, and share a tradition of anti-Russian nationalism. Today, Poland and Romania are avidly rearming, seek US/NATO reassurances against Russia, and increasingly perceive each other as security partners: just like in the 1920s/1930s period. The wheel of history has made a full circle.

Theoretically, convergence between the two ethnically unlike states has been a reality for many decades. Both challenged Soviet controls in the communist era. Poland's 1956 reform movement led to intense meetings with leaders from Moscow on Polish soil, and its 1980–1 comprehensive Solidarity reform package led to a Moscow-induced crackdown by the Polish military itself. Romania's independence from Cold War Warsaw-Pact controls was parallel to the Polish in time but very different in form. The Romanian leader Ceaușescu preserved unreformed, Stalin-like domestic controls but imitated Yugoslav leader Tito in his foreign policy independence from Moscow, helped in this respect by the removal of Soviet troops in 1958 (Gilberg 1990, 104–5). Alliance theory with its emphasis on closing of geographic and conceptual distances came to the fore for Poland after Russian aggression that followed the 2014 Crimean crisis. Poland, like its Baltic neighbors, worried that traditional Russian animosity would resurface in quite provocative ways. As a result, NATO moved a substantial amount of its military forces from Southern Europe to the North in an effort to protect the four states in that region. Alliance-induced closing of that geographic space was essential in order to fend off Russian intrusions, such as those in cyber-space. Defense policies of Poland and Romania also followed NATO- and US-led patterns in combating the Russian threat, as the two countries stepped up their armament efforts. While the US Missile Defense Proposal of the Bush administration in 2007–8 was ostensibly aimed against Iran, Poland and Romania clearly saw it as a part and parcel of their anti-Russian strategies. Later the Obama administration developed a new missile shield concept that incorporated NATO, and both Romania and Poland managed critical components of it (Peterson 2011a, 20–23). Thus, alliance and national interests coincided.

The special case of Moldova and its breakaway territory of Transnistria will be also discussed in Chapter 9, as the fate of this country cannot be discussed but in the context of its special relationship with Romania. Briefly,

Introduction 17

Moldova is the traditional Romanian province of Bessarabia, which was forcibly attached to the Soviet Union in 1940, pursuant to the Molotov-Ribbentrop Pact, and then reoccupied by the Soviets in 1945. After 1991, Moldova emerged as an independent state, but immediately faced a civil war and ethnic secession of Transnistria inhabited mostly by a Slavic "Soviet" (mostly Russian, Ukrainian, and Belorussian) minority. This conflict, together with Transnistrian ambitions for independence and a complex nexus of relationships with Russia and Romania involved in the conflict, remains to this day, as the first and oldest "frozen" conflict of the post-Soviet space.

In Chapter 9, these three jeopardized states will receive considerable attention.

Most security challenged NATO/EU Baltic states: Estonia, Latvia, and Lithuania

The northern Baltic states of Estonia, Latvia, and Lithuania were unique in having been republics in the Soviet Union for several decades but also in terms of their considerable economic development levels at the time of the collapse of the Soviet Union in 1991. Each one of them had a significant but different-sized Russian minority that had principally resulted from decades of Russianization during the Soviet period. Given their small populations and geographical vulnerabilities as well as advanced state of development, they sought security in both NATO and the EU. However, the Russian reaction to their proposed entry into the Western military alliance was highly combative in the 1990s. Admission of former Soviet republics so close to the Russian border appeared to be a very hostile anti-Russian move by the West. Russian expressions of discontent and anger continued through their admission to both multilateral organizations through the 2004 admission year. A sense of Baltic vulnerability increased after the Ukrainian-Crimean crisis of 2014, and commitments of NATO to the region strengthened in the immediate aftermath of the events. Today, the Baltics are rearming quickly and efficiently, all against potential Russian aggression.

Although each is distinct and possesses its own cultural make-up, the three Baltic states have experienced the forces of convergence in significant ways. While independent in the 1920s and 1930s, all became republics in the Soviet Union during the Cold War for a full five decades. During that period, they collectively stood out for their relatively high levels of economic development. That feature made them valuable to the Soviet leadership, but it is also true that they were subject to patterns of Russianization. The intent was to inject Russian influence into their midst but also to avail young Russians of the opportunity to benefit from jobs and income that may have exceeded standards further east in the Soviet state. After 1991, they were all targets of Russian anger as each quickly gravitated toward the embrace of Western alliances. One curiosity of defense policy in the region is the Russian hold on Kaliningrad Oblast, a geographic piece of their state that is not contiguous to Russia but instead nestled between Lithuania and Poland. This exclave is an important military island that Moscow has populated with both weapons and military personnel. On several occasions, its strategic location has served as a Russian propaganda weapon whose use has been part of threats to the West after perceived American provocations. For instance, efforts of the Bush administration to build a missile shield capability that rested on Polish and Czech geographic space led to Russian proclamations that they would arm and perhaps use the Kaliningrad defense capabilities in response (White 2011, 286). Similar outcries occurred after Western protests about the 2014 intervention in Ukraine as well as NATO's ensuing plans to buttress and expand their own military capabilities in Northern Europe. Finally, alliance theory is helpful in analyzing the NATO decision at its summer 2014 Wales Summit to move troops from the territory of its Mediterranean partners north to the Baltics and Poland (Kalb 2015, 235). Location of an actual NATO military base in Poland was also under consideration, but such a decision would have violated Russian understandings of the conditions of the Russia-NATO Founding Act of 1997. As NATO expanded its presence in the vulnerable area of Northeast Europe, the alliance was in effect closing the geographic space that had become more vulnerable to Russian moves after its takeover of Crimea.

Chapter 10 will offer important conclusions about the deep security challenges to these three Baltic states.

Conclusion

What do these anniversaries commemorate in terms of the future role of the former communist states within NATO and the EU? An answer will appear within the framework of the final Chapter 11.

On the one hand, in recent years both organizations have received sharp criticisms and rebukes from their senior alliance partners. President Donald Trump challenged NATO members to reach quickly the expected commitment of 2% of their GDP to defense, and at one point, he suggested that the United States might not fulfill Article 5 requirements that all members take military action to support any member that was subject to an invasion. The EU has been the target of a dual number of challenges as well. Following a close referendum vote, the United Kingdom under the heading of Brexit has left the European Union. In addition, the waves of refugees

Introduction 19

that flooded from points east into EU member nations throughout 2015 led to the strengthening of nationalist forces in many members, opposed to the EU-imposed refugee quotas. Given the newness of these organizations in the life of the former communist states, such controversies usually had strong repercussions within the domestic politics of each.

On the other hand, the reliance of relatively small states on two well-grounded organizations with activity that spanned more than half a century provided possibilities for stability in a tumultuous time. National security challenges emanated from North Korea, ISIS, Iran, and an increasingly aggressive Russia. Threats to domestic conditions centered on variables such as ultra-nationalism, rapidly changing governing coalitions, and the outreach of China into their region in terms of trade policy. Stability was what both the EU and NATO could potentially offer in looking toward a future that was full of uncertainties. The challenge was for the post-communist states to work with more senior members of the two organizations to build and strengthen new frameworks for preparing mutual decisions that could adjust to multiple threats as they emerged. However, possibilities of dramatic fissures among the "old" members of the two Western alliances, which began in 2002 over the war in Iraq and continued with Trump's truculence and Britain's Brexit, might create a situation in which, again, Eastern and Central European members of EU and NATO might have to confront a new and unstable world.

Notes

1 The introduction of the Martial Law in 1981 engaged at least 70,000 Polish soldiers and 30,000 policemen, and thus was larger, but this "internal stability" repressive operation is probably not comparable to the Polish deployments overseas. A more similar counter-insurgency operation, "Wisła" (Vistula) against Ukrainian nationalist resistance in 1947 engaged around 20,000 Polish troops.
2 Aggestam states that "a role reflects norms and ideas about the purpose and orientation of a state as an entity as and as an actor in the international system" (Aggestam 2004, 8).
3 Gray defines strategic culture as "the persisting (though not eternal) socially transmitted ideas, attitudes, traditions and habits of mind and preferred methods of operation that are more or less specific to a particular geographically based security community that has had a necessarily unique historical experienc." Furthermore, strategic culture can change over time, as new experience is absorbed, coded, and culturally translated. Culture, however, changes slowly (Gray 1999, 51–2).

2

Cold War security experiences
of Eastern European states

Jacek Lubecki

This chapter will center on the experience of the Eastern European states in the period preceding the fall of communist rule during the four decades of the Cold War (1948–89). Because communism, especially "late" communism, represents the immediate background to the countries' current military and defense policies, it is important to discuss this period in some detail. As we will see, there are important and surprising continuities in the respective countries' military and defense policies between pre-communist, communist, and post-communist periods. For one, the countries' post-communist militaries were initially simply late communist militaries under a new top leadership. Even with the passage of time, strategic cultures and institutional patterns established under communism continued under new institutional guises (Young 2017).

To start with the obvious; communism past created the region in question as a meaningful unit of analysis and the communist past defines the region for us as the topic of this book. The region is not defined by its prior subjugation to the external Soviet empire (even though most of the region was a part of this empire) as neither Yugoslavia (Yugoslavian Socialist Republic, YSR) nor communist Albania were subjugated by the Soviet Union. However, all countries in question became Marxist-Leninist republics, based on the Soviet institutional template created in the 1920s/1930s and modified in the 1950s/1960s. All of them, thus, faced institutional and cultural factors of convergence, based on the ideological commonality of their respective regimes. Based on alliance theory, we would expect a common ideology, bolstered by a membership – for most of the countries – in a common institutionalized alliance system to overcome distances between countries of East-Central Europe. Some form of it definitely took place, and will be analyzed later. However, there were also institutional paradoxes of the communist system which worked against closing of distances.

The way the Soviet government system emerged out of the maelstrom of the Russian Revolution and the subsequent civil war featured a strong, centralized communist party in charge of a prioritized and powerful military

Cold War security in Eastern European states 21

and security apparatus which defended "communism in one country" against a hostile capitalist world and, always looming, internal "enemies of the people." These enemies, more often than not, were "heretical," real or imaginary, leftists tempting the people to abandon the one and true path set by the party.

The template set by the "communism in one country" example of the Soviet Union was copied in all countries in question, whether subjugated by the Soviets as the result of World War II, or, communist as a result of internal armed struggles against Axis powers and their indigenous allies (like in Albania and Yugoslavia). Everywhere the same basic system was cloned, with the communist party and its centralized apparatus of power, a fair level of militarization of society, a political police in charge of enforcing the party orthodoxy, and subordination of all institutions, at least formally, to the party. The party, in practice, meant a centralized organization of power formally centered on either the party leader or a nebulous network of power-brokers in the executive committees of the respective Politbureaus. The overall design of the system was one of a besieged castle: it created powerfully defended autarkic political and economic states designed for self-protection and the occasional projection of power abroad (Jowitt 2013).

From the alliance theory perspective and for the countries incorporated into the Soviet empire the internal design of communist states posed a challenge: how could countries designed to be "castles" cooperate in a common imperial system? By design, the communist states were geared for conflict and autonomy, not complementarity and cooperation. At the same time, the mythos of a worldwide revolution and Soviet imperial purposes demanded "internationalist unity" of all socialist states, based on the common policy representing the one correct path to communist utopia. Whose prerogative it was to define the path for all countries of "real socialism" was inherently contestable. How to maintain "socialist unity" in the Soviet empire became a problem, not just because different subjugated nations and often their communist leaders often demanded independence, but because the internal institutional design of communist states militated against unity. The first conflict to come, was, predictably, between the Soviet Union and the most substantial European communist country that avoided the Soviet occupation, Yugoslavia.

The split between communist Yugoslavia and the Soviet Union was over power,[1] and specifically, Tito's plans to set up a unified Balkan communist federation or "greater Yugoslavia" that would include Albania, and, perhaps, Bulgaria (Perović 2007). What ticked off Stalin, besides the prospect of a "Yugoslavian" power which could defy the Soviet Union, was the fact that Tito did not consult enough about his plans with the "great leader." This, in the mind of paranoid Stalin, was a sufficient reason for a break. One result

22 *Defending Eastern Europe*

of the break was that anti-Yugoslavian communist Albania, temporarily, firmly fell under the Soviet sphere of influence – until a Soviet–Albanian conflict in 1961. Another fallout of the crisis was the solidification of Soviet control over all countries actually occupied by Soviet troops during World War II. Not just "bourgeois enemies of communism" but also communist leaders with the slightest suspicion of independence from the Soviet domination were purged and often executed for the sin of "nationalist deviation" or "Titoism." This also affected the militaries, which were brutally purged of any "deviationism" while Soviet military patterns were slavishly copied and subjugation to Soviet diktat took very crude, bilateral forms.

Consummated by 1948 through a famous public exchange of letters between the Soviet and Yugoslavian communist parties, the Stalin–Tito dispute soon turned into militarized hostility. By 1950–1 Stalin was not only stepping up a military buildup against the West, but also preparing for a possibility of war against communist Yugoslavia.[2] As a result of these trends, all countries of the Soviet bloc engaged in massive, messy, and ruinous military expansion.[3] This was countered by parallel movement by NATO, and by Tito, as the latter set up a powerful conventional military establishment, the JNA (Jugoslovenska narodna armija, Yugoslav People's Army), pragmatically backed by the United States with training and arms deliveries, alongside preparations of Territorial Defense/guerilla forces (Lees 2010). These forces were eventually (after 1968, in reaction to the Soviet invasion of Czechoslovakia) based on the doctrine of "Total People's Defense" (Opštenarodna odbrana) whereby the entire population was to resist the invaders (Medunarodna Politika 1970). Necessarily decentralized, these territorial forces later (after 1990) facilitated the breakup and militarized ferocity of the wars of Yugoslavian succession. The doctrine of "Total People's Defense" was also later adopted by nationalist communist Romania after 1968, when the maverick Romanian communist leader Nicolae Ceaușescu started to prepare the country to resist a potential Soviet invasion (Opriș 2004). Communist countries of Eastern Europe, were, thus clearly, not a bloc; fissures and divergences among these countries coexisted with forces of convergence.

The death of Stalin in 1953 began a period of turmoil and revolts in the Soviet empire, beginning with the East German revolt in 1953 and Czechoslovak strikes in the same year, and punctuated by Hungary's bid for liberalization and independence in 1956, and Polish "events" of 1956. In East Germany, the street revolt was put down by the occupying Soviet troops. In Hungary, where the communist party leader Imré Nagy and parts of the communist military backed the revolt, a mechanized invasion by 30,000 Soviet troops and a bloody struggle with Hungarian insurgents was necessary to restore the Soviet domination and establishment of a puppet

Cold War security in Eastern European states

regime of János Kádár. In Poland, however, the complex events of 1956 resulted in a compromise: a potential armed clash between Polish military forces loyal to a newly created nationalist-communist leadership of Władysław Gomułka and Soviet or Soviet-loyal forces was avoided, and the Polish communist leadership was allowed to proceed on an autonomous "Polish path to communism." This path included, among others, the departure of Soviet military officers from the Polish Armed Forces,[4] while Poland was allowed to create its own autonomous doctrine, structure of forces, and weapons systems.[5] To some extent, other countries of the Soviet bloc followed the same pattern. While the Soviet control was maintained, both through formal and informal means,[6] cruder forms of subjugation were terminated after 1956, and the country-members of the Warsaw Pact asserted their limited autonomy (Ross Johnson 1977; Jones 1981; Lewis 1982; Mastny and Byrne 2005).

What mattered for the development of Polish strategic culture as a result of the 1956 and the 1980–1 (more of which later) crises in Poland is that in both cases the country avoided (unlike Czechoslovakia in 1968 and Hungary in 1956) a direct Soviet military intervention, thus avoiding either a moral and material destruction (Hungary) or utter demoralization (Czechoslovakia) of its military. Moreover, even though the Polish communist-controlled armed forces were used by the regime (in 1956, 1970, and 1981–2) for internal repression, a persistent public perception in Poland was that the country's military was actually a patriotic force, reluctant to be used as a force of repression and potentially willing to defend the country against external enemies, be it revanchist Germany or even the Soviets. This perception mattered, as in the national culture in which a sovereign military force and armed struggle for independency were all-important, communist armed forces were still held in high regard, maintained their coherence and professionalism, and transitioned relatively easily into a post-communist reality where, as sovereign Armed Forces of the Polish Republic, they continued to enjoy public support and a high level of funding. The situation was diametrically different in Czechoslovakia and Hungary, where communist-era militaries were more compromised, perceived with more hostility by the public opinion than in the Polish case (Young 2017, 21), and where the post-communist period brought about relatively quick demilitarization, which, in the Hungarian case, actually continued the trend that began in 1953–6.

Around a decade of relative stability within the Soviet WTO bloc followed the Polish events of 1956 until 1968, and then, until the events of the 1980s in Poland, which began the final decade of communism. Among other things, the ruinous militarization characteristic of high Stalinism was pared down to a more manageable level. Still, the Soviet Union continued to insist on a relatively high level of military mobilization of the allies which the

Soviets required to augment their own huge forces in Central Europe. WTO joint forces were expected to wage a strategically defensive but operationally aggressive mechanized war against NATO.[7] As a result, the countries settled on fairly high (if much lower than during high Stalinism) levels of standing, albeit conscript-based forces, which for Poland numbered around 300,000, 200,000 for Czechoslovakia, 150,000 for East Germany, and 100,000 for Hungary. These forces were also fairly well (at varying levels, depending on the country) technologically modernized and featured, as contrary to Stalinist times, some level of professionalism, especially in more technical services (air forces, logistics, naval forces, etc.).[8]

Substantial upgrading of WTO equipment took place throughout the 1970s and 1980s, as evidenced by the high and growing military procurement budgets of the countries in question (Crane 1987). Weapons systems such as Mig-23 and Mig-29 fighters, T-72 tanks, BTR-70 armored personnel carriers, BMP-1 infantry fighting vehicles, and Mi-24 "Hind" attack helicopters were either imported (BMP-1s, Mig-29s and Mi-24s) or domestically produced (T-72s, in Poland and Czechoslovakia). Nevertheless, all countries in question resisted Soviet demands to further increase their military budgets and then, while formally agreeing to increased goals, never fully implemented them (Lewis 1982). Only East Germany completely fulfilled its promises to expand its military budget in 1980s, marking the country's status as the favored junior partner of the Soviets in the 1980s (Crane 1987). The countries' doctrines and militaries were all subordinated and coordinated with the Soviets, which in all cases envisioned a dual nature of the forces – highly mobile mechanized troops were to wage coalition warfare as a part of Soviet strike forces in Central Europe, whereas territorial defense forces were to defend the respective countries' land, air, and, in the case of Poland, also sea spaces. Coordination was maintained through multilateral and bilateral mechanisms of control.

However, factors of divergence were also in evidence, with Czechoslovakia (prior to 1968 seen as "the most trusted ally") leading with the highest levels of military spending which hovered between 5 and 6% of GDP in the 1960s, lowered to 4% in the early 1970s and climbing back again to over 5% in the early 1980s. Polish spending in the meantime was consistently above 4% in the 1960s and between 3 and 4% of GDP in the 1970s, climbing back up close to 4% in the 1980s. Hungary continued a pattern of relative demilitarization which made it an outlier in the communist camp – the country was spending below 2% of its GDP in the 1960s, and never exceeded 3% of its GDP throughout the period until the fall of communism. Characteristically, by the 1980s East Germany assumed the status of the "most trusted ally" among the northern tier countries of the WTO, with a high level of military spending of close to 4–5% of GDP.[9]

Cold War security in Eastern European states

A partial symbol of stability and institutionalization of the Soviet control was the growing institutional strength of the Warsaw Pact. The May 1955 Treaty of Friendship, Co-operation, and Mutual Assistance was signed in Warsaw (hence the "Warsaw Pact") between the Soviet Union and its seven Eastern European allies mostly as a purely political ploy by Khrushchev who wanted to create a bargaining chip to be traded for the potential dissolution of NATO and the withdrawal of US forces in Europe (Mastny and Byrne 2005, 3). When the ploy failed and tensions with the West over Berlin escalated in the early 1960s, the WTO was forced to become more and more a real military alliance, with a growing capacity for multilateral, albeit Soviet-centered and commanded, coordination and planning of the members' military strategies (Mastny and Byrne 2005).

Nominally, the purpose of the alliance was collective security against any external aggression (Article 4) by any country or group of countries. The country-members also nominally subscribed to the principles of independent sovereignty of member states, and mutual non-interference in their respective internal issues (Article 8) (Warsaw Treaty 1955). Institutions that were supposed to embody these principles included the ruling Political Consultative Committee (Article 6), a Committee of Ministers of Defense in charge of coordination of armed forces, and the Technical Committee in charge of military equipment, procurement, and modernization issues – this last committee was matched with a Military Industrial Cooperative Standing Commission in charge of military-industrial cooperation within the Council of Mutual Economic Assistance (COMECON, the Soviet bloc multilateral economic organization) (Germuska 2015). There was also a façade of unified joint military command structures (Article 5), but only for peacetime – during the war, the allied forces were to be fully subordinate to Soviet command structures (Ross Johnson 1977).

The chief crisis of the "middle-communist" period was the "Prague Spring." This Czechoslovak crisis of 1968 was a result of a liberalization episode analogous to Polish and Hungarian crises of 1956. Unlike in Poland and Hungary, Czechoslovakia did not undergo an explosive de-Stalinization around the mid-1950s, which meant that accumulating resentment over communist repression and self-destructive economic policies persisted with no partial release valve into the mid-1960s. When the Communist Party of Czechoslovakia tried to implement limited economic reforms in 1965, the process got out of control by early 1968, and resulted in a full-blown cultural liberalization by the middle of the year. Presided by popular, newly elected Communist Party Secretary Alexander Dubček the reform program was strictly internal, as Dubček was careful not to provoke a Soviet invasion through challenges to Soviet strategic priorities. Nevertheless, the prospect of "socialism with a human face" was a strategic threat of the Soviet system, if anything, worse than Romanian assertions of national sovereignty. Consequently, after repeated unsuccessful Soviet attempts to force Dubček to crack down on liberalization, a full-blown massive invasion of Warsaw Pact forces followed on the night of August 20–21, 1968. This invasion was actively cheered on and supported by East German (Ulbricht) and Polish (Gomułka) communist leaders, with Hungary's Kádár attempting to negotiate a compromise solution to the last moment (Bischof and Karner 2010). Significantly, the Soviet leader, Leonid Brezhnev, was reluctant to launch the invasion, fearing its domestic and international consequences (Navratil 2006). This did not prevent the subsequent term "The Brezhnev doctrine" to be applied to a broader principle underlying the invasion, expressed by Brezhnev himself at the 5th Congress of the Polish United Workers' Party on November 13, 1968:

> When … forces that are hostile to socialism try to turn the development of some socialist country towards capitalism … it becomes not only a problem of the country concerned, but a common problem and concern of all socialist countries. (Brezhnev 1968)

In other words, Brezhnev stated that the Soviet Union and the Warsaw Pact forces would intervene if the Soviet leadership decided that socialism – or whatever the Soviet leadership defined as socialism at any given moment – was threatened in any of the Soviet-bloc member countries.

While a massive civil-non-violent resistance was the Czechoslovak people's reaction to the invasion, the quite formidable (200,000 strong versus the initial invading force of around 250,000) Czechoslovak armed forces, as directed by Dubček, completely stood down (Windsor and Roberts 1968; Bischof and Karner 2010). The experience of the country's armed forces being completely irrelevant to Czechoslovak self-defenses twice in the period of 30 years (1938–9 and 1968) must have had a profound influence on Czech and Slovak strategic cultures – reflecting their relative pragmatism, but also, inevitably, contributing to the relative devaluation of the military as relevant to the country's security. Czechoslovakia and its successor states' relative demilitarization after 1989 – less extreme than Hungary's, but clearly distinctive from Poland's continuous existence on strong armed forces as a guarantee of the country's sovereignty – is clearly a reflection of this persistent historical pattern and the strategic culture it created.

While the 1960s–1970s was a time of stability and the assertion of Soviet control among the northern tier WTO countries, the same cannot be said for the Balkans, where the Soviet control further slipped away. Paradoxically, the post-Stalinist period in the Balkans began with a positive development for the Soviets, as by 1956 Khrushchev and Tito managed to patch up their relationship. Partially in function of this improving relationship,

Soviet troops were withdrawn from Romania in 1958.[10] Still, the Soviets established a naval presence in the Mediterranean with a submarine base in Albania, and with Bulgaria and Romanian being faithful Soviet allies, the Soviet Union could seemingly look forward to further expansion of their influence in the Balkans. This was not to be, as a long brewing Soviet break with Albania, whose Stalin-type leader, Enver Hoxha, accused Khruschev of "modern revisionism," was consummated between 1960 and 1961. The Soviet submarine naval base at Vlor was closed, Albania *de facto* left the Warsaw Pact (the formal break was in 1968) and concluded an anti-Soviet military alliance with communist China, in a bizarre development which defied geography, but made perfect sense for a communist-nationalist regime which feared subjugation by both communist Yugoslavia and the communist Soviet Union. By the 1970s even this alliance was broken over Albania's objections to China's post-Mao liberalization, and Albania, the poorest country in Europe, stood alone as perhaps the most wacky, militarized, and isolated Stalinist dictatorship in the world.

With Albania becoming an open enemy of the Soviets, and Yugoslavia maintaining its guarded, if friendly, strategic independence, the Soviets lost access to the Mediterranean and control over developments in Western Balkans. This seemingly left at least the Eastern Balkans under Soviet control, with both Romania under Gheorghiu-Dej and Bulgaria under Todor Zhivkov as loyal allies. However, the Soviet–Romanian relationship kept deteriorating, starting with the 1958 refusal by Gheorghiu-Dej to listen to Khruschev's dictates regarding the "socialist division of labor" (whereby Romania was to be relegated to an agricultural, natural resource, and light-industry oriented pattern of development) and punctuated by episodes such as Romanian Minister of Foreign Affairs Corneliu Mansecu's secret missive to Dean Rusk that Romania would stay neutral in a potential Soviet–US nuclear confrontation in October 1963 (Mastny and Byrne 2005, 25).

Indeed, throughout the 1960s to the 1980s Romania, which since 1965 was ruled by Gheorghiu-Dej's successor, Nicolae Ceauşescu, kept openly defying the Soviet Union's dictates. This included Ceauşescu's condemnation of the Soviet invasion of Czechoslovakia, and the gearing of Romania's defense capabilities toward countering a similar invasion by the Soviets. At the same time, while fiercely independent in foreign policy, Romania remained a member of the WTO, and openly fulminated against Soviet control and for the equal sovereignty of all member states at all and any WTO fora to which the country was invited. This must have caused much grief to the Soviets, who, in absence of their troops in Romania, and with an apparent failure of covert efforts to overthrow Ceauşescu, were unwilling to absorb the material and political costs of an open military intervention against this peculiar "ally." At the same time, however,

Ceauşescu maintained the strict Stalinist orthodoxy in his internal controls, modeling himself on Chinese and North Korean examples, so, unlike in the Czechoslovak case, no threat of domestic liberalism to the Soviet system emanated from Romania. Romania was also not particularly militarized – while Ceauşescu created Yugoslav-style popular-militia based territorial defense forces (the Patriotic Guards), and a military doctrine explicitly aimed to resist a Soviet invasion, the Romanian conventional military was marginalized, under-funded, and deprived of the newest Soviet equipment. Instead, Ceauşescu emphasized his peculiar vision of Romania's economic development, which by the 1980s resulted in a massive impoverishment of the population and discontentment violently repressed by Romanian political police, the dreaded Securitate.

All in all, by the late 1960s the Soviets and the WTO were left with only one faithful Balkan ally: Bulgaria.[11] While unfailingly, even slavishly, loyal under Todor Zhivkov, Bulgaria was also a relatively small and objectively weak country.[12] It partially compensated for its weakness with its zealous commitment to Soviet strategic interests,[13] balanced, however, by Zhivkov's undoubted, if eventually misguided, dedication to Bulgaria's own economic prosperity at the expense of the Soviets. Still, with the Soviets' very weak strategic position in the Balkans and Yugoslavia's wild card status in defense planning of both NATO and WTO, it is clear that in the Soviet strategic planning the Balkans became a backwater and a liability, relegated to a secondary theater at best or to strategic insignificance at worst (Baev 2008). Since NATO's military planning involved a fair degree of mirror-imaging, this was reciprocated, partially for similar reasons. With NATO's two Balkan members, Turkey and Greece, being constantly at each other throats, the region looked like a nightmare for the Western alliance too. The Cold War pattern of relative non-significance of the region where World War I started and which was still thought of as very important in World War II, is to be noted. This was clearly a part of the reason why, when the wars of Yugoslavian succession started, US Secretary of State James Baker said, "We have no dog in the fight." The Balkans seemingly lost its broader strategic significance during the Cold War. The region was to regain it, though, in the post-communist era.

In the 1980s Poland provided the Soviets with the most significant source of problems, the Polish crisis of 1980s being eventually unsolvable and leading to the demise of the entire communist bloc. The "Solidarity" crisis was brought about by a non-violent uprising of the Polish population in the summer of 1980, which was a culmination of a tradition of social protest and resistance against communism that resulted in crises in 1968, 1970, and 1976. This time the wave of strikes and protests involved a newly found ability of working-class/farmer masses to create an institutionalized

Cold War security in Eastern European states 29

form of interest representation in alliance with dissenting intellectuals and the Catholic Church. Unwilling to use force, the regime capitulated to the opposition demands, and, by fall 1980, authorized autonomous institution-alized forms of non-communist civil society, most importantly the Polish "Solidarity," which was a massive social movement with some ten million members, masquerading as a "trade union." While planning for the move-ment's disruption and eventual violent suppression, the Polish communist government and its military and police forces felt overwhelmed, while the Soviet leadership, beset by the ongoing crisis in Afghanistan, was extremely reluctant to intervene, pressuring the Polish communist leadership to sup-press the revolution internally (Paczkowski and Byrne 2008).[14] This marked an effective end of the "Brezhnev doctrine" which was exercised in precisely one case, in Czechoslovakia in 1968.

One peculiar characteristic of the Polish crisis was the ascendance of the Polish communist military, and its leader, General Wojciech Jaruzelski, who had been the minister of defense since 1968, became prime minister in February 1981 and the First Secretary of Polish United Workers Party in September 1981. This unique merger of military and political powers was solidified in December 1981, when Jaruzelski introduced a "martial law" in Poland. The crackdown was a massive,[15] country-wide, well-coordinated repressive operation which not only violently suppressed the "Solidarity" movement and destroyed the Polish liberalization episode, but also for-mally suspended the supremacy of the communist party, by proclaiming the Military Council of National Salvation (in Polish: Wojskowa Rada Ocalenia Narodowego, WRON) with Jaruzelski at its head to be the supreme state organ. This was followed up with a widespread militarization of all state institutions (Michta 1990; Dudek 2003). No communist country of the Soviet bloc ever underwent this type of formal institutionalization of mili-tary rule, the phenomenon being specifically Polish, and perhaps harkening back to Piłsudski's coup of 1926.

The militarization of Poland, and Jaruzelski's self-styled pose as a military-patriotic savior of the country from chaos and (implicitly) potential Soviet invasion, appealed to a nationalistic-authoritarian streak of the Polish public opinion and political culture which trusted the military as a patriotic institution. Significantly, resistance to martial law, while widespread, was also relatively shallow and the regime had no problem asserting control. Significantly, as late as 2001, so long after the fall of communism, around 50% of the Polish public saw the instruction of the martial law as a justi-fied necessity, thus implicitly accepting Jaruzelski's "patriotic" and nation-alistic excuses, which recent historiography largely dismisses (Paczkowski and Byrne 2008).[16] What matters for the purposes of this book is that the whole phenomenon testifies to the persistent militarized patriotism of Polish

30   *Defending Eastern Europe*

public opinion – in this case, even the communist military was mythologized by a substantial section of the public opinion to be a "savior of the nation."

The martial law was followed by a slew of American and Western sanctions against the Polish communist regime and the Soviets, and this further escalated hostilities between the Soviet Union and the West, culminating the (apparent) war scare of 1983 (Jones 1981; Paczkowski and Byrne 2008; Domber 2014). This period of high tension was accompanied by Warsaw Pact efforts of military modernization, as reflected in increasing procurement budgets of the member countries (Crane 1987). However, this effort was clearly unsustainable in the context of escalating economic crisis of all communist countries which were reaching a limit of their economic growth horizon. Torn between the insolvable dilemmas of a need for internal legitimacy, economic crisis, militarism, and the need for Western cooperation to foster the communist countries' economic growth, the Soviet leadership desperately looked for solutions.

Under Yuri Andropov (1982–3), a KGB head who became the first Secretary of the Soviet Communist Party after the death of senile Brezhnev, the solution was to be found in a neo-Stalinist emphasis on law and order, militarism, and a crackdown on both dissent and corruption, accompanied by relative pragmatism on select economic and political issues. Under senile Konstantin Chernenko (1983–4), who was terminally ill when ascending to the office, late Brezhenevian orthodoxy and corruption seemingly returned. After Chernenko's death the ascent of Andropov's protégé Mikhail Gorbachev to the highest office finally marked a full and final attempt to restore dynamism to the decadent system.

Initially Gorbachev's solutions seemed to follow his mentor's emphasis on law and order and militarism, but this soon led to liberalism, opening to the West, and the encouragement of liberalization among the bloc countries. A search for arms-control agreements/détente with the West and demilitarization was a part of the reform package that soon brought about cuts in military spending and demilitarization of the Warsaw bloc countries. By 1988–9 Poland and Hungary were in full turn toward liberalization, encouraged by Moscow. By the end of 1989, through either peaceful negotiated transitions in Poland and Hungary, or massive upheavals from below accompanied by the internal collapse of the regimes in Bulgaria, Czechoslovakia, and East Germany, the communist regimes in East-Central Europe ended. This was encouraged by Moscow through an explicit repudiation of the Brezhnev doctrine and its replacement by the jokingly formulated "Sinatra doctrine."[17] In Romania, though, Ceaușescu was overthrown by an internal revolt in December 1989 supported by the Hungarian minority, the military (unsurprisingly, given its demoted status under his rule), and sections of popular masses, with the Securitate

Cold War security in Eastern European states 31

bitterly and bloodily supporting the regime to the end.[18] Shortly thereafter, Yugoslavia disintegrated into constituent parts, and soon descended into vicious and bloody wars. In Albania, finally, there was a protracted process of transition which ended up with the communist party losing power in 1992. By 1997, however, the country disintegrated into chaos and civil war, which Albania's weak and corrupt military was unable to contain. Stability was only restored through an international UN-authorized armed intervention featuring some 10,000 soldiers.

Importantly, though, the end of the Cold War in Europe was accompanied by Western guarantees that NATO/the US would not expand (with the exception of East Germany) into the strategic space left behind by the retreat of the Soviet empire (Beschloss and Talbott 1993). Thus, the countries of East-Central Europe were left happily liberated from the Soviet imperial yoke, but also left in a strategic vacuum between the West and Russia, where they needed to (re-)construct their post-communist defense policies and establishments. A period of ambiguity and instability was to follow.

Notes

1 The conflict was not about institutional design or forms of communism – the peculiar "Yugoslav path to communism" developed later as the result of the conflict.

2 Until recently, based on testimonies of Béla Király, commander of Hungarian infantry during the Stalinist period, there was a widely accepted notion that the Soviet Union with its allies was preparing a massive military invasion of Yugoslavia. New evidence from open communist archives (chiefly the Hungarian Ministry of Defense) debunked this notion (Ritter 2005).

3 The Polish communist military personnel in 1952 were 356,000 soldiers, while the country devoted at least 15% of its GDP toward military spending. The equivalent Hungarian figures were around 200,000 soldiers and up to 25% of GDP. In Czechoslovakia, the military personnel in 1953 were around 297,000 soldiers, and military spending reached 20% of GDP.

4 The most prominent symbol of this control was Soviet Marshall Konstantin Rokossovsky (albeit of Polish ethnic origins) who was the Polish Minister of Defense and head of the armed forces between 1948 and 1956. In 1956 he was sent packing back to the Soviet Union.

5 Poland developed its own military doctrine starting in 1961. Pursuant to this doctrine, the country developed fairly substantial internal/territorial defense troops. Presumed to be used against NATO, these forces could also be used against a potential Soviet intervention. In terms of equipment, since the early 1960s Poland and Czechoslovakia co-produced a wheeled armored personal carrier (APC) SKOT, superior to its Soviet BTR 60/70 equivalent.

32 *Defending Eastern Europe*

6 The formal and informal mechanisms of Soviet control over Polish military were described by Col. Ryszard Kuklinski, a high ranking Polish General Staff officer who was recruited by US intelligence and late defected to the United States. See "Soviet Penetration of the Polish Military," declassified document, at http://bi.gazeta.pl/im/5/6056/m6056505.pdf, accessed March 26, 2017. The mechanisms included the existence of a Soviet liaison mission with high-level access to all the relevant documents, a constant Soviet supervision over and formal ability to evaluate the performance of Polish officers and units in terms of "military readiness," and access to information from social and friendship networks, wiretapping, and use of intelligence agents among Polish military. Clearly, similar mechanisms were used in the Czechoslovak and Hungarian cases.

7 The so-called "Seven Days to the Rhine" 1979 war plan/hypothetical scenario was typical of these plans. Czechoslovak troops were expected to co-participate in the Soviet strike against southern West Germany, the Poles were to attack northern West Germany, Denmark, and Holland in a strike supportive of the Soviet main offensive on the right flank, and Hungary was to attack Austria alongside with Soviet forces stationed in Hungary. This war plan, presumably a counter against a NATO nuclear first-strike against Poland, also involved the lavish use of Soviet nuclear weapons against targets in Germany, Belgium, Denmark, and Austria (Mizokami 2016). This war plan was revealed by Polish Minister of Defense, Radoslaw Sikorski, in 2005, with the actual documents released in 2006.

8 Polish armed forces were the largest, with around 347,000 troops and 15 mechanized or armored divisions (in 1988), and included specialized Air Forces, Naval Forces, and Air/Territorial Defense Forces. The Czechoslovak military was the second largest with 201,000 troops (in 1987) and ten divisions, and was by far the best equipped (for instance, it had 4,585 tanks as opposed to Poland's 3,300, and the best aircraft, including Soviet Mig-23s and Su-25s). The East German military was similar to Czechoslovakia's plus the Navy. Finally, the Hungarian military, with approximately 106,000 soldiers and six divisions was by far the smallest and the least well-equipped among the East-Central European militaries on the eve of the transformation. Also, the Hungarian military merged its Air and Air Defense Forces into one service.

9 By Western standards a stunningly high percentage of the respective countries' military budgets were devoted to equipment procurement, especially in the high-spending Czechoslovakia, where in 1983 an astonishing 59% of the military budget is presumed to have been devoted to procurement, most of it from domestic manufacturers. Poland was a middle-level spender, which systematically increased its military spending as compared to the 1960s in the 1970s and continued to increase the military budget in the early 1980s, with procurement constituting 46% of the spending, most of it (53%) from domestic manufacture. While Hungary was a low-spender, it also devoted 46% of its budget to procurement, with the crushing majority of it (81%) devoted to imports of military equipment.

Cold War security in Eastern European states   33

10 See Verona (1989). More recent historiography indicate Gheorghiu-Dej's enduring quest for Romania's autonomous nationalist-communist development free of Soviet tutelage as deeper motivation for his crafty diplomatic game leading to Soviet withdrawal (see Mastny and Byrne 2005, 12).

11 Even in Bulgaria, in 1965 Zhivkov had to face an attempted pro-Chinese military coup led by a Stalinist-nationalist faction of Bulgarian communist party – essentially, an attempt to establish a Romanian-style communism (see Crampton 2005, 193). A prospect of a Chinese-led Bulgarian-Romanian-Albanian-Yugoslavian anti-Soviet bloc apparently worried the Soviets no end (Baev 2008).

12 Bulgaria was second to Hungary as the weakest member of the WTO by any objective measures of military power. In the 1985 World Power Index classification, Poland was 29th, Romania 42nd, GDR 44th, Czechoslovakia 49th, Bulgaria 68th, and Hungary 71st. The USSR had second place in the world, after the United States. Notice that WTO members featured one superpower, the USSR, one middle-size power, Poland, and, essentially, the rest were small powers (Nelson 1986, 59–60).

13 Nelson (1986, 116).

14 Several myths surround the Solidarity crisis, including a widespread notion that the Soviets planned an outright military invasion of Poland in December 1980, only to be deterred by a threat of US political retaliation. More recent research shows that that there was no imminent Soviet/Warsaw Pact invasion threat either in December 1980 or in December 1981.

15 The operation involved at least 70,000 soldiers, and 30,000 police personal. Around 10,000 people were detained, and 56 killed. This was by far the largest operation conducted by the Polish military since World War II.

16 Most recent research indicates that Jaruzelski, far from trying to avoid the Soviet invasion, which was actually not on the cards, begged the Soviets to intervene to prop up his crackdown, which succeeded way beyond expectations.

17 On October 25, 1989 referring to the Frank Sinatra song "My Way," the Soviet Foreign Ministry spokesman Gennadi Gerasimov retrospectively expressed Soviet approval of the then ongoing transition to liberal democracy in Poland, Hungary, and presaged Soviet approval for incoming revolutions in East Germany and Czechoslovakia.

18 The revolt was undoubtedly supported by Gorbachev. In a telling development, in the middle of the revolt the United States encouraged the Soviets to intervene in Romania to overthrow Ceauşescu (Mastny and Byrne 2005: 68).

3

Anti-communist revolutions and the emergence of states responsible for their own defense

Jacek Lubecki

When the shackles of communist ideology and subjugation to the Soviet Union were thrown off, the initial thrust of defense and security policies of the newly liberated countries was not toward joining NATO and the EU.[1] Two ideological themes which initially dominated the post-communist narratives, nationalism and idealistic, anti-militaristic liberalism, were not friendly to highly institutionalized forms of security and defense cooperation represented by these two organizations. This was a (brief) age of either fragmentation or dreams of a liberal-internationalist utopia.

Nationalism was the subtext of the entire process of the collapse of communism, which, for the publics in question, was conceived as a rejection of an alien ideology, foreign domination, or both. The latter was definitely the case for all of the non-Russian WTO members and seceding republics of the Soviet Union, where the collapse of the Soviet empire was celebrated as an opportunity to exercise true national self-determination in terms of both domestic political order and international sovereignty. In Yugoslavia, the constituent nations asserted their sovereignty against a domestic order perceived as repressive of them all. As attempts to restructure the state on a confederal and liberal basis crumbled, a long nightmare of "wars of Yugoslavian succession" followed.

Significantly, in ambiguous cases of "national communism" in Albania and Romania, the transition to post-communism was also more abstruse and longer than in other countries of the region. In Albania, ousting of the ruling party was not accomplished until 1992, only to be followed by an internal collapse of the state in 1997 and restoration of order through foreign intervention. In Romania the collapse of communism was a murky and violent affair which featured a genuine popular upheaval from below, elements of a military coup/mutiny and ambiguous foreign interference.[2] What followed was the hegemonic rule of a former communist apparatchik, Ion Iliescu, who, as the head of the Social Democratic Party, dominated Romanian politics until 2004, creating a system which did not feature a clean break with

Revolutions and the emergence of states 35

the communist past. Even more ambiguous was the special case of the ex-Soviet Socialist Republic of Moldova, which became independent with the collapse of the Soviet Union in 1991, and immediately had to confront an ethno-secessionist conflict in the breakaway region of Transnistria.

In the "normal" cases of post-communist transformation, which included all of the northern tier of WTO members (East Germany, Poland, Czechoslovakia, and Hungary), the Baltic republics, and Bulgaria, nationalism was a subtext of the process which sought to create liberal polities featuring free elections, free markets, and civil rights and liberties. Since the break from communism in all these countries avoided major outbreaks of organized violence, and the countries faced no clear prospects of an armed aggression or conflict, the liberal imperative was also attached to an assertive anti-militaristic and anti-power politics ideological streak, typical of the aftermath of all liberal revolutions.[3] This was especially the case, since communism featured extreme forms of militaristic power politics, which the ideology of anti-communist dissent identified as a part of a "global coalition of aggressive imbecility," or warmongering militarism, East and West (Konrád 1984, 217). Rejection of militarism was universal and with this came suspicion of military institutions, alliances, and preparations for war. As just exemplified by the largely bloodless collapse of the Soviet empire, the power of ideas and "human spirit" was considered superior to material power of coercion (Havel and Keane 1985, 21).

Liberal dreams were confronted with a devastating reality and seeming superiority of military power in the former Yugoslavia. After a decade-long process of institutional decay in the 1980s, and a failure of efforts to negotiate a transition into a loose liberal-democratic confederation in the first half of 1991, the country's formal break-up began on June 25, 1991 with Slovenia and Croatia proclaiming independence. The Yugoslav federal military (Yugoslav People's Army, Jugoslovenska narodna armija, JNA), was the one institution of the failing state with a pre-existing will, plan, and means to coercively resist the breakup. Accordingly, JNA 5th Military District troops attempted a muddily conceived massive show of force by deploying to key strategic points of Slovenia to intimidate the secessionists. Faced with the determined and well-planned asymmetric armed resistance of the Slovene Territorial Forces (Slovene: Teritorialna Obramba Republike Slovenije, TORS) the JNA actions failed miserably during a "Ten Day War" between June 27 and July 7, 1991. This was, in essence, that last and only "war" fought by the JNA, which was soon wrecked by desertions of conscripts and officers from constituent nationalities, and set adrift among political forces which sought to create separate states out of the six republics of the quickly disintegrating Yugoslavia. Dominated by Serbian and Montenegrin officers and Non Commissioned Officers, the JNA ended

36   *Defending Eastern Europe*

up putting most of its formidable skills and equipment at the service of the Serbian nationalistic project led by Serbia's Machiavellian leader Slobodan Milošević (Hadic 2002; Niebuhr 2004).[4]

The Slovenian war of independence, with around 70 killed and 200 wounded, was just an opening salvo for a series of "wars of Yugoslavian succession" which were waged in Croatia (mostly in the second half of 1991 and then in mid-1995), then in Bosnia (1992–5), Kosovo (1996–2000, mostly in 1999), and Macedonia (2001). By the end of the horror, these wars had killed around 140,000 people (most of these, some 100,000, in Bosnia, many of them civilians executed as a part of Serbian campaign of mass killing)[5] and generated around two million refugees and two million internally displaced people, mostly in and from Bosnia. All of this amounted to the largest armed conflict in Europe since World War II, which, while smaller in terms of human suffering than the earlier European conflicts,[6] or compared to wars occurring simultaneously in the Global South,[7] was a sobering reminder of the importance of military power and weakness of liberal institutions and norms in the world. Especially, the impotence of Western European countries[8] and international institutions which missed firm elements of military power and political resolve, such as the EC (later, EU), CSCE (later, OSCE), and the UN was dramatically and serially exposed in the course of mostly futile and byzantine diplomatic negotiations and peacekeeping operations which failed to create peace and solutions to the conflicts.

Conversely, naked military force settled the Yugoslavian conflicts. Decisive armed confrontations occurred in 1994–5. First, Croat military forces, superbly re-organized and armed after their humiliating defeat by JNA/Serbian troops in 1991 crushed the Serbs in Kraijna in a series of fast mechanized offensives (operations "Flash" and "Storm," the largest military operations in Europe since World War II) in Croatia. Then, in 1995 combined Croat and Bosniak forces systematically defeated and pushed back Bosnian Serbs, which were also selectively bombed by NATO aviation, and were forced to accept a compromise peace offered in the Dayton Accords in November 1995. Finally, in spring 1999, the Serbian counter-insurgency campaign against Kosovo Albanians was stopped by the Albanian guerilla force of Kosovo Liberation Army backed by a massive NATO air campaign. What followed was a negotiated Serb withdrawal from Kosovo and deployment of heavy NATO/KFOR troops in the summer of 1999, leading to eventual Kosovo independence in 2008. In all cases, "NATO" operations were decisively led, manned, and equipped by the United States. Only in the 2001 case, the armed revolt of Macedonia Albanians against the government led by Macedonia's Slavic majority, the EU-sponsored negotiations and attempts at compromise peace seemed to have been of importance, eventually leading

Revolutions and the emergence of states 37

to a political settlement and (uneasy) cessation of hostilities. However, even in this case the ability of the Macedonian government – supported and partially armed by Bulgaria – to mount a vigorous military response to the insurgency, forced the Albanian fighters to a negotiated solution.

The effect and lessons of the Yugoslavian conflict on the world, but especially the West and post-communist Europe, were in many ways decisive in conveying the imperative of NATO expansion into the former communist countries. In the case of the Western Balkans (former Yugoslav countries and Albania), the countries most aligned with the West during the wars of Yugoslavian succession (essentially, all of them except Serbia and Republika Srpska in Bosnia), had an obvious motivation to pursue membership in Western security institutions, especially NATO, which offered "hard" security guarantees backed by force. Still, these countries had to overcome external and internal legacies of the armed conflict,[9] and had to wait until the 2000s to be considered for NATO and EU memberships.[10] The former WTO member countries, though, faced no such strong imperative and legacy, and it was up to domestic political processes – mostly democratically negotiated – to establish a political consensus on the quest for NATO and EU memberships. These processes developed differently in each of the countries, influenced by both international factors of divergence and convergence, and domestic variables encompassed by the various defense policy formation frameworks. All of these countries embraced the goal of NATO membership relatively early in the 1990s. Ambiguities of the process that led to these decisions, first in East-Central Europe, then in the West (the United States), in the Western Balkans, and, finally, among the Baltic countries, are examined below.

The first East-Central European entrant to NATO was East Germany, admitted in 1990 as a result of German unification and international treaties associated with it. These included a formal agreement that unified Germany would be a member of NATO, in exchange for informal but clear German and US pledges to the Soviet Union that NATO would not expand further to the east. Instead of NATO the United States promised to make CSCE the centerpiece of all-European security architecture that would also incorporate the Soviet Union.[11] As a result of German unification, the West German military (the Bundeswehr) inherited the impressive military forces and equipment of the East German Military (Nationale Volksarmee or NVA), which by the 1980s were considered the best equipped and trained forces of the WTO (Trainor 1988). Tellingly, the challenge of integrating the NVA into the Bundeswehr proved to be formidable because of totally different conceptual, cultural, and material matrices underlying the respective armed forces, but the lessons of this experience for the later expansion of NATO were largely ignored (Young 2017, 50). Also, with Germany unified, the

38 *Defending Eastern Europe*

West seemingly lost interest in decisively managing security issues in post-communist Europe, mired in political and economic complexities of transition (Asmus 2002, 20). This inward turn of the West was highlighted by the electoral victory of Bill Clinton in the United States in November 1992, as he promised to focus on US domestic issues, especially the economy. A similar inward focus in Western Europe was symbolized by the signing of the Maastricht Treaty in February of the same year. This treaty, which created the EU out of the EC, was a victory for the French-led project of European "deepening" rather than its "widening."

In the meantime, between roughly 1990 and 1992, the former WTO members had to focus on asserting their defense autonomy, securing the withdrawal of Soviet troops (which did not leave Poland until September 1993), and the dissolution of the WTO (formalized in July 1991 at a ceremony in Prague). They also had to resist attempts by Russia to secure residual rights and constraints on their sovereignty, including formal pledges not to join NATO or the EC – the only country to sign (but not ratify) this type of a treaty, was, bizarrely and characteristically, Iliescu's Romania, but the treaty was nullified by the collapse of the USSR by the end of 1991.

As mentioned earlier, at the beginning of post-communist transformation the zeitgeist was not to enlarge NATO but to create a new, all-inclusive and idealist security architecture for Europe. Such was, after all, the nature of Western (US) promises to the Soviet Union, the dominant ideology of dissenters in Eastern Europe, and the nature of Soviet/Gorbachev's expectations. Accordingly, in the early spring of 1990 Czechoslovak Foreign Minister Jiri Dienstbier formally put forward a proposal to reform the CSCE and create a "European Security Commission" which would replace both NATO and the WTO – an idea seconded by Czechoslovak President Václav Havel at an April 1990 meeting of Polish, Hungarian, and Czechoslovak leaders, and in May 1991 during a speech at the Council of Europe (Wallat 2001/2, 15–16). The November 1990 Paris Summit of the CSCE seemingly confirmed the continuous expansion of this diplomatic idea by issuing a "Charter of Paris for a New Europe" which promised a reform of the CSCE to become a meaningful pan-European security organization.[12] This, however, was probably the high tide of CSCE dreams. As 1991 brought in the outbreak of wars of Yugoslavian succession in June, and the Soviet coup in August, elites and peoples of post-communist countries were exposed to the stark realities of nationalist violence and authoritarian backsliding. Manifestly, neither the CSCE nor the EC – just experiencing a bout of "deepening" led by the Franco-German tandem – were in position to provide hard security guarantees for the newly liberated countries.

Faced with risky and costly prospects of defense autonomy and, perhaps, long-term neutrality, sections of new political elites in East-Central European

Revolutions and the emergence of states   39

countries soon embraced the notion of a possibility of NATO membership or, at least, NATO security guarantees for their countries. If one is to believe in Ronald A. Asmus' accounts (he was one of the intellectual parents of the NATO expansion idea), as early as June 1990 during a RAND co-hosted sub-ministerial level security conference in Warsaw[13] (so, when the WTO was still formally in existence and Soviet troops were in Poland), Polish anti-communist civilian politicians, and communist-trained uniformed military officers serving under the Polish Minister of Defense, communist General Florian Siwicki,[14] openly asked their US interlocutors[15] about possible prospects of Polish membership in NATO and/or US troops being stationed on the Polish soil as a "security guarantee." Interestingly, while the civilians justified their request by referring to shared values of freedom and democracy "defended by NATO," the military officers were uninterested in values or NATO, simply asking for "US troops" – a stark reminder of their way of thinking in terms of hard power and bilateral alliances. This episode, however, was apparently isolated – during their later contacts with the West in 1991 both the Polish President Lech Wałęsa (elected in December 1990) and Foreign Minister Skubiszewski did not mention NATO membership, referring to neutrality as Poland's official strategic stance, and the CSCE as their preferred institutional platform for security and conflict resolution in Europe.

In the meantime, however, the thinking of both Hungarian and Czech foreign policy elites, both firmly in the hands of anti-communist forces, was evolving very quickly. As early as late 1990 and early 1991 the Hungarian Prime Minister József Antall and Alexandr Vondra, Czechoslovak foreign policy advisor to President Havel, were exploring prospects of NATO membership or a "special" relationship between NATO and Czechoslovakia and Hungary respectively. By spring 1991 the Polish center-right Center Alliance Party (led by the Kaczyński brothers)[16] made Poland's membership in NATO a part of their electoral platform. Since right-wing parties won the first fully free Polish parliamentary elections of fall 1991, by 1992 Poland had a right-wing government of Jan Olszewski openly and officially calling for Polish membership in NATO. Membership in NATO also became institutionalized as the goal of Polish foreign and defense policy in the Polish National Security Strategy *Principles of Polish Security Policy, and Security Policy and Defense Strategy of the Polish Republic.*[17] However, Polish President Lech Wałęsa, almost perennially in conflict with Poland's parliamentary governments[18] did not support the idea at the time, instead floating (in March 1992) a notion that all former members of the WTO minus Russia should form a new military alliance organization called "NATO-bis." Mercurial Wałęsa changed his mind by May 5, 1992, when in Prague, Wałęsa, Havel, and Antall jointly declared that the quest for NATO membership was on their countries' official diplomatic agendas.

40 *Defending Eastern Europe*

The May 1992 Prague declaration did not settle the issue, but was just an opening salvo in the "battle for NATO" of the East-Central European trio, soon to become (after the split of Czechoslovakia) the "Visegrád Four." On the one hand, the West, the United States, and NATO were not ready to even begin the process of accession, but responded with vague positive statements of encouragement. On the other hand, post-communist countries were volatile new democracies and their consensus of May 1992 reflected simply the leadership in place at the time. In the subsequent years the guard in charge of the countries was to change, and the goal of joining NATO had to survive the leadership changes.

By 1993, battered by difficulties of economic reform pursued simultaneously in the fairly developed Czech and much poorer Slovak parts of the country, Czechoslovakia split, and the governments of newly established countries had to re-establish their own separate consensus on foreign and defense policy goals. The consensus on the desirability of joining NATO was quickly continued in the Czech Republic in 1994, but not in Slovakia, where under the rule of authoritarian nationalist-populist Vladimír Mečiar (1993–8) the country became shunned by Western institutions and toyed with pro-Russian or neutralist foreign policy orientations, while maintaining a nominal push for NATO membership (Radio Free Europe/Radio Liberty 1997). As a result, Slovakia was not allowed to enter NATO in the first tranche of the candidate countries in 1999, and was only admitted together with the Baltic countries, Bulgaria, Slovenia, and Romania in 2004, after anti-Mečiar opposition took power and led the country into a firmly pro-NATO and pro-EU direction.

In Poland, the pro-NATO center-right government of various former anti-communist forces was defeated, humiliatingly, in the fall 1993 parliamentary elections by an electoral alliance SLD (Sojusz Lewicy Democratycznej – Alliance of Democratic Left) representing ex-communist political forces and an electorate with a positive view of the communist past. The new government elite in their electoral and other pronouncements was initially skeptical about the goal of NATO membership for Poland. Indeed, SLD leader Aleksander Kwaśniewski called NATO "a relic of cold war" (Lis 1999, 249–51). It took a victory of a pro-Western and pro-US faction (led by Jerzy Wiatr and Longin Pastusiak, long-time communist-era Polish experts on the United States) among the SLD leadership in late 1993/early 1994, for the ex-communist to embrace NATO membership as a Polish national security goal. Later, in 1999, Kwaśniewski, as president of Poland, enthusiastically led the country into NATO, and then presided over Poland's outsized participation in US- or NATO-led expeditionary deployments to Iraq, Afghanistan, and a dozen other locations.

Revolutions and the emergence of states

Similarly to Poland, in 1994 Hungary the ex-communist left organized in the Hungarian Socialist Party (MSZP, Magyar Szocialista Párt) defeated, overwhelmingly, the ruling Hungarian Democratic Forum party of former dissidents, and took power. However, unlike in Poland, the political unanimity on seeking membership in NATO was not a matter of dispute in Hungarian politics, where a consensus on this issue among the otherwise bitterly competitive six main political parties was achieved already in 1993, and was institutionalized in the "Basic Principles of the Defense Policy of the Republic of Hungary" (Peterson and Lubecki 2019, 86).

Clearly, by early 1994, the pursuit of NATO membership was firmly established as the foreign policy goal of three East-Central European countries. By then, this idea was also accepted by the West – chiefly the United States, but also Germany, two pro-NATO expansion champions – as a question of not "whether" but "when."

The US decision to expand NATO was made by President Clinton's cabinet and foreign policy-making bureaucracies based primarily on strategic considerations. Fear of Europe adrift and of loss of US leadership was the central motivating factor here, and it began to be clearly articulated in 1993, as the initial confusion following the end of the Cold War gave way to a growing understanding that NATO must find new members and new missions or face institutional atrophy, and, ultimately, extinction. Articulated in Senator Richard Lugar's famous adage "out of area or out of business," first expressed on June 24, 1993, the geostrategic imperative of expansion was originally coined by three RAND Corporation analysts, Stephen Larrabee, Ronald Asmus, and Richard Kugler, in late 1992 and widely disseminated in 1993, culminating in their famous *Foreign Affairs* article in the fall of 1993 (Asmus et al. 1993). Their ideas were embraced by key personalities in the National Security Council (Anthony Lake and his speechwriter Jeremy Rosner) and the State Department (Lynn Davis and, later, Richard Holbrooke) (Sperling 2001, 125).[19] However, the Pentagon's opposition and Ambassador Strobe Talbott's concern about Russia's reaction led to a considerable slowdown in the process and compromises embodied in the 1993 Partnership for Peace[20] and Russia-NATO "Founding Act"[21] ideas (Waller and McAllister 1997, 58). These institutional detours, however, could not stop the momentum for expansion that by January 1994 became an officially proclaimed policy, which included a "dual-track" component: conciliation of Russia and NATO expansion.

A romantic story that we find in some accounts tells us that Clinton made up his mind alone, after Havel's and Wałęsa's pleading during the opening of the Holocaust museum in April 1993 (Waller and McAllister 1997). Strobe Talbott, however, does not mention this story in his memoirs (Talbott 2002). More credibly, the president responded to the pre-expansion voices

42 *Defending Eastern Europe*

at the NSC and State Department in the middle of 1993, while Talbott's and the Pentagon's objections, in the fall of 1993, led to the Partnership for Peace (PfP) idea accepted at the Travemünde NATO summit of October 20, 1993. While Yeltsin loved the PfP, Wałęsa hated it, expressing his displeasure to Madeleine Albright in January 1994, and leading the United States to an official reformulation of PfP goals from substitute for, to an entry hall into, NATO. The pro-NATO expansion cause found additional US allies with the Republican Party ascendancy in US politics in 1994.[22] Indeed, the GOP added a pro-NATO expansion item on the 1994 electoral "Contract with America" platform. That the decision that NATO expansion was not a question of "if" but of "when and where" was announced publicly by Clinton in January 1994 in Prague at a summit meeting with leaders of the Visegrád countries. Given bipartisan and decisive bureaucratic support for NATO expansion into East-Central European in the United States, the rest of Western members of NATO were sure to follow.

In the Balkans – the countries of Romania, Moldova, and Bulgaria; and in Yugoslavia's neighbor Albania – the post-communist formulation of the respective countries' foreign and defense policy strategies was a reflection of these countries' internal characteristics which differed significantly from the ones in East-Central Europe. All four of them were relatively poor and small countries. Albania was, in 1990, the poorest country in Europe, featuring the worst type of a Stalinist regime, a delayed transition to democracy, and, after the fall of communism, a weak state, hardly able to maintain internal control. Impoverished Romania was recovering from the last years of Ceauşescu's insanity, and, under Iliescu, featured a regime akin to Mečiar's Slovakia. Bulgaria, with its close ties with the Soviet Union and Russia, and a near-absence of anti-communist opposition prior to 1989, featured a public opinion and elites severely split between pro-Western liberal orientation, and pro-Russian conservatives, who shunned NATO. Moldova, alike the Baltics, emerged from the break-up of the Soviet Union as country deprived of any military power, and, unlike the Baltics, Moldova had to immediately face the armed secession of the country's Slavic minority in the region of Transnistria. This conflict, unresolved to this day, immediately complicated Moldova's security situation – just like Ukraine and Georgia, Moldova has remained as a country too weak and internally torn to pursue NATO membership vigorously, or to be desirable by the West/the United States as a stable security partner.

The Bulgarian case is an interesting one, as the country featured, essentially, no organized anti-communist opposition with the exception of the Turkish minority, victimized by Todor Zhivkov's regime during 1984 and 1988–9 anti-Turkish nationalist campaigns (Rossi 2002). The regime therefore fell as a result of an intra-communist factional struggle and a

Revolutions and the emergence of states 43

palace coup, whereby an anti-Zhivkov reformist faction of the Bulgarian Communist Party (Bëlgarska Komunističeska Partija, BKP) led by Petar Mladenov took power in early December 1989, and liberalized the country from above (Petrescu 2014, 254–74). Only subsequent to this coup oppositional movements, united mostly in an electoral alliance called the Union of Democratic Forces (SDS, Sayuz na Demokratichnite Sili), materialized and contested democratic elections, which, in a context of parliamentary democracy, and proportional electoral rules, resulted in a fairly volatile pluralistic political system featuring shifting party alliances and a good level of governmental instability.

Soon, Bulgarian politics became torn in a constant electoral back-and-forth between the SDS and "reformed" ex-communists of the Bulgarian Socialist Party (Bulgarska Sotsialisticheska Partiya, BSP), with the former embracing a clear pro-Western orientation, while the latter, unlike Polish and Hungarian ex-communists, were against Bulgarian membership in Western security institutions (Dimitrova 2001, 35). In that last respect, the Bulgarian Socialist Party enjoyed a determined and numerically strong support of fairly Russophile and anti-Western sections of Bulgarian public opinion (Alexe 2016). With a lack of a firm domestic political consensus or prior efforts at preparation for NATO membership Bulgaria was rejected to be a member of a first tranche of newly admitted NATO members in 1999, and was only admitted in 2004 (Simon 1998). By then, the country was ruled by a new political force – a liberal populist party led by the former Tzar of Bulgaria (1943–6) Simeon the 2nd (Simeon Sakskoburggotski) who returned from exile and won a crushing victory at 2001 parliamentary elections as a head of a new National Movement Simeon the 2nd (Nacionalno Dviženie Simeon Vtoroi, NDSV). Today, Bulgaria is a part of NATO, but Western suspicions of the country's strong ties to Russia remain.

While Romania avoided the political volatility and lack of consensus characteristic of Bulgarian politics, it did so at the expense of democracy. The National Salvation Front (Frontul Salvării Naţionale, FSN) was an alliance of second tier communist apparatchiks which emerged from the muddy and bloody maelstrom of the 1989 revolution and gained the endorsement of mutinied Romanian military, to win the 1990 elections, and emerge, under Ion Iliescu, as the hegemonic force in Romanian politics until 2004. Claiming a "social democratic" ideology as head of a "social democratic" (Partidul Social Democrat, PSD) party, Iliescu and his semi-authoritarian clique presided over a corrupt political order which left already impoverished and decaying Romania without a clear sense of political direction. While defeated in 1996 presidential elections by a pro-Western/pro-liberal Romanian Democratic Convention (Romanian: Convenţia Democrată Română) led by Emil Constantinescu, Iliescu and his party managed to

44   *Defending Eastern Europe*

return to power in 2001, after Constantinescu's "shock therapy" economic reforms led a to a mass public backlash. In this case, both Iliescu (since 1993) and Constantinescu (after 1996) expressed a Romanian desire to join NATO, backed by a majority Romanian public opinion and political forces, but both Romanian will and resources to implement the needed defense reforms, and the Western acceptance of Romania as a desirable security partner, were not there to allow Romania in the first tranche of entrants in 1999 (Berdila 2005). In the end, Romania's defense sector was reformed, and the country was admitted into NATO under the second Iliescu administration in 2004. Today, as we will see in subsequent chapters, Romania is the Eastern Balkans' "Poland" – a country suspicious of Russia, and with a strong commitment to its military buildup and membership in NATO and alliance with the United States, and membership in the European Union Common Security and Defense Policy.

Moldova is included in this study because of the country's connection to Romania, as Romania's hostility to Russia cannot be understood without a discussion of Moldova. Moldova, or its part west of the river Dniester, which is the majority of Moldova's territory, is a part of historical/cultural Romania, constituting the geographical core of the principality of Moldova since the fourteenth century. However, most of the area (also known as Bessarabia) was included in Russia in 1812, after a Russo-Ottoman war. In 1917–18 the area's mostly Romanian-speaking population demanded independence, and, then, became unified with Romania in the 1920–40 period. However, the Soviet Union never recognized the "loss of Bessarabia" and proclaimed their own "Molodovian Socialist Republic" as a part of USSR, creating (from scratch) a territorial unit East of Dniester (so, not a part of historical Moldova) as an expression of Soviet territorial claims. Then, in 1940, pursuant to the Molotov-Ribbentrop Pact Stalin annexed Romanian Moldova, creating a "Moldovan Soviet Socialist Republic" as a part of the USSR including the eastern enclave, where the majority of population were not Moldovan/Romanian speakers. By 1945, as a result of victory in World War II, the Soviet Moldova – an uneasy matchup of actual historical Moldova and areas east of the river Dniester (Transnistria) – was finally made a part of the Soviet Union.

When the Soviet Union started disintegrating and fell, and Moldova proclaimed independence, the country was stuck with artificial ethno-cultural boundaries, and an impossible political dilemma – the country's Romanian majority wanted its own state and perhaps reunification with Romania, while the Slavic (mostly, Russian) speaking majority of Transnistrians did not want to be a part of independent Moldova, but the boundaries of the country followed the Soviet administrative diktat. The obvious solution (autonomy for Transnistria) was not successfully negotiated, and brief but

Revolutions and the emergence of states   45

very violent (around 1,000 dead, 3,000 wounded) war between Moldovan armed forces (quickly created out of former Soviet soldiers and equipment) and Transnistrian separatists backed by the heavy weapons of the Russian 14th Army and Russian volunteers from the rest of former USSR erupted between March and July 1992. In the conflict Moldovan forces were supported by Romanian weapons, officers, and volunteers.

While the ceasefire was negotiated in July 1992, the conflict over Transnistria was never settled, and the Pridnestrovian Moldavian Republic (PMR) continues to exist, not recognized by any member of the UN (including Russia), but recognized by other similar units in the post-Soviet space, including republics of Abkhazia and South Ossetia. In the meantime, post-communist Moldova emerged as the poorest country of Europe (replacing Albania in that role), burdened with dramatic economic problems, corruption, and an unstable political system dramatically split between pro-Russian and pro-Western forces. Moldovan politics featured, among others, an electoral victory of the (unreformed) Communist Party of the Republic of Moldova (Partidul Comuniștilor din Republica Moldova, PCRM) in 2000 elections, and a recent (2019) constitutional crisis with two competing prime ministers, both claiming legal authority. Most importantly from our point of view, while some progress on Moldovan integration into the EU has been made, the country achieved no internal consensus or, seemingly, public majority in support for Moldovan membership in NATO,[23] even though the country joined the PfP in 1994, and signed an association agreement with the EU in 2014. Finally, the Moldovan Constitution (Article 11) states that "The Republic of Moldova proclaims its permanent neutrality. The Republic of Moldova does not allow the deployment of armed forces of other states on its territory" (Moldova 2006). This seems to formally preclude NATO membership for Moldova, barring a change in its constitution.

Moving on back to the Western Balkans, the fact that Albania finally achieved NATO membership in 2009 borders on a miracle, given what the country was in 1989/90. Albania emerged from the worst Stalinist dictatorship in Europe as the poorest country on the continent, and, by 1997, became the continent's weakest when it essentially fell apart in the wake of the collapse of financial pyramid schemes and the collapse of organized government in the early part of the year. This was the result of the country's failed democratic transition between 1992 and 1997, when the anti-communist government of Democratic Party leader and president of Albania Sali Berisha, tried, unsuccessfully, to reform the country. The anarchy that followed in January–March 1997 featured multi-pronged violent clashes between various (mostly, tribal, regional and local) armed factions and gangs, which eventually killed around 2,000 people and

46   *Defending Eastern Europe*

devastated the entire country. Order was only restored by a multinational armed intervention organized by the UN and led by Italy (operation "Alba"), enforcing order with a force of 7,000 troops between April and August 1997. These forces were replaced by West European Union police units afterwards.

While tragic, the events of 1997 allowed the Albanian state to be reconstructed under international tutelage, essentially from scratch, and launched in a more positive direction. Most importantly, the country's armed forces were reconstructed, turning them into a small, professional light infantry force, supported by minimal air force and navy, actually serving the country's interest of internal stability/border control and international cooperation (Kubiak 2019). Under a more stable government, Albania was able to successfully begin the process of NATO accession in 1998, when the country received a Membership Action Plan, and formally joined NATO in 2009, after amply proving Albania's usefulness to NATO/the United States in deployments to Iraq, Afghanistan, and cooperation with Western security operations in Europe and the Middle East.[24] What helped was the near unanimity of Albanian political forces and people on the desirability of NATO membership, which in a country scarred by instability and facing potentially hostile neighbors (Serbia, Macedonia) was not surprising.

Likewise, it was not surprising that the domestic will to join NATO materialized fairly quickly in the Baltic countries of Estonia, Latvia, and Lithuania. These three countries were swallowed by the Soviet Union as a result of the Molotov-Ribbentrop Pact and then, Soviet conquest in World War II, but their sense of national distinction led them to secede from the Soviet Union in 1990,[25] even before the country collapsed in 1991. Being small countries, with initially no armed forces, and featuring the presence of large Russian-speaking minorities (up to 30% in Latvia and Estonia, with a smaller ethnic Russian presence in Lithuania) and a giant Russian neighbor to the East and West (the Kalinigrad Oblast) it was natural for the Baltics to, as soon as possible, seek the closest possible association with the West and Western security guarantees, including NATO membership.[26] Lithuania, led by President Brazauskas,[27] made clear that it was seeking NATO membership when it joined the PfP in 1994 (Rupp 2002). Likewise, Estonia expressed the same will when it joined in the PfP in the same year (Luik 2019). Latvia, with the largest Russian minority in the region, also joined the PfP in 1994, but the firm domestic course to join NATO membership was only established with a victory of pro-Western forces in 1998 parliamentary elections (Urbelis 2003, 3). For the West, it was not so much the Baltics' will or efforts at defense reform and cooperation, but the consideration of Russian hostility to the Baltic membership in NATO which delayed their membership until 2004.

Revolutions and the emergence of states

All in all, two of our broad theoretical frameworks help with understanding the early communist period: the convergence and divergence framework, and the policy formation framework.

Realism and the security imperative felt by ex-communist countries in the early post-communist period is clearly an obvious explanation of a convergence of foreign and defense policies of most post-communist countries in question – their need to seek powerful allies in the West, in the suddenly insecure environment of Europe. Importantly, in that early period it was not so much a threat of Russia that drove these countries to NATO, but a general fear of instability and wars as illustrated by wars of Yugoslavian succession. Manifestly, the same fear, plus a will to preserve US hegemony, seems to have driven the US decision-makers, reflecting President G.H.W. Bush's statement that in the post-Cold War era the enemy was "chaos."

The second factor of convergence was ideological: a widespread public consensus on the desirability of the liberal-democratic model of development felt by the people in post-communist countries. Just as in the case of security issues, initial dreams that ex-communist countries would pursue some type of "third way" model of development were very quickly discarded in favor of adopting the tested Western model. In this respect, the desire to join the "West" found its natural expression in joining the key European and North Atlantic security and economic institutions: NATO and the EU. Countries where this feeling was at the forefront, East-Central Europeans (except Slovakia) and the Baltics, had the least problems in finding a domestic consensus on NATO/EU membership.

It is within the realm of different domestic defense policy formation processes that we find most factors that explain divergences between different post-communist countries in their process of finding consensus, or lack thereof, in their search for NATO (and EU) memberships. These factors can be briefly conceptualized as a dialectic between forces of conservatism: either nationalistic or neo-communist, and pro-Western forces that sought quick integration into Western institutions. The process was the quickest where communism collapsed most thoroughly, leaving few political remnants capable of resistance against forces of Westernization: East Germany and Czechoslovakia (the Czech Republic) were the crown examples in this respect. Where ex-communists reformed and became, essentially, pro-Western forces (Poland and Hungary, and, perhaps, Lithuania and the rest of the Baltics), the will to join NATO/EU was equally strong. However, where powerful ex-communists were openly hostile to NATO (Bulgaria, Serbia) or initially sabotaged the prospects of NATO membership (Romania) the situation was different. Moldova, where ex-communist forces and public opinion remain opposed to NATO membership, illustrates the pattern vividly. Albania, where the domestic

48 *Defending Eastern Europe*

popular will and reconstructed state after 1997 were both pro-NATO, shows that the pattern of NATO expansion does not necessarily have to follow levels of political and economic development. Finally, the countries of former Yugoslavia follow the general pattern, with the caveat that each of them has had to face special considerations flowing from their varying legacies of the war of Yugoslavian succession, and different levels of political and economic development.

Finally, the alliance theory: institutional factors of convergence kick in when the countries in question started participating in the process of coming into Western defense and security institutions, which is the subject of our next chapter.

Notes

1 The EU did not exist under that name and form in 1989. It was only created by the Maastricht Treaty of 1992.

2 The revolt was undoubtedly supported by Gorbachev and the KGB. In a telling development, in the middle of the revolt the United States encouraged the Soviets to intervene in Romania to overthrow Ceauşescu (Mastny and Byrne 2005, 68).

3 For instance, after the eighteenth-century American Revolution, the dominant early Republican ideology rejected both militarism and traditional power politics (Gilbert 1961).

4 There were two nations in the former Yugoslavia who sought to revise the pre-existing administrative borders: the Serbs, who had a huge presence in Croatia and Bosnia, and the Albanians, present as a large majority in the province of Kosovo in the Republic of Serbia, and as a large minority in Macedonia. Both nations were mobilized and fought to either establish their own states and/or national unity or recognition against the other nations: the Serbs battled again Croats in Croatia and against Bosniaks (Bosnian Muslims) and Croats in Bosnia-Herzegovina; while Albanians fought against Serbs in Kosovo and against Slavic Macedonians in Macedonia. Both Serbs and Albanians failed in their project of national unification, but succeeded in carving out their own states or autonomous entities: a sovereign Kosovo for Albanians, and Republika Srbska as an autonomous constituent unit of the Bosnian Confederation in Bosnia. The one nationalist project which completely failed was the one of Serbs in Croatia, in the region of Kraijna. Their incipient state was destroyed in the course of Croat military operations in 1995, and the Serbs were forcibly removed or fled from Kraijna. The last, bloodless, act of Yugoslavian fragmentation was a secession of Montenegro from the Republic of Serbia and Montenegro in 2006. Thus, out of six constituent republics of communist Yugoslavia seven states emerged, all based on pre-existing administrative boundaries: Slovenia, Croatia, Bosnia, Serbia, Montenegro, Kosovo, and Macedonia.

Revolutions and the emergence of states 49

5 The hallmark of this campaign was a systematically planned and executed mass killing of around 8,000 Bosniak men and boys around Srebrenica, in Eastern Bosnia in July 1995. Srebrenica was one of the UN "safe zones" protected by Dutch peacekeepers who stood down when Bosnian Serbian troops overran the enclave, thus illustrating the UN's weakness in the face of atrocity. A similar drama had happened in 1994 in Rwanda, where genocide of Tutsis by Hutus were carried out in presence of UN peacekeepers who were ordered to stand down (Lebor 2006). As a side note, I am deliberately using the term "mass killing," preferring to use this neutral descriptive term instead of a legalistic and therefore controversial concept of "genocide."

6 In Yugoslavian territories World War II resulted in some one million victims (Ramet 1992, 255).

7 The Iran-Iraq War resulted in some one million dead, the series of interconnected conflicts in Democratic Republic of Congo-Rwanda-Burundi ("the African World War") between 1994 and today is estimated to have killed between 2.5 to 5 million people, the genocide in Darfur (2004–today) killed some 300,000, conflicts associated with "Global War on Terror" (Afghanistan, Iraq, etc.) resulted in between half a million and 1.5 million dead, and 250,000 to half a million dead is an estimated number of victims of the Syrian civil war.

8 Besides being typically feckless, Western Europeans were hopelessly deadlocked between vaguely pro-Serbian Great Britain and France, and pro-Croat/Slovenian Germany, Austria, and Italy. Besides paralyzing Western European/EC diplomatic efforts, this alignment dangerously reproduced World War I and World War II patterns of alliance (Ramet 1996, 243–74).

9 The wars of Yugoslavian succession are often misconstrued as "ethnic civil wars" fueled by pre-existing mass ethnic hatreds from below. In truth, these were often wars between established states or para-states, while ethnic nationalist projects were often imposed on reluctant populations by ex-communist reactionary elites who sought to remain in power and stifle democratic and liberal forces. As a result, with the partial exception of Slovenia and Macedonia, full-blown democracies and functioning economies emerged very slowly from the ruins of Yugoslavia. For the concept of reactionary nationalism see Synder (2000) and Gagnon (2004).

10 See subsequent chapters. On the plus side, these countries had substantial armed forces bloodied in recent armed conflict and carrying a positive legacy of Yugoslavian military culture (see Young 2017). Slovenia entered NATO in 2004, Croatia and Albania in 2009, Montenegro in 2017, and Macedonia in 2020.

11 At the same time, in private thinking and conversations, US policy-makers disdained CSCE and discussed the possibility of expanding NATO in the future. Still, there is zero evidence that the United States, or any actor, was actively planning to expand NATO at that early period. For the debate about the "broken pledge" see Itzkowitz (2016, 36–7 and 39).

12 Pursuant to the Charter, a Conflict Prevention Centre in Vienna was established in 1992, while consultative and conflict resolution/peacekeeping mechanisms

and institutions were created, etc. See, "Charter of Paris for the New Europe" at www.osce.org/mc/39516?download=true, and the website of the OSCE at www.osce.org/. In 1995, corresponding to its increasing institutionalization, the CSCE was renamed OSCE, and the organization remains in place as an important and, indeed, the largest regional security organization in the world, but, still, a poor shadow of what it was expected to become in the early 1990s projections that envisioned CSCE's own armed forces and a pan-European security scope.

13 To add to the irony, the conference was, apparently, hosted in the Presidential Palace in Warsaw, the building where the original WTO was signed in 1955. This building also hosted the NATO Warsaw summit of June 2016 (Asmus 2002, 15).

14 At the time, Poland was under a hybrid communist/post-communist government resulting from Polish negotiated transition and compromises reached in the early 1989 Roundtable Agreements. The compromise gave the presidency and "power" ministries of defense, foreign affairs, and the interior to communist officials. As a result General Jaruzelski, the author of the martial law of 1981, became the first president of post-communist Poland. The rest of the government, however, including prime ministership under Tadeusz Mazowiecki, was in the hands of anti-communist opposition.

15 Who included Supreme Commander of US Forces in Europe, Gen. John McCarthy and future Chair of the Joint Chiefs of Staff, Warsaw-born John Shalikashvilli.

16 By 2001 Jarosław and Lech Kaczyński were to become the unquestionable leaders of Poland's dominant right-wing party, Law and Justice (Prawo i Sprawiedliwość), which ruled Poland between 2005 and 2007 and has ruled it since 2015.

17 See *Security Policy and Defense Strategy of the Polish Republic 1992*, "Poland strives to gain membership in NATO" (Rzeczpospolita Polska 1992, 11).

18 Poland, like most post-communist countries, is a semi-presidential republic featuring a divided executive, with a popularly elected president and a prime minister based on parliamentary majority. This created a possibility of cohabitation – presidents and prime ministers of different parties. Lech Wałęsa tended to quarrel with prime ministers of whichever party, though.

19 Warren Christopher, Secretary of State in the first Clinton administration, was lukewarm to the idea of NATO expansion, but went along with it. Madeleine Albright, Clinton's Secretary of State in his second administration, was an enthusiastic and skilled architect of NATO expansion.

20 Partnership for Peace is a NATO program, formally created in 1994 and intended to build trust between NATO and non-NATO members in Europe and the former Soviet Union through joint military exercises, exchanges, and other acts of cooperation. The program is still in existence. See the program's website at www.nato.int/cps/en/natohq/topics_50349.htm, accessed January 1, 2020.

Revolutions and the emergence of states   51

21 The NATO–Russia Founding Act is a diplomatic agreement (not a formal treaty) between NATO and Russia, signed in 1997, to reassure Russia that NATO's actions in Europe are conducted in a spirit of friendship and cooperation, not hostility. The Act, contains, among others, mutual assurances that the agreeing parties do not see each other as enemies. For the text of the Founding Act, see www.nato.int/cps/en/natohq/official_texts_25470.htm?selectedLocale=en, accessed January 1, 2020.

22 In the mid-term 1994 elections, in response to Clinton's failed health reform push and other domestic issues, the Republican Party crushed the Democrats and took control of Congress.

23 A June 2018 poll found 43% of Molodovan respondents against NATO membership for the country, and 22% in favor of the membership. See Baltic Surveys/Gallup Organization for Republican National Institute 2018.

24 Albania is the only European country with a clear Muslim majority and the second such NATO member after Turkey. The perception of Albanian troops as Muslims apparently has helped tremendously in their deployments to Muslim-majority countries.

25 These secessionist moves were answered by violence and repression by Soviet forces, leading to tense standoffs and clashes – which, however, never degenerated into mass mutual organized violence.

26 According to Urbelis, in the 1991–3 period the Baltics took a strategic posture of "neutrality" because Russian armed forces were still present in the countries. "Neutrality" was thus just an expedient (see Urbelis 2003, 1–2).

27 Brazausakas was an ex-communist leader, who represented ex-communist political forces in Lithuania, analogous to Polish SLD and Hungarian MSZP. Just like in Poland and Hungary, and unlike in Bulgaria, both former dissident and former communist political forces in Lithuania had a consensus on seeking membership in NATO.

4

NATO: Partnership for Peace (PfP) and a staggered admission process

James W. Peterson

Alliance theory is vital in comprehending the admission process to NATO, the key Western defense organization dating back to 1949. The alliance offered a measure of reassurance to a Western world that was somewhat surprised by the eruption of an intense Cold War by the late 1940s. After the Cold War, the NATO alliance preconditions and requirements became a substitute for Soviet controls and a critical element for overcoming distances within the East European region. Additionally, the alliance has always struggled to integrate states with diverse ethnicities and political histories. Economic differences between states in the north and south of the European continent were apparent in the early days of the alliance, while a parallel regional division characterized the admission of former communist states in recent decades.

Alliance planners hoped for a convergence of capabilities and objectives among the many states that they admitted over time. However, divergences among 29 members were at times difficult to overcome. EU leaders also wrestled with factors such as the wide economic disparity between Estonia and Slovenia, on the one hand, and, on the other, Romania and Bulgaria.

Designing meaningful defense policies toward the new Russia became a major challenge for NATO leaders, especially given the shifts and uncertainties of the steps taken toward the region by President Boris Yeltsin. Realism, encompassed by convergence and divergence theory, would tell us that countries faced with different geopolitically defined positions vis-à-vis Russia will diverge with respect to their respective commitment to NATO, levels of defense spending, and perceptions of Russian threat. In turn, defense policy theory, with its heavy emphasis on the domestic variables that influence policy choices, is essential in understanding NATO successes and failures. For example, public attitudes and elite perspectives help inform conclusions about which states are adversaries and which allies. Devising fair and balanced defense policies toward and for the entire East European region required a sensible blend of insights derived from all three theoretical perspectives.

Organizational history of NATO and the postwar global order

Organizationally, NATO emerged in 1949 with membership admissions, an Allied Command Structure, and a new strategy to confront the aggressive Soviet posture in its immediate neighborhood to the east. Expectations centered on concern about Soviet leaders as a psychological threat whose tactics would center on blackmail of the traditional Western powers (Sayle 2019, 11–22). Significantly, French President Charles de Gaulle proposed that France, the United States, and United Kingdom manage the postwar security order, with NATO as a secondary tool. However, that tripartite concept died with construction of the Berlin Wall in 1961 (Sayle 2019, 50–75). Thus, the alliance in the next few decades became, in US eyes, the primary force in preserving a European power balance that supported American interests (Sayle 2019, 100). In the late 1960s, détente became a new theme that distilled a certain degree of hostility between the Cold War superpowers. What was the justification for the continuing existence of NATO, if the accords signed as a consequence in the 1970s sunk new roots of true cooperation between the Soviet Union and the United States? The American-led Western response indicated a decision to preserve the military strength of NATO but to provide it with a strong and new political role (Sayle 2019, 148–53). This was a prophetic decision in two ways. First, hostility returned on both sides in the 1980s, and the genuine military strength of the alliance was once again treasured. Second, the development of a meaningful political role prefigured the steps taken after 1991 to include a broadened set of new members that expand that political role.

Partnership for Peace (PfP) in the immediate post-Cold War period

In the 1990s, the Clinton administration worked with NATO leaders to develop a fully effective PfP that could be a path to full alliance membership for states that had just emerged from the cocoon of the loosely organized communist empire. The partners would take part in many alliance activities but not have a formal vote in decisions and proceedings. There really were four categories of states that were active in this process and that eventually did become full alliance members. The Baltic states of Estonia, Latvia, and Lithuania constituted the first category. Possessing a relatively high level of economic performance, they had actually been republics in the Soviet Union and subject to an influx of Russian citizens during Soviet times. They were restive and very prepared to move toward Western institutions (Eglitis 2008, 236). In the second category were Slovenia and Slovakia, two small new states that had emerged from larger federations. Slovakia had negotiated with the

54   *Defending Eastern Europe*

Czechs prior to joining the Czechoslovak federation in 1918, while Slovenia had worked with a number of ethnic groups to form Yugoslavia in 1920 (Banac 1984, 404). However, both felt betrayed by their experiences within their respective federations. Czech dominance over the Slovaks became apparent within a decade, although they were accorded an upgraded status during and after the 1968 Prague Spring reforms (Leff 1997, 64–6). Serb ambitions subordinated all non-Serb groups within Yugoslavia, and this reality was most apparent in personnel positions within the governmental and military organizations. For these two states, membership in NATO and the EU offered the prospects for a more co-equal status as well as mutual respect.

The third category of alliance partners included the most advanced states in the region, and they were the first to formally enter NATO as members in 1999. The Czechs had built up an extensive industrial system under the Habsburgs, and this economically developed infrastructure continued through communist times (Golan 1971, 13). Hungary had enjoyed a similar position of strength within the Austro-Hungarian empire, and the passage of the New Economic Mechanism in 1968 brought increased prosperity to all regions of the country (Heinrich 1986, 143, 160). The Polish situation was different, for its reputation relied on a willingness to challenge Moscow on more than one significant occasion (Ost 1991, 138–41). The fourth category of PfP alliance candidates included the unlikely and dissimilar duo of Romania and Bulgaria. Both possessed lower levels of economic development than East European states to the north, and both had succumbed to despotic and authoritarian leaders during communist times (Ratesh 1991, 1–16). However, the 9/11 attacks on the United States made their entry into NATO quite important. They were closer to the front lines of Iraq and Afghanistan, and NATO member Turkey's ambivalence about American intervention in Iraq demonstrated the need for a fortified alliance in the Balkans.

All ten of these PfP members achieved entry into NATO within 15 years of the 1989 anti-communist revolutions in East Europe. The third category of states moved to formal membership in 1999, and the first, second, and fourth categories entered the alliance in 2004. Each new member had met the formal alliance admission criteria, but the Balkan wars of the 1990s as well as the war against terrorism early in the next century surely accelerated that process.

NATO's containment of Serbia, 1992–9

The Western military alliance planners had downplayed the significance of the Balkans after the end of the Cold War. The more economically and politically developed states in the northern sector of East Europe offered more to the West in terms of economic and military capabilities. However, the aggressiveness of Milošević and the Serbs to recapture at least influence and perhaps control in former Yugoslav space led to a series of Balkan wars that began with a two-week struggle for power in Slovenia in 1991. The turmoil continued and war escalated in the same year in Croatia, but the major struggle in the mid-1990s occurred in Bosnia-Herzegovina (Magstadt 2004, 185–6). Serbs constituted 33% of the population in that new country but eventually captured 70% of its territory. The Clinton administration was reluctant to call upon NATO to play a containment role against Serbian forces but finally did after revelations of the terrible Serb massacre of innocent Muslims at Srebrenica in 1995 (Chittick 2006, 226). The eventual NATO bombing campaign halted Serb aggression and the United States hosted the Dayton Conference that established a shaky peace under UN and NATO supervision.

In 1998–9, the Serbian-Albanian conflict in the region of Kosovo generated an eventual NATO intervention in the former Yugoslavia. Unlike Slovenia, Croatia, and Bosnia, Kosovo was not an independent state at that time but an ethically Albanian region within Serbian-dominated rump Yugoslavia, which included the former Yugoslavian Republics of Serbia and Montenegro (Hook and Spanier 2004, 313). Western leaders were thus reluctant to intervene in an internal conflict that did not include aggression across any territorial border. In a careful way, alliance planners committed no ground troops to the successful operation but managed the brief conflict with a nearly three-month air war that drove the Serbs out of Kosovo (Papp et al. 2005, 209).

More recent new NATO members from Southeast Europe: Albania and Croatia (2009), Montenegro (2017), and North Macedonia (2020)

The logic for admitting Albania differed sharply from the rationale for bringing in Croatia. With the Albanian ethnic insurgencies in Kosovo and Macedonia, some observers had expressed concern about an effort to consolidate a new Greater Albanian state that included the 90% Albanian population of Kosovo and the 40% Albanian minority in Macedonia with their own people. However, Tirana did not make any serious efforts to promote greater Albanian nationalism, and therefore was perceived as factor of stability in the region. Moreover, after the outbreak of the twin Western-sponsored wars in Afghanistan and Iraq, there was a logic, based in dispatching contingents with nominally predominantly Muslim military personnel from Albania, to those particular cultural settings (Goldman 2009, 110–11; Ministry of Defense of Albania 2011).

56   *Defending Eastern Europe*

Croatia was a very different kind of candidate for full membership in the Western military alliance. With Slovenia, Croatia had been one of the more economically advanced territorial units in Yugoslavia. As a target of Serbian incursions shortly after the acquisition of independence, the Western embrace of the burgeoning state was apparent (Remington 1984, 238–82). However, its delayed entry paralleled that of Slovakia in some ways. Authoritarian leadership under Mečiar postponed Slovak admission into NATO for a full five years after that of their Czech former federation partner. Similarly, the dictatorial Tudjman leadership of Croatia in the last years of the 1990s put off its admission until five years after the entry of the big class of seven states in 2004. However, Croatia's willingness to contribute to key overseas missions in Iraq and Afghanistan, and its evolution in a democratic direction made eventual admission a certainty (Ministry of Defense of Croatia 2011).

Montenegro became a state in 2006 and a full alliance partner a little more than a decade later in 2017. During the life of the Yugoslav state, the republic had been relatively isolated in its mountainous terrain but also had the reputation of being very close to the Serb Republic in both geography and culture. Some observers were surprised by its declaration of independence so many years after the other non-Serb republics formed their own states. However, it moved quickly to embrace Western partnerships and made small but important commitments of troops to Afghanistan. For example, 33 of Montenegro's military personnel helped to secure the base in Panonia in Pol e Khomri Province in 2011. Prior to official membership in NATO, Montenegro worked to standardize its military equipment so that it meshed with the infrastructure of the alliance (Ministry of Defense of Montenegro 2011). Although a small state, it had taken the needed steps to move to full membership in 2017.

Macedonia had done much to contribute to NATO missions as a PfP member. Just as Serbia was an albatross around the neck of Montenegro, so NATO member Greece was a major barrier to Macedonian full membership. The northern province of Greece was also labelled Macedonia, and so, from this vantage point, the status of the new state of Macedonia was questionable. However, as a PfP member, it dispatched nearly 800 troops to Afghanistan between 2002 and 2011. Medical specialists were an important part of the personnel sent, and so it had carved out a niche specialty like many other smaller new NATO members such as the Czech Republic. This medical specialization also played a role in Macedonia's assistance in the protection of nearby Kosovo, and the connection between its own substantial Muslim minority and the population of Kosovo was significant (Ministry of Defense of Macedonia 2011). By 2020, it had contributed far more to the Western military alliance than expected, and the name change

NATO

to North Macedonia ameliorated some of the Greek anxiety and concerns and guaranteed the step up to full NATO membership.

Membership issues and potential puzzle pieces from Southeast Europe: Bosnia, Kosovo, and Serbia

Bosnia has been more of a project or concern for both NATO and the EU than an active PfP participant, and this situation is rooted in its ethnic complexity and tragic war in the mid-1990s. NATO airstrikes had helped immensely in pushing the Serb encroachers out of Bosnia, and the EU took over management of the peacekeeping forces at the end of 2004. At the same time, Bosnia committed peacekeeping forces to Afghanistan and Iraq. For example, in 2010 it sent a full rotation of infantry troops to Afghanistan, and connected with a Danish mission in Helmand Province in providing security to two NATO bases for six months. Further, it sent nearly 300 troops to Iraq between 2005 and 2010, and these forces both provided security at Victory Camp/Baghdad and participated in a combat mission in Tuzla (Ministry of Defense of Bosnia-Herzegovina 2011).

The strategic situation of Kosovo displayed even more vulnerability than that of Bosnia. NATO forces and airstrikes provided protection from Serbian attacks in 1999, and subsequent alliance introduction of protective forces continued after and beyond the assertion of state existence. Its leaders after 2008 aimed at PfP membership, but that was a long shot, given its small size, vulnerability, and Russian resistance. Instead, the official program of its Ministry of Foreign Affairs called for special outreach to Albania, Macedonia, and Montenegro (Ministry of Foreign Affairs of Kosovo 2011). If the internal situation stabilized, then a formal move of a small but independent state toward more formal connections with Western defense organizations may have become a possibility.

Serbia had been the provocative state that had guaranteed NATO responses in 1995 in Bosnia and in 1999 in Kosovo. At the same time, the Western alliances reached out to Serbia early in the new century in hopes of establishing a communications link that would make stability in the region a possibility. One result was a NATO invitation to become a PfP member at the 2006 Riga Summit. In mid-December of that year, Serbia did become a PfP member. The expectation was that it would then play a role in multilateral operations that would be anticipated in that capacity and role (Ministry of Defense of Serbia 2011). Some of those considerations about NATO underwent reconsideration after the Western recognition of the independence of Kosovo in 2008. Serbian ambitions to join the EU in effect replaced its pursuit of NATO membership.

58 *Defending Eastern Europe*

NATO, the war in Afghanistan, and East European contributions, 2001–19

Initially, the United States guided the war in Afghanistan after September 2001, and a number of Western allies volunteered their military support. However, on September 6, 2006, the "Declaration by NATO and the Islamic Republic of Afghanistan" supplanted that voluntary arrangement (*Declaration by the North Atlantic Treaty Organization and the Islamic Republic of Afghanistan 2007*). NATO management of much of the Afghan operation ensued, while the United States continued to control the rest of it, until complete NATO piloting took place in 2010. This was a major step in the self-definition of the Western military alliance, for it pulled the alliance into a project far from its original orbit of the European continent. The name of the operation continued to be International Security Assistance Force (ISAF), and that label covered the mission from 2001 to 2014. Thus, it is no surprise that many of the new NATO members chose to devote military personnel to that alliance operation.

Each of the three states admitted to NATO in 1999 made important contributions to the war in Afghanistan. In 2004, Czech meteorologists provided weather reports from Kabul Airport to Czech field hospital and chemical units that had entered Afghanistan soon after the 9/11 attacks (Ministry of Defense of the Czech Republic 2007). Later, it took part in helicopter missions, patrols in the mountainous terrain of Fajzabad, and work with the Rapid Reaction Force (Ministry of Defense of the Czech Republic 2007, 2010). In 2011 and 2012, it sent 100 special forces troops to remote locations, while, at the end of 2016, it supplied 264 personnel from its 14th Task Force to help protect Hamid Karzai International Airport (Ministry of Defense of the Czech Republic 2016).

By 2009, Hungary had contributed a full 315 troops to Afghanistan, and their work centered on infrastructure development projects. Hungary also carved out a specialty in civil–military relations, and this resulted in recruitment of local workers into alliance projects (Ministry of Foreign Affairs of Hungary 2010a). Overall, in the 2003–14 period, Hungary contributed 540 troops to ISAF, and special forces were among them. Resolute Force replaced ISAF as the NATO mission after 2014, and Hungary dispatched a training unit of 100 personnel to Afghanistan in those years (Simon 2002; Szenesz 2007).

Poland's large population and commitment to NATO projects sparked it to contribute 1,955 troops to overall alliance missions in Afghanistan. Many took part in the Multinational Corps North East (MNC NE), while the protection of the Kabul Airport also remained a mainstay of its commitment. In the years from 2015 to 2017, Poland provided 200 forces to

Resolute Support, and its principal contribution was a training/advising company (http://en.mon.gov.pl/missions).

Overall, NATO had made a solid start by admitting these three states as early as 1999, as their steady and firm commitment to the alliance enabled them to make significant contributions to ISAF.

The group of East European states admitted to NATO in 2004 all contributed in measured and important ways to the mission in Afghanistan. Among the ten new members admitted between 1999 and 2004, Slovenia sent the smallest number of troops to Afghanistan, but it did total 70 military personnel. Slovaks fulfilled several niche missions that centered on provision of airport security as well as healthcare. They worked at Bagram Airport, Kabul Airport, Uruzgan Province, and Kandahar. By 2009, they had a total of 240 military personnel in the country (Ministry of Foreign Affairs of Slovakia 2010). Later, Slovak troops sent mine-clearing specialists to be part of an engineering company of the Kabul Multinational Brigade (Ministry of Defense of the Slovak Republic 2016). Both of these new NATO members had broken away from big federations but discovered within NATO something of an enlarged geographic living space.

The three Baltic states were similarly quite small and anxious to move away from the Moscow hold that had restricted their aspirations and activities for a full half century. Estonian troops participated in a quite risky mission with others in Kandahar Province in mid-2006 (Bush 2007, 5–10). By the close of 2009, it had 150 soldiers in Afghanistan, and they did joint work with British and French troops in the dangerous Helmand Province. Estonian financial assistance also supported health care projects, education, and the new Afghan National Archives (Ministry of Foreign Affairs of Estonia 2010). Latvia's contributions to the mission were comparable, as its forces numbered 175 by 2009. Mainly they were regular troops but did also include a few police specialists (Ministry of Foreign Affairs of Latvia 2010). With 165 soldiers in Afghanistan by 2009, the role of the Lithuanian military paralleled that of the other two Baltic states. In particular, they led a Provincial Reconstruction Team (PRT) in Ghor Province that helped prepare the ground for later work by the UN (Ministry of Foreign Affairs of Lithuania 2010). Additional projects in the provincial capital of Chagcharan centered on public service activities in areas such as education and parks (Ministry of Defense of the Republic of Lithuania 2010). It is noteworthy that the three Baltic states made about the same levels of commitment to NATO operations in Afghanistan, but they each made contributions unique to their own capabilities and resources.

Bulgaria's closer proximity to the theater of operations enabled it to offer valuable overflight and stay rights to American forces, while it also permitted usage of its own Sarafovo Airport by incoming troops at the

60 *Defending Eastern Europe*

beginning of the war (Ministry of Defense of Bulgaria 2017). Specific contributions included provision of 540 troops in 2009 alone, weapons and ammunition, and financial support for humanitarian purposes (Ministry of Foreign Affairs of Bulgaria 2010). In 2006, the Romanian military forces took part in an actual battle against Taliban forces in Kandahar Province. Mostly, this entailed operational support rather than full combat (Gates 2007, 36–9). Romanian forces totaled 940 in 2009, and its 280th Maneuver Battalion had been located there twice for six-month rotations (NATO 2010). Overall, these two Balkan states provided considerably more troops to Afghanistan than did the other five states admitted to NATO in 2004, and that offered a promised of their potential should other defense crises arise.

The war in Iraq, Coalition of the Willing, and the role of new NATO members, 2003–11

Military contributions of the class of 1999 far exceeded those of the group of states admitted to NATO in 2004. Poland was clearly the leader, for it managed a large occupation zone south of Baghdad for some time with 2,400 of its own troops. By the close of 2004, Poland had sent a full three rotations of troops into the combat zone (Michta 2006, 37). Czechs played a smaller but still significant role with 100 military personnel who trained 12,000 Iraqi police officers as well as another military police unit that worked at the UK's Al Shaiba base near Basra from late 2003 until November 2006 (Velinger 2006). The third member of the 1999 NATO new member class was Hungary, and it maintained a 300-soldier battalion in Iraq from 2003 to 2004. In 2007–8, Hungary also made the second largest commitment to the Military Advice and Liaison Team (MALT), and that unit provided valuable training for Iraqi military forces (Ministry of Foreign Affairs of Hungary 2010b).

Military contributions in Iraq were considerably smaller for the NATO class of 2004. Slovakia offered 70 soldiers at the beginning of the war, and they helped monitor the risks of chemical, biological, and radiation risks. Importantly, a Slovak Engineer Company of 100 soldiers worked in the Polish sector on demining as well as on the liquidation of arms and munitions (Ministry of Foreign Affairs of Slovakia 2010). The Baltic nations of Latvia and Lithuania also provided some services. The former sent 125 military personnel who took part in the initial invasion in 2003, and then later on it provided funding for the training of security forces (Ministry of Foreign Affairs of Latvia 2010). Lithuania took part in several NATO training schools which Iraqi soldiers attended (Ministry of Foreign Affairs of Lithuania 2010). Similarly, the Balkan state of Bulgaria helped train Iraqi security forces at its own military schools as well as providing funding for training at other locations (Ministry of Foreign Affairs of Bulgaria 2010). Romanian contributions as well centered on the training of Iraqi military personnel (Ministry of Foreign Affairs of Romania 2010).

New alliance member contributions to the Iraq War were less than they were for Afghanistan. Part of the reason was the fact that the war in Iraq was much more controversial for their populations and leaders than was the Afghan War that was the direct response to the 9/11 attacks. Another vital fact was that Afghanistan was a NATO operation, for it took over a substantial portion of that mission in 2006 and then the entire operation in 2010. NATO refused to endorse or take part in the Iraq War at its origin in 2003. Later on, NATO managed the National Training Mission-Iraq (NTM-I), and it is no surprise that the smaller new alliance partners from East Europe chose to contribute in that program rather than in more controversial and dangerous combat or combat-related operations. However, in both cases these ten new NATO members all began to learn from and interact with a strong Western military organization that came to substitute for the very different Moscow-led Warsaw Pact that directed their military operations during Cold War times.

NATO after 70 years: renewed defense priorities after the 2014 Crimea crisis, budgetary issues, and responses by new NATO members from Eastern Europe

The Wales Declaration was an important and immediate NATO response to the 2014 Ukrainian crisis with the resultant Russian annexation of Crimea. The alliance meeting in Wales occurred in September 2014, and member states were clear in their conclusion that criticized "Russia's illegal self-declared annexation of Crimea." The Declaration also called for establishment of a new Readiness Action Plan that would enable quick dispatch of military forces of the alliance to regions that exploded in turmoil in sudden and unexpected ways. The new procedure would also provide an additional tool to enforce NATO's Article 5 that called for mobilization of the whole alliance should invasion into a member occur. Further, the Wales Declaration set a target through which each member state would commit 2% of GDP to defense within a decade. Goals were not just confined to military operations but also included accelerated "defence industrial cooperation." NATO also would welcome strengthened defense capabilities of the EU that could supplement those of the military alliance ("The Wales Declaration on the Transatlantic Bond," September 5, 2014). Overall, the Declaration was a

62 *Defending Eastern Europe*

wake-up call to the alliance to actively defend its members against future Russian provocative moves.

By 2017, Donald Trump was the American president, and NATO looked ahead to its Brussels meeting on May 25, 2017. In addition to the recommended increase in defense budgets to 2% of GDP, they were now also prepared to challenge member states to increase the proportion of military funds devoted to equipment to 20%. The rationale for this goal was partly to counteract the natural tendency of all militaries to spend most of their budget on personnel. Additional goals included an increase in the proportion of troops that are "deployable and sustainable." NATO had set up many planning targets, and goals now also entailed measurements of the degree of implementation of such goal clusters. There was also a sense that alliance planners sought to balance understandable aspirations of each alliance partner with stronger commitments to "collective defense," pools of forces, and putting together the national pieces for a mutual and joint military operation. In order to have well-trained military forces, it was also imperative to focus on enhanced personnel recruitment and retention strategies. At a point that was three years after the Ukrainian crisis, NATO planners centered their recommendations on concrete expectations such as the ability of larger countries to maintain a division and smaller ones either a brigade or a battlegroup. While it may be tempting for observers such as President Trump to look solely at state behavior in terms of compliance with NATO guidelines such as the 2% or 20% targets, much more important is the actual increase in capabilities, as contrary to mechanical increases in inputs (Mattelaer 2017).

NATO established very clear budget recommendations in 2019, and they centered in quite concrete ways on the types of threats that had emerged in the five years since the 2014 Russian intervention in Ukraine. They called for increased financial commitments to capabilities such as airborne early warning and control forces, ground surveillance, and cyber defense. They also underlined the importance of continued funding of the NATO Mission-Iraq (NTM-I) as well as the Resolute Support Mission in Afghanistan. Additional funding for the relatively new Readiness Action Plan was imperative at this point five years after its birth ("2019 Military Budget Recommendations Executive Summary" 2019). Military planners also focused on related civilian needs of the organization. They had moved NATO headquarters to a new location in 2018, and its funding was a continuing need. In their civilian component, they set a limited target of a 1.9% increase over general civilian spending in comparison with 2018 ("2019 Civil Budget Recommendations" 2019). For each member state, there was a corresponding need to mesh large increases in military spending with corresponding attention to its civilian component.

NATO 63

Table 4.1 Military capabilities of new NATO states in 2019

State	Defense expenditure as share of GDP (%)[a]	Equipment expenditure as share of defense expenditure (%)[b]	GDP Defense Expenditure per Capita (in thousands of US $s)[c]	Military Personnel (in thousands)[d]
Albania	1.26	14.4	58	6.8
Bulgaria	1.61	25.1	132	25
Croatia	1.75	11.6	238	15
Czech Republic	1.19	14.5	236	26
Estonia	2.13	19.4	429	6.3
Hungary	1.21	23.5	178	20
Latvia	2.01	25.3	325	6.4
Lithuania	1.98	28.7	336	15.9
Montenegro	1.68	14.3	126	1.6
Poland	2.01	23.9	296	123
Romania	2.04	24.8	225	69
Slovak Republic	1.74	41.7	322	13
Slovenia	1.04	8.0	253	6.8

[a] Graph 3: "Defence Expenditure of NATO Countries (2012-2019)" nato.int.
[b] Graph 4: "Defence Expenditure of NATO Countries (2012-2019)" nato.int.
[c] Table 6: "Defence Expenditure of NATO Countries (2012-2019)" nato.int.
[d] Table 7: "Defence Expenditure of NATO Countries (2012-2019)" nato.int.

How did the Eastern European nations respond to these calls for increased attention to defense spending in the aftermath of a crisis that brought Russian foreign policy much closer to their own doorstep? Overall, the European NATO partners and Canada collectively increased overall defense spending by 1.6% in 2015, by 2.9% in 2016, by 5.8% in 2017, by 4.0% in 2018, and by 3.9% in 2019 (see Table 4.1). The countries of Eastern Europe were part of that financial increase, and the data indicated a heightened level of defense alertness.

In terms of the targeted 2% of GDP devoted to defense, the states in the Eastern European region that met that goal included four of the 13, one on the edge, and eight below the goal. The five at the top of the list included all of those most challenged states that Chapters 9 and 10 will cover (Estonia, Latvia, Lithuania, Poland, and Romania). Clearly, they perceived the new

64   *Defending Eastern Europe*

threat from Russia to have great pertinence to them and took appropriate measures (see Table 4.1).

In measuring the related alliance goal of 20% of the defense budget devoted to equipment, there were seven states in the region that met the goal and six that did not. Estonia was a bit below the 20% threshold, but all the others that had met 2% of GDP were above it. In addition, the Slovak Republic, Bulgaria, and Hungary also met the 20% challenge in the area of purchased equipment (see Table 4.1).

It is also interesting to factor in the population of the various Eastern European states, and a way of doing this is to look at GDP Defense Expenditures per capita in US dollars. The Baltic states held the top three slots on this indicator, while Slovakia was fourth, Poland fifth, and Slovenia sixth (see Table 4.1). Again, the ranking includes four of the five most challenged states, while the other two are quite small states in the region. These data demonstrate that most of these states compensate for their small size with strong efforts to do all that their populations can support in the defense area.

Finally, how large are the military forces of the Eastern European states, and what does that reveal about capabilities to make a response in case of a threat? Population does matter on this indicator, and the rank order of top states in the region includes Poland, Romania, the Czech Republic, Bulgaria, and Hungary. It is noteworthy that several East Central European states become visible in this indicator, although they were not in the previous ones. Clearly, the Czech Republic and Hungary maintain sizeable armies, in spite of their reserved posture on the matter of deterring Russian aggression (see Table 4.1). Altogether, these four sets of data round out the picture of the defense responsiveness of Eastern European states in impressive ways.

In conclusion, the NATO alliance has evolved through the immediate post-Cold War years in impressive ways that include responses to the emergent crises of each of the three decades since the fall of communism in the region in 1989. In the 1990s, the alliance took firm action in Bosnia-Herzegovina in 1995 as well as in Kosovo in 1999. After 9/11, in the 2000s, the alliance invoked Article 5 for the first time and commenced a two-decade involvement in Afghanistan. In the 2010s, the NATO Wales Summit was effective in setting tangible goals that would strengthen the defensive posture of the entire region against future Russian aggressive moves. Taken together, these three sets of ongoing military and peacemaking operations, over time, reveal a responsive and flexible organization that has met the expectations and mandates of its founding in 1949.

5

The EU as a security provider in Eastern Europe

Michael Baun

For a book on collective security in Eastern Europe, it makes perfect sense that the primary focus should be on NATO and matters of military defense, or hard security. It is also necessary to consider, however, the security role of the EU, to which many of the states of this region belong, and most of those who do not would like to. This despite the fact that the EU at present, and probably for the near future, is not much of a military actor. In fact, it can still be described relatively accurately today, as it was nearly 30 years ago, as an "economic giant but a political dwarf (and military worm)."[1] In the years since these remarks were made, the EU has increased military cooperation among its member states by creating a Common Security and Defense Policy (CSDP), and it has deployed more than two-dozen CSDP missions in its own neighborhood and around the world. These have mostly been civilian or civil–military operations, however, such as police and rule-of-law training, border monitoring, and humanitarian assistance, and the EU has not been able to form military units larger than battalion-sized (1,500 troops) multinational "battle groups." After an initial burst of activity from 1999 to 2004, EU military cooperation has enjoyed a resurgence since 2016, in response to increased security threats in the European neighborhood and uncertainty about the Trump administration's commitment to NATO. However, the EU remains far from achieving its announced goal of becoming an autonomous security and strategic actor, let alone being capable of providing on its own hard security for Eastern Europe.

Nevertheless, this chapter argues that the EU is an important security provider in Eastern Europe. In various ways, the EU protects its member states and enhances their capacity to withstand all manner of security challenges, including economic, political, and even military pressures. For lack of a better term, we can conceptualize the EU's role in this regard as being a provider of soft security, to distinguish it from the hard security provided by NATO. The concept of soft security, as used here, refers not just to the nature of security threats, as is commonly the case, but instead to civil

66 *Defending Eastern Europe*

or non-military means of protection against threats to security, especially those of a non-military or soft nature. While the hard security provided by NATO is obviously important for the Eastern European (EE) states, the soft security role of the EU is equally vital. This is perhaps even more the case at a time when the main threats to European security are of a soft variety concerning such issues as energy, the economy, migration, climate change, cross-border organized crime, the cyber sphere, and social cohesion. For the EE states in particular, the EU is important for the protection it offers against Russian economic and political pressure, which for many of them is among their greatest security challenges.

Precisely because of the different nature of their security roles, the EU and NATO are complementary and mutually supportive entities. Both organizations are vitally important for the security of the EE states, who would be much more vulnerable and exposed without the existence and effective functioning of either one of them. However, in the emerging new world disorder of post-2016, just as the future of NATO is called into question by mounting uncertainty about the US commitment to European security, the EU's capacity to be a soft security provider is endangered by new threats to EU unity and cohesion posed by both external and internal political forces.

The remainder of this chapter proceeds as follows. The next section discusses the distinction between hard and soft security and the EU's role as a provider of the latter for the EE states, especially when it comes to offering protection against Russia. The chapter then examines two key cases in which the EU was asked by the EE states to protect them against Russian pressure, the first concerning Moscow's economic and political campaign in 2005–7 against several of the new member states, and the second the important issue of energy security, and in particular the Nord Stream 2 pipeline. While in the former case the EU demonstrated solidarity with its new members and helped them resist Russian pressure, in the latter the EU's response has been weaker and more divided. The two cases thus demonstrate both the potential and the limits of the EU's ability to be a provider of soft security for the EE states. The final section before the conclusion examines new threats to EU unity, and thus to its capacity to be a soft security provider, posed by the efforts of external powers like Russia, China, and the United States to divide and weaken the EU, and by the growth of illiberal nationalism within the EU and Eastern Europe in particular.

The EU and soft security

The concepts of hard and soft security generally center on the distinctive nature of security threats. While the former refers to threats to the physical

The EU as security provider 67

security of the state and its citizens posed by military conflict and terrorism, the latter concerns non-military threats, challenges, and risks posed by economic, environmental, societal, and other problems. However, it is widely agreed that in today's world the distinction between these two categories is rapidly dissolving (Lindley-French 2004, 2). According to Ordzhonikidze (2009), "Much of what has traditionally been classified as 'hard threats,' such as inter-State war, or terrorism, can – and often is – fueled or exacerbated by 'soft threats' such as lack of development, massive human rights abuses, humanitarian emergencies, or even climate change."

There is another way to conceive of hard and soft security beyond the nature of threats, however, and that is in terms of the nature of protection against threats. In this regard, hard security is provided by military power, especially the capacity to deter others (both state and non-state actors) from attacking you. Soft security, by contrast, concerns protection against security threats via non-military or civil means. While soft security protection has implications for defense against military or hard security threats, for instance by enhancing a state's political cohesion and resilience, it is most important and effective for protecting against threats of a soft security nature, such as economic, energy, environmental, and societal threats.

Soft security, in this protective sense, has both internal or domestic and external dimensions. The former concerns the internal strength of a state – the economic, societal, and political stability, cohesion, and resilience that allow a state to withstand and surmount external pressures, including even military threats or terrorist attacks. The latter includes good and cooperative relations with other states, which reduces fear and uncertainty and mitigates or eliminates the "security dilemma" with respect to these states. Taken to its furthest extent, cooperative relations between states can lead to the formation of pluralistic "security communities" – groupings of interdependent and like-minded states between whom war has become unthinkable (Deutsch et al. 1957; Adler and Barnett 1998). Soft security can also take the form of diplomatic support and the promise of economic and other assistance if states are threatened or attacked, a form of protection that also comes from being part of a broader alliance or cooperative grouping of states. Soft security (non-military) protection, in other words, can involve the internal strengthening of a state and the reduction of both internal vulnerability and external uncertainty, and the provision of external reinforcement and support, which can be diplomatic, economic, and moral as well as military.

As a highly integrated and prosperous community of democratic states, the EU is in good position to provide these various elements of soft security to its EE members. EE states can use the trade and investment opportunities that come from being part of the huge EU single market to strengthen and grow their economies and create greater prosperity for their citizens. The integration of EE states into a larger economic bloc should also make them less vulnerable to external economic pressure, blackmail, or disruption. EU membership also requires the adoption of democratic norms and institutions, and provides valuable external support for democratic reforms in the EE states and adherence to core democratic principles, including good governance and rule of law. In theory, at least, EU membership should increase the internal strength, stability, and resiliency of EE states by making them more prosperous, economically secure, and democratically legitimate.

EU membership also enhances the security of EE states by enmeshing them in a network of cooperative relations with fellow member states, and through their incorporation into the EU security community. It also offers EE states the promise of diplomatic and other forms of support from the EU and other member states should they be threatened or pressured by outside powers. Enhanced security for the EE states, in other words, even against potential hard security threats, derives from the soft security benefits of being part of a larger and more influential economic and political bloc.

Finally, the EU provides soft security protection to the EE states by helping them deal with threats to their security of a soft or non-military nature. These include threats in the realms of energy security, economic instability, cyber security, cross-border organized crime, the environment and climate change, and disinformation and public opinion. Through its capacity for collective action to help deal with these and other soft security problems, the EU provides value-added for its member states, who acting individually or in smaller sub-groups would be less capable of addressing these increasingly serious threats to their security.

For the EE states, the security benefits of EU membership are of primary relevance for protection against renewed pressure from Russia, which poses the main security threat to most of the EE states, especially those that are geographically closer to their former master to the east – chiefly Poland, the Baltic states, and Romania. Indeed, protection against Russia and permanent escape from Moscow's geopolitical orbit was a primary reason the EE states sought to join the EU as well as NATO after regaining their freedom in 1989. Thus for the EE states, as much as for the Western European member states, the EU is ultimately a security project: for the latter, "The EU is a guarantee against war and fascism (or the cause of war). For the Eastern European member states, the EU is a guarantee against Russian occupation and political [vassalage]" (Debeuf 2018). While Russia poses the main security threat to the EE states, the EU also provides valuable soft security protection against pressure and intervention by other external powers, including China and, in Southeastern Europe, Turkey.

The security benefits of EU membership would also be greatly welcomed by those EE states that are not members of the EU, and are thus even more vulnerable to Russian pressure and aggression – Ukraine, Moldova, and Georgia (Belarus being in a different category). For the Western Balkans states that are not yet members, but have been promised eventual membership by the EU – Montenegro, North Macedonia, Bosnia-Herzegovina, Serbia, Albania, and Kosovo – the security benefits of EU membership would be useful mainly as protection against renewed regional and civil conflict. In this region as well, however, intervention by both Moscow and Ankara has the potential to destabilize and generate conflict.

Highlighting the EU's role as a provider of soft security for the EE states does not diminish the need for, or importance of, hard security, such as that provided by NATO and potentially in the future a more militarily capable EU. Indeed, the existence of hard security guarantees makes soft security means of protection more viable, and soft security alone without the backing of hard security would be insufficient to guarantee a state's survival or independence. However, it would be a mistake to overlook or ignore the soft security benefits of EU membership or the EU's role as a security provider, which nicely supplements and complements the hard security provided by NATO. The EE states themselves were certainly aware of these benefits, as they made the transition from communism and, beginning in the mid-1990s, undertook the long and difficult path from being candidate states for EU membership to accession.

But how effective has the EU been as a provider of soft security for the EE states, especially when it comes to resisting economic and political pressure from Russia? The next two sections examine to key cases in which the EU was asked by its EE members to protect them against Russian pressure and potential security threats emanating from Moscow, with divergent results. The two cases thus demonstrate both the potential and the limits of the EU's ability to be a provider of soft security for the EE states.

Russian pressure on the new member states, 2005–7

Shortly after joining the EU in May 2004, several of the EE states came under economic and political pressure from Russia, which sought to test the EU's willingness to show solidarity with its new members. The EU passed this initial test with flying colors, showing the value of EU membership and diplomatic support as a form of soft security protection against Moscow.

The Russian pressure campaign against the new member states began in November 2005, when Moscow imposed a ban on the import of Polish

70 *Defending Eastern Europe*

meat, claiming it was of low quality and unsafe. However, the government in Warsaw claimed the import ban was politically motivated, and it retaliated the following year by vetoing the beginning of negotiations between Russia and the EU on a new Partnership and Cooperation Agreement (PCA). At about the same time, Lithuania, another new member state, was also experiencing problems with Russia, after Moscow decided in July 2006 to shut down a branch of the Druzhba pipeline, through which Lithuania received most of its oil. While the Russian pipeline company Transneft blamed a leak for the shutdown, the Lithuanian government claimed it was a politically motivated action to punish the country for selling a domestic refinery to a Polish company rather than a Russian bidder (Reuters 2007). In response, the Lithuanian government also threatened to veto the PCA negotiations with Russia. The Lithuanian and Polish prime ministers also sent a joint letter to European Commission President José Manuel Barroso in March 2007 demanding EU support on the Druzhba pipeline issue, to which the Commission President responded by promising to raise the issue with Russian President Vladimir Putin at the EU–Russia summit in May (Rettman 2007).

Before the summit, a third new member state came under pressure from Moscow. Beginning in April and continuing into May, Russian government-sponsored hackers launched a massive wave of cyber-attacks on Estonian government, media, and business targets, in response to the decision of Tallinn city authorities to move a monument to Soviet World War II soldiers from a square in the capital city center to a more obscure military cemetery. Ethnic Russian youths rioted in Tallinn, and in Moscow, a Kremlin-supported youth organization blockaded the Estonian embassy and attacked the ambassador. In response to the latter incident, the EU issued a strong statement reminding Moscow of its obligation under the Vienna Convention to protect diplomatic premises (Kasekamp 2013, 105).

The EU–Russia summit on May 18, 2007 gave the EU the opportunity to show solidarity with its new member states, which it did by informing President Putin that increased economic and energy cooperation between the EU and Russia could not take place until Moscow had resolved its bilateral disputes with the EE states. At a press conference following the summit, Commission President Barroso, sitting next to Putin, declared "that a difficulty for a member state is a difficulty for the whole European community." This demonstration of EU solidarity visibly frustrated the Russian leader, who complained, "We often hear about the need for solidarity. Are there any limits to solidarity? Are there any questions that should be decided internally?" (Euractiv 2007), by which he presumably meant by EU authorities and Moscow alone, without consideration of the interests of the EU's smaller and weaker members.

The EU's demonstration of solidarity with the new member states had a positive effect in all three countries. In the words of an Estonian analyst, "For the first time, the EU publicly demonstrated solidarity in the face of Russian pressure on the new member states" (Kasekamp 2013, 105). This demonstration of solidarity, in turn, bolstered the Estonian population's support for the EU, helping them realize that "the EU is not just a single market, but has much broader value in political and security terms" (Kasekamp 2013, 103). As for Poland, in return for EU support on the meat issue, the new government of Prime Minister Donald Tusk (2007–14) adopted a more cooperative policy in the EU, dropping its threat to block an agreement on voting procedures in intergovernmental negotiations on the Treaty of Lisbon. The Polish government also began viewing the EU more positively as a potentially valuable means for achieving Warsaw's foreign policy objectives, especially in its Eastern European neighborhood (Kamińska 2013, 28–33).

The Lithuanian government was also grateful for the EU's support. For Vilnius, however, of more importance than summit statements were EU efforts to develop a new energy security policy, including measures to link Lithuania to the energy networks of other member states, thereby ending its status as an "energy island in the EU" and reducing its dependence on Russian energy. These steps included EU financial support for construction of an energy bridge from Lithuania to Sweden, and the EU's adoption in June 2009 of the Baltic Energy Market Interconnection Plan (BEMIP), which aims at integrating the Baltic states into the EU energy market. Vilnius also welcomed subsequent efforts to develop an integrated internal EU energy market (Vilpišauskas 2013, 132–3). Nevertheless, in the area of energy security the EU's actions have not always matched its rhetoric and ambitions, thereby leaving the EE states potentially vulnerable to Russian pressure. It is to a closer examination of the issue of energy security, and the case of the Nord Stream 2 pipeline in particular, that we now turn.

Energy security: the case of Nord Stream 2

Energy security is an issue of vital importance for the EE states, and one in which the EU can play an important role as a security provider. As a legacy of the communist era and a product of geography, the EE states remain highly dependent for their energy needs on Russian oil and natural gas, most of it supplied through pipelines that traverse Ukraine and Belarus. In 2019, eight EE states received more than 75% of their natural gas imports from Russia, while two others – Poland and Lithuania – received more than 50%. For many of the EE states, Russia is a major source of oil imports as

Table 5.1 Share of Russia in national extra-EU imports, first semester 2019 (share (%) of trade in value)

Country	Oil	Natural gas
Bulgaria	50–75	75–100
Czech Republic	25–50	75–100
Estonia	75–100	75–100
Hungary	50–75	75–100
Latvia	0–25	75–100
Lithuania	75–100	50–75
Poland	50–75	50–75
Romania	25–50	75–100
Slovakia	75–100	75–100
Slovenia	0–25	75–100

Source: Eurostat (2019).

well (see Table 5.1). This energy dependence keeps the EE states vulnerable to Russian pressure should Moscow decide to use energy as a geopolitical lever, as the governments of Poland and Lithuania claimed it was doing by shutting down the Druzhba pipeline in 2006. Ending this state of energy dependency is thus a necessity if the EE states are to escape permanently from Russia's orbit.

The Druzhba pipeline shutdown highlighted the vulnerability of the EE states to Moscow's decisions, as did Russia's suspension of gas flows to Ukraine, and thus much of the rest of Europe, in the winter of 2006–7 because of a dispute between Moscow and Kiev over energy prices. For this reason, in negotiations on the Lisbon Treaty in 2007, Poland and other EE states pressed for the inclusion of provisions (Title XX, Article 176a) requiring EU solidarity in energy supply matters and calling for the creation of a more comprehensive EU energy policy (OJEU 2007, 88). Agreement on the Lisbon Treaty was followed by new EU legislation aimed at promoting the liberalization and integration of national energy markets, most notably the Third Energy Package in 2009 (European Commission n.d.). In March 2015, the European Council endorsed plans to create an Energy Union, which included the goals of enhancing EU energy security through the diversification of energy supplies and the creation of a more integrated internal energy market (European Council 2015, 1–3). By design, an Energy Union would reduce the dependence of the EE states on Russian energy by linking them to an EU-wide energy network fed by diversified sources and suppliers.

Given their energy security vulnerability, the concerns of the EE states regarding the Nord Stream 2 (NS2) pipeline are understandable. This German–Russian project entails the construction of a new system of pipelines under the Baltic Sea to transport Russian gas to Germany and Western Europe. NS2 would accompany a first set of pipelines, Nord Stream 1 (NS1) – constructed in 2011 and operational since 2012 – and would double the capacity of Russia to supply gas to Europe via the undersea Baltic route. A second pipeline system to the south, Turkish Stream, is also planned by Moscow, and when completed would supply Russian gas to Southeastern Europe via Turkey through pipelines under the Black Sea. Both pipeline systems bypass Ukraine and Belarus.

The Nord Stream and Turkish Stream projects have generated considerable unease among the EE states, who argue that the new pipelines undermine the EU's strategic efforts to diversify energy supplies away from Russia. The EE states are deeply concerned about the geopolitical implications of NS2 in particular, fearing that enhanced direct energy connections between Russia and Germany would enable Moscow to cut off oil and gas flows through pipelines traversing Belarus and Ukraine, as a means of pressuring or punishing these former Soviet states, and thus increasing Russian influence over them. The possibility of such cutoffs also increases the insecurity of the EE states, who remain heavily dependent on Russian energy despite efforts to diversify supplies and develop energy links to other EU countries. Indicative of the security fears generated in some EE states by the pipeline projects, as well as the historical prism through which they are viewed, in 2006 Polish Defense Minister Radek Sikorski compared plans for NS1 to the 1939 Molotov-Ribbentrop Pact, the secret agreement between Nazi Germany and the Soviet Union to destroy and carve up Poland (Beunderman 2006).

Gazprom, the Russian state energy company, and four European energy concerns signed an agreement to construct NS2 in June 2015. In March 2016, before work on the new lines had begun, the leaders of eight EE states – the Czech Republic, Estonia, Hungary, Latvia, Lithuania, Poland, Slovakia, and Romania – signed a letter addressed to Commission President Jean-Claude Juncker. In the letter, they claimed that NS2 would generate "potentially destabilising geopolitical consequences," and that it would "pose certain risks for energy security in the region of central and eastern Europe" (Sytas 2016). The EE states thus asked the Commission to block NS2, claiming that it endangered EU energy security and contradicted the bloc's commitments to diversify energy sources. They also argued that the project violated EU energy rules, specifically provisions of the Third Energy Package (Natural Gas Directive) requiring the separation of energy production and transmission and that each be managed by separate entities (Rettman 2016).

The Commission also expressed strong misgivings about NS2, citing its threat to European energy security and the divisions it was generating within the EU (Łoskot-Strachota et al. 2018, 5). Also strongly opposed was the US government, with the Obama administration claiming that NS2 would undermine EU energy security and deprive Ukraine of much-needed transit revenues (Crisp 2016). After coming into office in January 2017, the Trump administration increased US pressure on Germany to abandon the project, citing not only the threat it posed to European energy security, but also the prospect of increased sales of US liquefied natural gas (LNG) to European markets as a replacement for Russian energy. The Trump administration also threatened to impose sanctions on European companies involved in the project if it proceeded (Wilkes 2018). Germany and several other Western European states, including the Netherlands, Austria, and France, strongly supported the project, however. The governments of these countries rejected criticism of the security implications of NS2, claiming it was a purely commercial venture that could help improve political relations with Moscow (Łoskot-Strachota et al. 2018, 5).

Despite its concerns about NS2, the Commission decided it was unable to block the project because it did not comply with EU energy rules. According to the Commission's legal services, EU rules on the "unbundling" of production and transmission applied only to land-based pipelines within the EU, leaving the offshore Nord Stream pipelines, which entered the EU from a third country, in something of a "legal void" (Malvout 2017). Instead, the Commission sought to limit the negative security and geopolitical impacts of NS2 through legislative changes that would place the pipeline within the EU regulatory framework and give Brussels more control over its operation (Łoskot-Strachota et al. 2018, 5; Rettman 2018). Based on Commission proposals, in April 2019, the Council of the EU approved amendments to the Gas Directive, including the requirements that import pipelines should not be owned by gas suppliers and third parties should be able to use them. The effect of these amendments would be to reduce Gazprom's control over the NS2 pipeline and limit the amount of gas it could ship through it, thereby reducing Moscow's ability to use energy as a geopolitical weapon (Łoskot-Strachota 2019).

The Commission also sought to mediate negotiations between Moscow and Kiev on a new transit agreement, to replace the one expiring at the end of 2019, in order to ensure that Ukraine would not lose transit revenues because of NS2. The German government, responding to fierce criticism of its support for the project, also supported this effort, and in April 2018 Chancellor Angela Merkel pledged that Germany would not receive gas through NS2 unless Russia agreed to continue to transit gas through Ukraine (Euractiv 2018). Berlin then helped broker a deal between Moscow and Kiev over a new transit agreement, with agreement in principle on a new deal reached in late December 2019 (Gotev 2019). Under the terms of the five-year deal, however, Russia will reduce the amount of gas it transits through Ukraine by half, thus partly achieving Moscow's goal of re-routing energy shipments to Europe around Ukraine (Isachenkov 2019).

Construction of NS2 began in 2018. In late 2019, with Denmark giving its approval to construction of a final section of the pipeline passing through its exclusive economic zone, the main remaining threat to the completion and launching of NS2 was the prospect of US sanctions (Łoskot-Strachota et al. 2019). In December 2019, the US Senate approved legislation that would penalize European companies doing work on the NS2 and Turkish Stream pipelines, as part of a larger defense bill which President Trump then quickly signed (BBC 2019). The US sanctions produced an immediate effect, with Allseas, a Swiss-Dutch energy company announcing later the same day that it would cease laying pipe for the project, while both the Russian and German governments condemned US interference and promised to complete the project (Scott 2019).

In the end, the cases of the 2005–7 Russian pressure campaign and the NS2 pipeline illustrate both the potential and the limits of the EU's ability to be a provider of soft security for the EE states. The potential lies in the EU's capacity for unity and its ability to show solidarity with the EE states. In the case of the 2005–7 pressure campaign, the EU did precisely this, and thus fulfilled its potential as a security provider. In the case of energy security, the EU's potential as a security provider stems from the prospect of an Energy Union, which would reduce the dependence of EE states on Russian energy and their resulting geopolitical vulnerability. However, the EU's inability to stop the NS2 project, which undermines many of the bloc's energy policy goals and could make the EE states even more vulnerable to Russian pressure, shows the limits of the EU's role as a security provider. While the Commission was able to gain some regulatory control of the pipeline through changes to EU energy legislation, thus limiting its potential use by Russia as a geopolitical lever, it did not go as far as the EE states wanted by blocking the project altogether. If the EU's ability to be a soft security provider depends ultimately on its capacity for solidarity and unified action, as the NS2 issue shows this may not always be possible due to divergent national interests, especially when the interests of the EE states conflict with those of other influential member states. The next section discusses a number of new threats to EU unity that could further undermine the bloc's potential to provide security in Eastern Europe.

76 *Defending Eastern Europe*

New threats to the EU as a security provider

There are currently a number of threats to EU unity and cohesion, including Brexit, the differential impact of increased migration from the Middle East and Africa, and the continued economic and political fallout from the Eurozone debt crisis. This section, however, focuses on two threats in particular that are of special relevance for Eastern European security, the growing efforts of external great powers – Russia, China, and the United States – to sow division and exert influence within the EU, and the growth of illiberal nationalism within the EU, and Eastern Europe in particular.

Concerning the first of these threats, dividing, and weakening, the EU has been a long-standing strategic goal of Russia, and before it, the Soviet Union (along with severing the transatlantic relationship).[2] As the NS2 issue shows, Moscow is able to do this by playing upon the different economic and geopolitical interests of EU member states. Especially pertinent in this regard is the division between Western and Southern European states, who being more geographically distant from Russia are less fearful of it and more desirous of closer economic and political ties, and the EE states, especially, the "frontline" states who for reasons of both geography and historical experience, are more wary of Moscow and vulnerable to its geopolitical influence. Those states sharing a physical border with Russia or that are geographically closer – Poland, the Baltic states, and Romania – are more fearful of Moscow and take a harder stance on relations. However, EE states that are more geographically distant from Russia – for example, the Czech Republic, Slovakia, and Hungary – or as in the case of Bulgaria also have close historical and cultural ties to it, feel relatively less exposed to Russian pressure and are more open to positive relations (Zaborowski 2019).[3] In recent years, just as Moscow has stepped up its efforts to divide and destabilize politics throughout Europe – for example, through disinformation campaigns, interference in elections, and financial support for far-right populist parties – it has also increased its efforts to exploit divisions within the EE states, including by cultivating closer ties to states that are less reflexively hostile to Russia. For example, the Putin regime has fostered close ties to the illiberal government of Prime Minister Viktor Orbán in Hungary, who in turn has sought to use special ties to Russia, China, and other non-EU powers to counterbalance Brussels and expand his room for maneuver within the EU (Apuzzo and Novak 2019; Euractiv 2019).

Also threatening to divide and undermine the EU is China's growing economic and political presence in Europe, and the economically weaker countries of Eastern and Southern Europe specifically. China has become a major trade partner of the EU, its second largest after the United States in terms of the overall volume of trade. It has also become an increasingly important source of foreign investment for Europe, especially in the wake of the 2008 Global Financial Crisis and subsequent Eurozone debt crisis. Chinese foreign direct investment (FDI) in the EU has surged in recent years, reaching a record €37.2 billion in 2016, compared with only €2.1 billion in 2010,[4] although Chinese investment subsequently dropped to only €17.3 billion in 2018 because of stricter scrutiny by European governments (Hanemann et al. 2019). While most Chinese FDI has gone to larger and more prosperous Western European countries, an increasing amount has flown to Eastern and Southern Europe, including many of the EU's new member states. Much of this investment is linked to Beijing's ambitious "Belt and Road Initiative" (BRI), aimed at constructing a transport infrastructure network (roads, railways, ports, etc.) connecting China and Europe. To facilitate these investments, Beijing has also promoted the creation of a new diplomatic forum – the 16+1 framework – which brings together on a regular basis the representatives of China and 16 Southern and Eastern European states, including all 11 EE states (Godement and Vasselier 2017, 64–74; Valášek 2017).[5]

While welcome as a source of investment and economic opportunities, China's increased economic presence in Europe has also generated concern about the Chinese acquisition of strategically important industries and technologies, and about how Chinese investments might evade or undermine strict EU rules and standards concerning such things as tendering procedures and protection of the environment. It has also given China growing political influence, especially over economically weaker Southern and Eastern member states that are large current or potential recipients of Chinese investment, thus threatening to divide the EU and make it even more difficult to forge common policies toward Beijing (Godement and Vasselier 2017, 64–74; Seaman et al. 2017, 11–13). As an example, strong lobbying by Hungary, the largest recipient of Chinese investment in Eastern Europe, was reportedly a key reason for the EU's ambivalent response to the July 2016 ruling of the UN Permanent Court of Arbitration against China, in a case brought by the Philippines against Beijing's territorial claims in the South China Sea (Godement 2016). Hungary's ambassador to Beijing also refused to sign a statement critical of the BRI that was agreed to by the other 27 EU national ambassadors to China in April 2018 (Heide et al. 2018).

Intra-EU differences have also hobbled EU efforts to forge common trade and economic policies toward China. For example, different national positions affected the debate in 2017 about creating an EU system for screening and regulating Chinese investments in Europe. While the Commission's proposal for new legislation was strongly supported by France, Germany, and Italy as well as other Northern and Western European states, it was opposed by Greece, Portugal, and the EE states, all of which have become, or seek to become, major recipients of Chinese investment in their finance or infrastructure sectors (Godement and Vasselier 2017, 56).

China's increased economic presence in Europe, and the growing dependence of some European states on Chinese capital and markets, thus undermines a common EU approach toward China. It also allows Beijing to exploit intra-EU differences and play member states off against each other according to the strategy of "divide and rule." By dangling lucrative economic deals and investments, or at least the potential for these, before individual governments, Beijing is often able to break or prevent a common EU front against it, thereby leaving the EU vulnerable to Chinese influence and weakening it overall. In the words of former German Foreign Minister Sigmar Gabriel, "if [Europe does] not succeed in developing a common strategy towards China, then China will succeed in dividing Europe" (Reuters 2017). A divided EU, easily influenced and manipulated by Beijing as well as other external powers, would be a weaker EU, and one less able to be a provider of soft security for the EE states.

While the efforts of Russia and China, two non-Western authoritarian powers, to divide and weaken the EU are perhaps not surprising, the attempts of the United States to do so are. While past US administrations have not been above using "divide and rule" tactics to exert influence in Europe on key issues, they have generally been supportive of the EU as an entity and viewed a strong and united Europe as a good thing and a key US ally and partner. However, the Trump administration departs markedly from this tradition, and seems determined instead to sow discord and division within Europe in a manner that is at times oddly consonant with the efforts of Moscow and Beijing. As has been well documented, President Trump is openly skeptical about the continued value of NATO, and he has publicly mused about the possibility of US withdrawal from the transatlantic defense alliance. He has also expressed antipathy toward the EU, making it clear that he views it only as an economic competitor that was formed to take advantage of the US in trade. He is a vocal supporter of Brexit, and he has urged other member states to follow the British example and leave the EU. While criticizing and attacking, at times in very personal terms, the leaders of key European democracies like Germany, France, and Britain, he has cultivated friendly relations with the illiberal and Eurosceptic governments of Poland and Hungary, as well as with other populist nationalist European politicians.[6]

Uncertainty about the US commitment to NATO have led some EE states, especially those closest to and most threatened by Russia, to hedge their bets by developing special bilateral security ties to Washington. The most prominent example of this is Poland, which has expressed a strong interest in a permanent US military base in the country. While the centrist

Tusk government made the initial request for a US base, the conservative Law and Justice government, which took power in 2015, has made the idea a major objective of its foreign and security policy. Polish President Andrzej Duda formally submitted Warsaw's request to host a US base during a White House visit in September 2018, offering to contribute at least $2 billion to build the facility. In an attempt to play on the president's famously large ego, he also suggested that the new base could be called "Fort Trump" (Taylor 2018, 29). Aside from Poland, Romania and the Baltic states may see opportunities for new bilateral security deals with the US (Gotkowska 2019), while a joint statement released following the White House visit of Czech President Andrej Babiš in March 2019 also floated the possibility of bilateral defense cooperation outside the NATO framework (Gearan 2019).

Any such efforts to cultivate special bilateral ties between individual EE states and Washington are bound to be highly divisive within both NATO and the EU, however, with other European governments opposed to steps that could further antagonize Russia. The idea of a permanent US base in Poland has not been discussed within NATO, for example, precisely for this reason (Taylor 2018, 29). More generally, efforts by the EE states to seek bilateral side-deals with the United States undercut the alliance's common strategy. According to a senior NATO official, "If you start doing that, the whole system of collective defense starts to unravel" (quoted in Taylor 2018, 30). Such efforts also undermine EU unity and cohesion. Indeed, according to one analyst, some Western European officials even believe that hardliners in the Trump administration may seek to use special ties to the Polish government "as a wedge to weaken or even break up the EU" (Taylor 2018, 42). Such suspicions are reinforced by the Trump administration's support for the "Three Seas Initiative," a Poland-promoted project launched in 2016 that seeks to build closer infrastructure ties among 12 EU states along a north–south axis stretching from the Baltic to the Adriatic and Black Seas. All 11 EE states as well as Austria are members of this project, whose membership closely overlaps with that of the Chinese-led 16+1 forum (Gotev and Brzozowski 2018). Despite fears to the contrary, US officials portray Washington's increased engagement in Central and Eastern Europe as an effort to check growing Russian and Chinese influence in the region rather than an attempt to divide the EU (Wemer 2018). Even if not intended, however, US engagement in the region may end up achieving precisely that.

A final major threat to EU unity and cohesion, and thus to its ability to be a soft security provider for Eastern Europe, is of a more internal nature, and that is the growth of illiberal nationalism in many countries and parts of Europe, but in particular the EE states. This development not only corrodes the normative basis of the EU – centered on liberal-democratic values, the

80 *Defending Eastern Europe*

rule of law, open borders, and transnational cooperation – it also holds the potential for increased friction and antagonism between European states, and between individual states and EU institutions, that could also weaken and divide the EU. Hungary and Poland are at this point the primary examples of the strength of illiberal nationalism in the EE states, which have proven particularly susceptible to these trends for a number of reasons (Krastev 2018). Illiberal governments hold power in both countries. Both Budapest and Warsaw also face Article 7 (of the Treaty on European Union, TEU) procedures within the EU, which can be launched against member states found to be persistently in breach of the EU's founding liberal democratic values, and which could eventually lead to the suspension of a state's voting rights within the bloc's decision-making institutions. However, illiberal tendencies are also evident in other EE states, including Romania, Slovakia, and the Czech Republic.

The continued growth of illiberal nationalism in the EE states also threaten to infect the rest of Europe and corrode the EU's unity and cohesion from within. One speculative future scenario discusses what could happen if present trends continue:

> The sovereigntist and illiberal trend that is particularly pronounced in Central European politics becomes mainstream across the EU. European norms of democracy and rule of law are hollowed out in more and more EU member states, while their further political integration as a bloc is first halted and then gradually reversed. As a result, the European project degrades until it constitutes little more than a free trade zone among what are, essentially, only nominal democracies. (*Visegrad Insight* 2018, 6)

Even if illiberal nationalism does not spread throughout Europe, the EE states affected by this trend could become increasingly alienated and divided from the rest of the EU. They would thus be more vulnerable to the pernicious influence of outside powers like Russia, China, and even a more nationalist United States, which seek to divide, weaken, and even destroy the EU.

Conclusion

This chapter has argued that the EU is an important provider of security in Eastern Europe. While the EE states are primarily reliant on NATO for their hard security, the EU is also vitally important as a provider of soft security in the region. EU membership bolsters the economic prosperity and political stability of the EE states, thus enhancing their internal strength and resiliency, reducing their vulnerability to external pressures, and increasing their capacity to withstand all manner of security threats. Integration into the EU security community has mitigated or eliminated the security dilemma vis-à-vis fellow EU members and provided the EE states with the protective benefits of being part of a much larger and more influential economic and political bloc. EU membership has helped the EE states to escape from Russia's geopolitical orbit, and at times, the EU has provided them with valuable diplomatic support against economic and political pressure from Moscow. Moreover, the EU's role as a soft security provider could become increasingly important going forward, as threats to European security in the future are more likely to be of a soft or non-military nature, such as those concerning energy, economic stability, climate change, the cyber sphere, and social cohesion.

While the soft security benefits of EU membership are of a fundamentally different nature than the hard security protection provided by NATO, the two types of security are complementary and mutually supportive. Whether one could be effective without the other is doubtful, and each is therefore dependent on the other.

The EU's ability to be soft security provider is greatly dependent on its capacity for unity and solidarity. As the case of the NS2 pipeline shows, however, in a decentralized polity of 27 member states such unity is not always a given, and is sometimes difficult to achieve because of divergent national interests and priorities. The energy security issue thus demonstrates both the considerable potential but also the limits of the EU's ability to be a soft security provider. Moreover, the EU's capacity for unified action, and hence its ability to be a security provider, is currently faced with a number of new challenges. These include the increased efforts of external great powers – Russia, China, and the United States – to sow division and exert influence within the EU, as well as the growth of illiberal nationalism in Europe and the EE states in particular. Whether the EU is able to surmount these threats to its unity will largely determine its future capacity as a security provider, including its potential someday to be a provider of hard security should that become necessary.

Notes

1 As famously expressed by Belgian Foreign Minister Mark Eyskens in January 1991, in reference to the EU's inability to contribute to the international military coalition put together by the United States to push Iraqi forces out of occupied Kuwait in 1990–1; quoted in Whitney (1991).
2 For an analysis of the efforts of Russia, as well as China and Turkey, to exert influence in Central and Eastern Europe, see Szicherle et al. (2019).

3 The analysis in this paragraph excludes the non-EU states of the former Yugoslavia, especially Serbia, which have a more friendly view of Moscow, for both historical (Tsarist Russia's support for their liberation from Ottoman rule) and cultural (religious and linguistic) reasons.

4 Although Chinese FDI still represents only a small share of the EU's total FDI stock, amounting to only 2% in 2015 (Seaman et al. 2017, 9–10).

5 In April 2019, the 16+1 became the 17+1 with the addition of Greece (Yu 2019).

6 For an overview of the Trump administration's views of Europe and impact on transatlantic relations, see Stelzenmüller (2019).

6

Secure East-Central European NATO members: the Czech Republic, Hungary, and Slovakia

James W. Peterson and Jacek Lubecki

It is clear that the Russian takeover of the Crimean Republic from Ukraine in 2014 had a major impact on security perceptions of the three Baltic nations and Poland. However, what was the reaction of Central European nations such as the Czech Republic, Hungary, and Slovakia? In this chapter, the authors will explore those perceptions in an effort to determine how broad were the ripple effects of the events further east into the neighborhood of the EU. Initially, the commentary will focus on a brief assessment of five theoretical perspectives that help explain the reasons for the decision of President Putin and the Russian leadership to react to the turmoil in Ukraine connected with the Euromaidan Revolt. Second, attention will turn to common factors in the Czech, Hungarian, and Slovak security preparations in the years prior to the tumultuous events connected with the takeover of Crimea. Third, it will be important to identify separately the foreign policy themes of the three in the same time frame before early 2014. Fourth, it will be vital to look at their contrasting defense preparations after 2014, with an understanding that the three nations do differ in significant ways, for example, that its larger population enables Czechs to build up defense capabilities to a greater degree than is true for Slovaks. Finally, there will be an assessment of what the impact of the 2014 events was in changing or maintaining defense preparedness and perceptions of security threats in Hungary, Slovakia, and the Czech Republic. Linkage of the findings back to the key models of Russian behavior during the events will help demonstrate how the discovered conclusions about the Czech, Hungarian, and Slovak reactions impinged on theories of Russian foreign policy behavior.

Motivations for the Russian takeover of the Crimean Republic

There are five perspectives that endeavor to explain the motivations behind the Russian willingness to absorb the Crimean Republic after the turmoil connected with the Euromaidan demonstrations and eviction of

President Viktor Yanukovych in 2014 (Treisman 2018, 279–80, 295). These approaches can be the starting point for developing models of Russian foreign policy behavior both within this crisis area and in the broader Central and Eastern European region. It may be that one or more of these perspectives explain Russian policy better than the others, or it could be that, combined, they all assist in understanding this explosion in the region. In turn, our analysis of Czech, Slovak, and Hungarian defense policies before and after the Crimean events of 2014 has the potential to illuminate the relevance of these five perspectives in concrete detail.

First, a tradition of imperial expansion in the Black Sea area may have driven Russian policy toward Ukraine in 2014. In the 1790s, Catherine the Great had moved the border of the old Russian empire in that direction through conquest, and this was a result that Russians celebrated in verse and ensuing traditions. In fact, an early Russian anthem commemorated this expansion into an exotic area and the role of Catherine the "Mother" in that addition to the Russian Empire. The Crimean Peninsula remained a valued part of the Russian and Soviet state until 1954, when First Secretary/Premier Khrushchev awarded it to the Ukrainian Republic within the Soviet Federation. Russian vacations often centered on this beautiful location, while Soviet leaders usually repaired to their official summer dachas or residences during the August vacations. In that sense, it was not a surprise that prominent Russians such as Mikhail Gorbachev expressed great joy at the recovery of this state treasure that had been accidently lost after the breakup of the Soviet Union and emergence of Ukraine as a nation-state in 1991.

A second model of Russian behavior in 2014 was fear that the new Ukrainian leadership might push for or accept membership in NATO or the EU. In fact, the matter of admission to NATO had materialized in a serious way at the organization's Bucharest Summit in 2008, but Kiev's desire for that development did not materialize. Efforts to prevent Ukraine from a greater embrace by the EU was clearly one factor in the events of late 2013 and early 2014. President Putin offered his Ukrainian counterpart Yanukovych a $15 billion loan to woo him away from signing and ratifying an Association Agreement with the EU. Through the Russian takeover of Crimea in 2014 and secession of Russian-speaking areas of Eastern Ukraine, perhaps the new Ukrainian leadership would understand the need to balance West versus East in a more even-handed way.

Next, there existed many Russian populists or extreme nationalists who resented the expansion of NATO into the region that Moscow had dominated during the Cold War. Incorporation of the Baltic nations of Estonia, Latvia, and Lithuania was particularly troubling, for they had indeed been actual republics in the Soviet Union for half a century. The positioning of NATO troops in a variety of traditional alliance partners such as Germany as well as new allies such as Poland fueled the Russian nationalists in their belief that encirclement of Russia was the prime objective of such military tactical moves. Officially, Russian military leaders had put the proposed Missile Defense System of the George W. Bush administration in the same category. The possible emplacement of pieces of that system in Poland and the Czech Republic led them to react with counter-proposals to build up missile capabilities in their own exclave of Kaliningrad. Such important regional debates fueled the conclusions of Russian populists about the nefarious intent of such NATO and American military activities.

Fourth, there is evidence that the rational actor, President Putin, in the early years after rising to the presidency on the first day of 2000, had become a very different kind of decision-maker more than a decade later. Models of incremental decision-making that became strong alternatives to the rational actor model may have been more characteristic of Putin in the years leading up to the Crimean crisis. Incremental decision-making meant that bureaucratic politics had taken over from the cost–benefit approach that was at the heart of rational decision-making. From that perspective, Putin and his advisors may have decided on tactical moves in the heat of a crisis that were not wide departures from previous stands. In the words of incrementalism and the bureaucratic politics model, he may have "muddled through" the Crimean crisis on a day-to-day basis. Attempting to decipher an overall vision of the president through the entirety of it may have been a futile task.

A fifth and quite persuasive explanation is one that centers on the significance of Sevastopol in Russian strategic calculations. The Russian military base there of about 20,000 troops was a post-Cold War anomaly in the sense that it had its life in the midst of territory of the independent state of Ukraine. Ships from that base took a key part in the containment of the Georgian military moves against Russia in 2008, and they were part of an immediate and strong Russian military overreaction afterwards. Would the new post-Euromaidan leaders of Ukraine attempt to deny Russian access to that base and thus make it part of the Ukrainian military strategy and set of capabilities? In the uncertainty that surrounded the protests and regime change in Ukraine, the plans for a referendum in Crimea, and extreme Western concern about the resulting fragmented security picture, the future of the Sevastopol base was an open question and source of both Russian anxiety and concern.

Common security factors in Czech, Hungarian, and Slovak pre-2014 preparations

For all three states, Atlanticism with NATO responsibilities has been the driving factor behind their individual security considerations and policy

86 *Defending Eastern Europe*

moves. However, Europeanization with an emphasis on EU obligations was moving into a more prominent position, especially for the Slovak defense leaders and managers (Kříž and Chovančík 2013, 49–52). There were a number of reasons that guided this important shift in emphasis. Following the Lisbon Treaty of 2009, there was a decision by all three states to take part in additional EU military operations. At that conference, the EU replaced the European Security and Defense Policy (ESDP) with renewed emphasis on collective action through its Common Security and Defense Policy (CSDP). Without a major threat to either nation in the early part of the twenty-first century, Central European states in general were moving to postures that were "more continentalist in their strategic orientation" (Mitchell and Havranek 2013, 42–3). At the same time, a number of challenges had emerged and they had the result of pulling Hungary, the Czech Republic, and Slovakia away from the Atlanticist–NATO priorities. The emphasis of the Obama administration on a pivot or rebalance toward Asia, his cancellation of the Missile Shield Program in 2009, the rise of nationalist leaders like Orbán in Hungary and Trump in the United States, and Russia's increased interest in the East-Central European region all served to unbalance the relationship toward which Czech, Slovak, and Hungarian (prior to 2010) leaders were working. As a result, for states in question there was a disruption to their efforts to achieve a balance between the "geopolitics from without" and "nationalism from within." The importance of "pragmatic groupings" like Visegrád 4 (V4) might become more significant in the future (Mitchell and Havranek 2013, 42–8). In general, preparedness was an important priority, but the emphasis seemed to be shifting to a more European focus that was less reliant on US leadership.

Czech and Slovak military units also worked together in particular theaters in ways that underlined their common security concerns. For example, they formed a joint battalion that became part of the KFOR peacekeeping operation in Kosovo in January 2002. Further, in 2003–5, they cooperated with the Polish military in the Topolčany Brigade. Each of the three militaries maintained a presence related to the Brigade on their own territory. For example, the Czech 46th Artillery Brigade stayed in its home base in Pardubcice, while the headquarters of the unit remained in Slovakia (*Military Technology* 2003, 87, 92). Such operations reinforced the Atlanticist theme of their policy, for it was the attack on American soil in 9/11 that activated the need for enhanced and collective preparedness by Central European nations. Further, the need for the Kosovo operation was precipitated by NATO attacks on Serbian incursions into that republic in 1999, and so NATO interests continued to be relevant and prominent.

Perceptions of Czech Republic defense leaders prior to the 2014 crisis

In 2002, the Czechs passed a Constitutional Amendment that consolidated power in the executive branch for making decisions about commitment of troops to NATO and EU missions and deployments. The Amendment centered power in the executive branch alone to make such decisions for a period of 60 days without consultation with the legislature. Such a decision was complementary to preferences of both NATO and the EU (Kříž and Chovančík 2013, 55). Another important decision emerged at the beginning of 2005 when the Czech leaders ended military conscription and transformed their military into an all-volunteer force. Linked with this decision were two critical assumptions. First, future military operations would be outside the region and entail mainly peacekeeping and humanitarian projects. Second, the Czech armed forces would operate exclusively under NATO command and not be unilateral operations (Kříž and Chovančík 2013, 53–4). Taken together, these assumptions became guides for Czech defense policy in the midst of the Afghan and Iraqi campaigns, but they did incorporate an unexpected combat potential as well.

In the early part of the twenty-first century, NATO was the most important factor in Czech national defense considerations. For example, the Minister of Defense Jaroslav Tvrdik, in an interview in 2003, described the collective military alliance as "the best international collective security system there is today." In addition, he noted that the Prague NATO Summit worked with the Czech military to focus on a role in "specialization" that included Nuclear/Biological/Chemical (NBC) protection and surveillance. In fact, the NBC Battalion was active in Operation Enduring Freedom in Afghanistan, as it operated in support of civilians threatened by weapons of mass destruction. He expressed pride in Czech contributions to Balkan security but did observe that the floods in 2001 in the Prague area had made it difficult to meet budget objectives in defense and other areas. In enumerating important defensive capabilities produced by the Czechs, he mentioned electronics and its engineering counterpart, manufacture of NBC protection equipment, production of medical support equipment, and construction of small arms. At the same time, Chief of the General Staff Lt. General Pavel Stefka described the battalion-sized units that were actively deployed to Kuwait and Kosovo. In his view, such contributions reflected the rise of a professionalized military at a time of considerable post-Cold War military downsizing ("Interviews" in *Military Technology*, April 1, 2003). Thus, Czech military capabilities meshed with and contributed to the NATO missions at the transition point between the Balkan wars of the 1990s and the War on Terror of the early twenty-first century.

88 *Defending Eastern Europe*

At about the same time, the Czech military had set certain goals that helped ease the transition from the territorial defense priority of the Cold War to deployments into a variety of peacekeeping operations in both combat and non-combat zones. For instance, their 2001 defense reform pointed to an objective to deploy an army or air forces unit of 3,000 personnel to a location for at least six months. Alternatively, the same units should be prepared to dispatch 1,000 troops for six months while keeping another 250 in readiness for a different deployment. However, the 2007–8 economic recession took a toll on such military plans, and so the Czech 2011 White Paper on Defense eliminated concrete goals of that type. However, the document did call for regular participation both in the NATO Response force (NRF) and in the planned EU Battlegroups that were part of its ESDP thrust (Kříž and Chovančík 2013, 57–8).

The focus on preparedness for defense missions was not the sole preoccupation of Czech national security and foreign policy architects. Concern about the evolving trade imbalance with China was a concern that originated in the 1990s but continued on into the new century. By 2009, the trade deficit with them was the equivalent of $9.6 billion and a matter of increasing concern. This disturbing figure was even more surprising, given that Czech exports to China increased by 70% in 2007 alone. However, goods sent to China constituted only 0.7% of overall Czech exports, and so there was much room for substantial increases. For its part, China endeavored to make amends partially by cultural outreach to the Czechs. In 2008, they opened a Confucius Institute at Palacký University in Olomouc and doubled stipends for student exchanges between the Czech Republic and China (Fürst and Pleschová 2010, 1370–6).

Another way of reacting to the Chinese challenge has been activity in Africa by Central European nations connected with the V4. In a sense, the leaders of those nations have sought to counter-balance the overtures from distant Asia, and the Czechs have been the most active of the V4 states in that effort to upgrade development in sub-Saharan Africa. Prior to the 2014 Ukrainian-Crimean crisis, Czech assistance also expanded into Ethiopia, Ukraine, Belarus, and Georgia (Kopínski 2012, 39–41). Such work in development assistance within the framework of the V4 balanced somewhat the heavy military obligations that were part and parcel of full membership in NATO.

Perceptions of Hungarian defense leaders prior to the 2014 crisis

Perhaps the most significant fact of Hungarian defense policies between 1999 and 2014 is how thoroughly the country embraced the liberal-internationalist ethos of both NATO and EU in terms of institutional and doctrinal adjustment, following, in this respect, the Czech Republic. Just like the Czechs, however, the Hungarians, and this includes both the pre-2010 governments of ex-communist MSZP and of the centrist-populist "right," and the post-2010 populist-nationalist governments of Victor Orbán, pursued a course of systematically shrinking defense budgets and therefore shrinking military capacity. Indeed, during the decade between 2004 and 2014, the Hungarian defense budget shrank from 1.7% of the Hungarian GDP to roughly 0.85% of it, which represented a loss of around 50% in real value (Peterson and Lubecki 2019, 89). This made Hungary, alongside with Spain and Belgium, into a "chronic under-spender" in NATO (Kufčák 2014). Indeed, when referring to the post-communist Hungarian military Lt. Gen. Ferenc Végh (Chief of General Staff, 1996–9) and Minister of Defense Fenrec Juhász (2002–6) used terms like "operetta military" and "army of a banana republic" (Simon 2002, 38, 92; Kufčák 2014).[1] Only in 2012 has the inadequacy of Hungarian military spending been acknowledged by Minister of Defense Csaba Hende. In 2012 he, and later his successor Istvan Simicsko promised to increase military spending, and substantial increases have indeed occurred since 2015 (Hungarian Republic Ministry of Defense 2012; MTI 2014; Than and Szakacs 2017).

The paradox of Western liberalism being a mix of anti- and pro-military values explains the paradox of Hungary's success in being admitted to NATO in the first tranche of countries in 1999. Inasmuch as liberalism meant the rejection of both communist and nationalist militarism, Hungary's public and elite found no problem adjusting to liberal institutional and policy requirements such as subordination of the military to civilian leadership and demilitarization. Indeed, Hungary's political and institutional success in adjusting itself to Western democratic liberalism was so conspicuous that the country appeared as a leader in terms of post-communist transformation. The country's admission into NATO (1999) and the EU (2004), coupled to a general transformation of Hungary's neighborhood into a zone of liberal peace and stability solved the country's strategic dilemmas and allowed it to focus on internal economic development. One way to conceptualize the absence of Hungary's robust defense policies is to understand its security policy as a victim of its own success.

Liberal internationalism, indeed, promised a way to solve the challenging strategic predicament of displaced Hungarian minorities in neighboring countries. This security dilemma, coupled with neighboring countries' fear that Hungary would seek to revise their borders, or otherwise undermine the countries from within, had the potential to generate a mutual cycle of national oppression and state-to-state hostilities insolvable in a realist-nationalist world. In a liberal-internationalist world, though, Hungarian

90   *Defending Eastern Europe*

minorities could enjoy the constitutional rights and autonomy guaranteed to all citizens because integration into a Western security (NATO) and socio-economic (EU) community meant a diminishing importance of national borders and accompanying security dilemmas on all sides. Post-communist Hungary, indeed, rejected militaristic realism and nationalism,[2] and explicitly chose liberal internationalism as a logical way to solve its strategic dilemmas. This strategy, from a 2020 vantage point, has succeeded wildly, with five out of seven of Hungary's neighbors also becoming members of either NATO or the EU. Only Ukraine and Serbia have formally remained on the outside of Western institutionalized national communities, though both have embraced liberalism and have been seeking membership in NATO/EU (Ukraine) and the EU (Serbia). Peace has been achieved – regardless of the persistence of tensions with Romania and Slovakia – in bilateral relationships between Hungary and all its neighbors, highlighted by friendly treaties with Ukraine (1991), Slovakia (1995),[3] and Romania (1996) (Nagy 1997). Indeed, liberal internationalism has remained the doctrinal basis of Hungarian foreign, security, and defense policies throughout the post-communist period, and was forcibly reasserted in the country's 2012 National Security Strategy and 2012 National Military Strategy, regardless of the nationalist-populist turn the country took during 2010 elections (Hungarian Republic Ministry of Defense 2012, 1–2; Republic of Hungary 2012, 20). Overall the Hungarian political elite, backed by a supportive public between 2004 and 2014, decided that what Hungary needed to do was to implement for defense policies token spending and loyal engagement with NATO in terms of "niche capabilities."

The Yugoslavian crisis presented both a risk and a strategic opportunity for Hungary. The risk of military spill-over into Hungary was real, and, if the government acted too brashly in an effort to protect its borders, ethnic Hungarians living in Serbia faced insecurity. In this respect, it helped that in the early 1990s, Hungary still possessed substantial conventional military assets, which were strengthened by Defense Minister Keleti's acquisition programs. Hungary's proximity to the conflict, more importantly, provided the country with an opportunity to demonstrate its utility as a new liberal-internationalist democracy. Hungary became a staging area for NATO military operations, deployed peacekeeping troops to former Yugoslavia without costly overseas logistics, and firmly upheld sanctions and embargoes in the region

Hungary utilized the mix of danger and opportunity resulting from conflict in the Balkans masterfully to gain NATO recognition and membership (Szenesz 2007). Indeed, the very fact that Hungary faced real dangers when cooperating with NATO, both in Bosnia and, later, in Kosovo, evidenced not simply its usefulness but, more importantly, its loyalty (Hendrickson 2002; Simon 2002). With the waning of the Balkan conflict, in turn, engagement in multilateral deployments overseas became Hungary's solution for national security in the face of its rapidly shrinking defense budgets and disintegrating military infrastructure.

The consequence of Hungary's shrinking defense budget was a loss of territorial defense capabilities. NATO, along with the promise of continued liberalization in the region, offered a solution through investment in multilateral deployments for peacekeeping and peace-enforcement. These missions required less costly capacities, such as light-infantry and special forces trained in civilian affairs and logistical/civil reconstruction. The practical ways Hungary contributed to NATO and EU alliance missions, to the US-led "War on Terror," offered to the country a role in an international network of "niche capabilities." As a result, under-spending on indigenous self-defense became much less relevant to national security,

After Hungary was admitted to NATO in March 1999, the country's new defense policies were formally enumerated in key documents. A new National Security Strategy was issued in 2002 and again in 2004. These developments culminated in the 2009 National Military Strategy of the Republic of Hungary (Republic of Hungary 2002, 2004). The doctrinal thrust of these documents was the assumption that Hungary, as a result of membership in NATO and the peaceful liberalization of Hungary's neighbors, is free from conventional military threats. The Hungarian Ministry of Defense was urged to adjust to a new era of utility through the establishment of quick reaction forces, easily mobilized for the type of missions Hungary executed in Yugoslavia, Iraq, and Afghanistan. In the words of the 2004 National Security Strategy:

> The Hungarian Defense Forces need to possess rapidly deployable and sustainable forces suited for flexible use and available also for expeditionary operations that are able to cooperate with allied forces and can be used in crisis spots without any geographical limitations. The necessary capabilities need to be developed in a way coordinated with NATO, coordinating force contributions committed in the NATO and EU framework and by making use of the opportunities lying in bi- and multilateral international co-operation and development programs. The goal is to develop an armed force that is new in the sense of operational philosophy, able to fulfill the commitments made to NATO, that is financially affordable, capability-based and specialized in the framework of the North Atlantic Treaty Organization, that constitutes an integral part of the society and enjoys the latter's support,

92 *Defending Eastern Europe*

that is placed under democratic and civilian control, and that is composed of members committed to their countries and profession, properly trained and motivated, commanding the respect of the society. Respective goals and tasks need to be set down in the National Military Strategy. (Republic of Hungary 2004, 22–3)

These transformative defense policies culminated in Hungary's first National Military Strategy in 2009 (Hungarian Republic Ministry of Defense 2009). They were accompanied by HDF structural reform throughout the 2000s. After an extensive Defense Review process conducted between 2001 and 2002, conscription was suspended in 2004 and an all-volunteer force created by 2006, which stabilized at around 20,000 troops and 10,000 civilian employees by 2009. The troops centered around at first three, and then two infantry brigades (comprised, altogether, of seven battalions), one intended mostly for collective defenses and one for international deployments, plus an Air Wing and support services for specialized tasks. Command structures were unified, comprising a General Staff and a Joint Forces Command integrated in the Ministry of Defense.

Modernization and capacity-building influence during the first decade of Hungarian membership in NATO is undeniable, albeit narrowly focused on "niche capabilities" (Biró 2005; Pécsvarady 2010; Racz 2012; Racz and Erzsebet 2012; Magyarics 2013; Matei 2013; Wagner and Marton 2014; Kufĉák 2014; Csiki 2015). Capacities such as special forces[4] and strategic lift capabilities were acquired, mostly in the course of multilateral or bilateral cooperation. Cooperation with the United States on issues such as doctrine and training was close, and it was the United States that provided Hungary with modern equipment necessary for foreign missions, such as MRAP mine-resistant and HMMW vehicles, communication equipment, and assault small arms used by Hungarian special forces in Afghanistan.

Without pressures from external allies, it is unlikely the Hungarian military would have taken on even the small-scale modernization efforts it did during its first two decades as a liberal-internationalist democracy. Hungarian public opinion is historically inclined to see all military spending as a luxury, and membership in NATO hardly changed the pervasive political culture of anti-militarism. In fact, widespread opposition to deployments in Afghanistan, Iraq, and the former Yugoslavia was likely aided by the fact that Hungary's small professional military operated somewhat detached from a wary public. Taking on missions unapproved by the public – like the one in Afghanistan – hardly contributed to building a culture of popular consensus and approval for defense policies as a part of Hungary's self-identity (Sherr 2000; Talas and Csiki 2013; Csiki 2015).

Perceptions of Slovak defense leaders prior to the 2014 crisis

Slovaks differed from Czechs in retaining a legislative role with its hold on troop commitments in other nations. They continued to require that the National Council approve such decisions as they pertained to either the sending of Slovak troops outside their nation or the bringing in of allied troops onto their own territory. Such a policy decision made it difficult for them to contribute to the NRF or to the EU's ESDP commitments. In addition, they ended compulsory military service in 2006, one year after the Czechs made a similar decision for professionalization of the personnel in the armed forces (Kříž and Chovančík 2013, 53–5).

Slovakia did not join the Western military alliance in 1999, the year of Czech admission to that organization. In its Defense Doctrine of that year, it gave equal importance in defense considerations to NATO and the Western European Union (WEU). Europeanization obviously played a stronger role in Slovakian perspectives than it did for the Czechs. In the defense strategy outlined in 2005, their policy designers put an equal value on the EU and NATO in protecting the Slovak state (Kříž and Chovančík 2013, 52, 59). However, the objectives of the transatlantic military alliance shone through in the 2004 Armed Forces Goal and Model 2015. In that document, the Slovak defense planners proposed a series of objectives that they would meet by 2010. Their short-range security goals included fulfillment of NATO's Article 5 obligations, contributions to two international crises at the same time, commitment of 8% of its troops to crisis management, and preparation of 40% of its military personnel in reserve to engage in military operations that were necessary (Kříž and Chovančík 2013, 56).

The Slovak Republic defense planners, like their Czech counterparts, also placed a priority on Asian connections. In the 2003–8 period, the Slovaks actively countered the Chinese on trade benefits, but their deficit with China in 2009 was 1.6 billion euros. Exports to China increased in each of those years but only amounted to 0.7% of their total exports by 2009. China did take positive steps to improve its image in Slovakia, outside the economic realm. Such moves included establishment of a Confucius Institute in the capital of Bratislava in 2007, re-opening in 2004 of the Department of Slovak Language and Culture in Beijing, and opening of a Chinese IT company in Bratislava in 2006 (Fürst and Pleschová 2010, 1370–7). All of these overtures balanced the heavy defense emphasis of missions connected with NATO and even the EU. In addition, the Slovaks earmarked specific aid packages for Kenya on the African continent and both Serbia and Montenegro in their Balkan neighborhood (Kopínski 2012, 39–41). Overall, Slovak perceptions entailed a much broader vision than one might expect from a relatively small state.

94   *Defending Eastern Europe*

Perceptions of Czech defense leaders after the 2014 crisis

One important component of the decision-making process was established in the year of admission to NATO, and it was called the Foreign Security Policy Coordination Committee (FSPCC). Among its key undertakings was coordination of significant "regional security matters" (mzv.cz 2018a). In the period after the outbreak of the 2014 explosion in Ukraine, the work of that committee included interactions with the Czech defense organizations and personnel on re-definitions of national security needs, interactions with NATO, work with the EU on its new and emerging defense plans, and coordinated activity with the other three nations that made up the V4. The latter was particularly important during the 2015–16 year of the Czech presidency of the V4.

Adoption of a new "Security Strategy" in 2015 made it possible for Czech defense managers to articulate a changed posture in light of the transformative events further east during the previous year. Renewed commitments to allies now made more sense in light of "the new security environment." While human rights and personal freedoms were still at the heart of that strategy, the document did underline "sovereignty, territorial integrity and political independence." Those latter features reflected the new reading of national security needs that followed perceptions of Russian aggressiveness toward Ukraine on the Black Sea. The document also contained an expression of hope for more "cohesion and efficiency" within both NATO and the EU. Such an outcome would provide a broader framework for and concrete security steps that would be required by the Central European powers (mzv. cz 2018b).

NATO held a number of important summits after the outbreak of unrest in Ukraine in 2014, and two of the most significant were the 2014 Wales Summit and the 2016 Warsaw Summit. Czechs were supportive of the action plans of the former with respect to creation of a new readiness military force and redirection of units to the now-threatened Baltic area and Poland. In connection with the goals of the latter, they agreed with the renewed priority on assuring enhanced stability and security in both the southern and eastern neighborhoods of Europe. Czech defense goals also included an increase in defense spending that would result in elevation to 1.4% of GDP by 2020. Given Russian capabilities in the hybrid warfare arena, there was a need for close work by Czech defense specialists and the personnel of the Western military alliance in that area. Inclusion of new NATO members was part and parcel of the firmed-up posture of the whole alliance toward continuing or future crises in the East. Czechs took on some of the work with PfP and alliance candidates such as Bosnia-Herzegovina, Georgia, and Macedonia. Eventual admission of such new members would strengthen the "stability zone" and make the alliance more prepared to cope with "possible security crises." In addition, Czech forces had deployed to crisis areas for two decades, and their personnel continued to play roles in Kosovo and Afghanistan (mzv.cz 2018c). All of these projects within the alliance were extensions of past Czech activity, but they all assumed a heightened urgency with new evidence of Russian willingness to violate border and territorial integrity when the opportunity presented itself.

The EU had taken a number of steps that better prepared its members collectively to deal with future instability in its eastern neighborhood. One move was the agreement in its 2009 Lisbon Treaty to rename its European Security and Defense Policy (ESDP) as the Common Security and Defense Policy (CSDP). While renaming an overall policy in this way was not a major shift, the implications were important in underlining the need for agreement and conviction by all when security threats developed. It is not a surprise that they made the change one year after the brief war between Russia and Georgia. A second initiative was the 2016 start-up of the European Global Strategy (EGS), and this might help to cement the links among member states in articulating a vision of future objectives and thus strengthen purposefulness with regard to security strategy. Further, Czech experts and specialists played a continuing role in a full array of 16 EU missions (mzv. cz 2018d). In the view of Czech leadership, an improved EU defense capability would be a vital supplement to NATO capabilities, as well as a better guarantor of outcomes, in a time of anxiety and uncertainty about future developments in the region.

Notable is the V4 program that accompanied and guided the Czech presidency of that organization in 2015–16. That program highlighted, in its opening passages, the urgent need for strengthened trust in light of the fact that "armed conflicts have returned to Europe." The V4 would continue, as well, its ongoing work in helping to resolve the perpetual economic conflicts in the region, but clearly security was now an issue at a level that it had not been before 2014.

The document selected out energy cooperation with Ukraine as a priority for the future, and modernization of that sector would receive V4 assistance. This thrust of the assistance was very important in the Ukrainian context, due both to its dependence on Russia for energy and to its role in maintaining a pipeline that transmitted oil and natural gas westward into the Balkans and also to its immediate north. Outreach to the potentially threatened Georgia and Moldova was part of the group agenda as well, for their territorial integrity was not assured in light of the Russian takeover of Crimea and its transformation into a republic in Russia. The V4 pledged to organize seminars for both but for "mainly Ukraine." When Slovakia chaired the organization in 2014–15, it had started a series of networking

96   *Defending Eastern Europe*

roundtables in Ukraine, and the Czechs intended to continue to build on that during their V4 presidency. More specifically, their assistance would center on "education, transport, environmental protection, and healthcare."

Discussion of security issues was at the heart of the 2015–16 V4 program, while increased readiness was its cornerstone. In that sense, the document reminded that goals in 2014 did include a plan to create a V4 military structure. As that would take some time, the near-term goal highlighted work within NATO to implement a Readiness Action Plan (RAP). Organizationally, RAP would eventually include a Very High Readiness Joint Task Force (VJTF). Preparedness to treat future crises or unexpected spill-over from the Ukrainian situation would benefit, and the merger between NATO and V4 work would be accelerated. Of course, contingent work on security with the EU and its programs would better prepare Central Europe for a future threat. The EU had been preparing a plan for a series of battlegroups that would possess combat capabilities to deter future threats. Under Czech leadership, the V4 decided to prepare one of those groups and set a deadline of 2019 for its completion. There would be flexibility in such a battlegroup, for it could be of use to NATO as well as to the EU (mzv.cz 2018e).

Perhaps this kind of common work among three related organizations would give Russian leaders second thoughts about any new plans for unexpected invasions. In that regard, there was outreach even beyond those units to additional nations that might have perceived increased threat. The V4 sponsored three meetings with the Western Balkan nations of Croatia and Slovenia, as well as with the Baltic state of Latvia. They also made plans for four bilateral meetings between their leadership and that of NATO. Such connections would provide leaders of the Western military alliance an opportunity to provide feedback to the V4 nations on their progress in meeting the defense objectives in their individual security plans.

Perceptions of Hungarian defense leaders after the 2014 crisis

As the Ukrainian crisis exploded in February 2014 with Putin's takeover of Crimea, Hungarian Prime Minister Orbán's response to the issue was unsurprisingly dual. On the one hand, his government, alongside other V4 countries, condemned the violation of Ukraine's sovereignty, and diplomatically supported and sustained EU sanctions against Russia (Kucharczy and Meseznikov 2016). On the other hand, in a display of political schizophrenia, Orbán publicly criticized the sanctions his government helped to draft (Kucharczy and Meseznikov 2016) and raised the issue of Hungarian minority rights in Transcarpathia in a display of inferred support for

Russian claims of Ukraine's Russian minority rights violations. Though Orbán's rhetoric painted the EU as an enemy and Russia as a friend, his political actions in many ways could not have been further from his words. This duality with respect to Hungarian defense policy is explained below.

The year 2010 was a watershed in Hungarian domestic politics, as the right-wing nationalist populist FIDESZ–Hungarian Civic Alliance (Fidesz – Magyar, KDNP), led by Orbán, won the country's parliamentary elections by a landslide, defeating the disintegrating left and liberal parties. FIDESZ won again in 2014, and again in 2018, and remains popular today, in contrast to Hungary's left and liberal opposition parties, whose continued weakness almost guarantees that FIDESZ will win the 2022 elections as well and remain in power for almost two decades Significantly, as of 2018, the second most popular party in Hungary was "Jobbik" (in Hungarian: Jobbik Magyarországért Mozgalom, JMM, Movement for Better Hungary) with an even more nationalistic and populist program than FIDESZ.

With its supermajority, FIDESZ created a new Constitution of April 2011 and passed over 200 new laws, thus modifying every aspect of Hungarian domestic politics. The Constitution and the laws have been criticized as nationalistic and anti-democratic. Victor Orbán, in particular, became famous with statements that proclaimed the exhaustion of liberalism as an ideology and liberal democracy as a political system. Orbán also praised authoritarian rulers like Putin, and engaged in an "opening to the East" policy, friendly to Russia. As a nationalist populist Orbán has asserted Hungary's sovereignty against the "global capitalist system" and depicted the EU as an oppressive institution that represents the interests of the globalist elite as opposed to the national interests of Hungary (Orbán 2014).

One would expect Orbán's self-proclaimed "national revolution" to immediately impact Hungary's security and defense policies, channeling them in a unilateralist direction toward a strategy of territorial self-defense. However, the essential structure, spending, and doctrine of Hungarian armed forces have stayed similar to the past policies in every essential national security document since the Constitution of 2011 until 2017. In fact, during that period the only concrete change that has resulted from Orbán and FIDESZ's rhetorical shift has been a modest increase in military spending in 2015, which was on track to matching the average spending of European NATO member states as a percentage of GDP by 2022.[5]

It was clear that without a substantial increase in funds allocated, Hungary would not be able to develop a military infrastructure capable of the unilateral territorial defense that FIDESZ was advocating. Therefore, it was only logical that Hungary continued to enjoy the historically unprecedented security of Euro-Atlantic defense alliances through policy that reaffirms its commitment to multilateral peacekeeping missions. Then, since 2017, and

98 *Defending Eastern Europe*

implementation of a new "Zrínyi 2026" defense program Hungary's military defense policies started shifting toward more robust funding, procurement, and defense preparations. Paradoxically though, and similarly to the Czech and Slovak policies, the direction of the procurement and acquisition effort pointed to clearly a Europeanist, as contrary to an Atlanticist or pro-US, direction, that one would expect from Orbán's ideological affinity to a fellow populist nationalist leader in the White House.

An early indication of a shift in defense planning can be found in the "Foreword" to the 2012 Hungarian National Military Strategy – a document still in place as of 2020:

> We have to abandon the previously denizened, comfortable, but altogether dangerous attitude that national defense is feasible without substantive military strength, relying on a bare minimum of own capabilities, and trusting solely in the solidarity of NATO and EU nations. This approach, which is a far cry from that of the Alliance, can only lead down the bitter path of further deterioration of our defense force. Only a strong, confident and proud defense force can be of service to Hungary, Europe, and Hungary's National Military Strategy. (Hungarian Republic Ministry of Defense 2012, 1–2)

However, only in 2015 did Hungary's military defense budget start increasing, clearly motivated by the twin 2013–14 Ukrainian and 2015–16 refugee/migration crises at the Hungarian border, during which the government made statements about "doubling the size" of the 20,000-strong Hungarian military. However, the chief way in which Orbán initially dealt with the personnel problem[6] of policing a large numbers of immigrants at the Hungarian border was recruiting a special 3,000-strong auxiliary force of Határvadász/Grenzenjäger, also called "Border Chasseurs" or "hunters" formation (Staff 2016a). To address the cultural problem of Hungarian anti-militarism, Orbán promised to increase military pay[7] and pursue "patriotic education of children focused on instilling military and patriotic values in school" (Staff 2016b).

In accordance with Dr. Csaba Hende's admission in the "Foreword" an increase in resources was set into motion by the 2012 Security Strategy. Specifically, by freezing the nominal value of the Hungarian defense budget until 2015, and then, starting in 2016, increasing the budget with "annual increases no less than .1 percent of the GDP." In reality, in 2014, Hungary's defense budget decreased to US$1.006 billion, marking the lowest real budget in the history of post-communist Hungary. However, in response to the Ukrainian crisis, Hungary lived up to its promise and increased nominal and real spending to fulfill and even slightly exceed the level of spending promised in the "2012 Military Strategy." This trend continued in 2016 and in 2017, thus raising Hungarian defense spending to roughly 1.21%

of GDP and \$1.21 billion real level (in 2015 constant dollars) by 2019. These budgetary increases financed a newly unveiled "Zrínyi 2026" defense development plan, which emphasized, in accordance with new defense doctrine, reserve and territorial defense forces, military pay increases, personal equipment and helicopter and armored vehicles procurement (Hungarian Republic Ministry of Defence 2017).

As the Hungarian military budget continued to increase with the direction of new procurement policies, far from purchasing expensive US weapons systems – a path taken by Poland and Romania – Orbán shunned the US and embraced European producers, purchasing an initial batch of 20 Airbus H145M (Caracal) helicopters in 2017, with an additional 16 H225Ms to be acquired, all for the value of around \$1 billion. This was followed in December 2018 by an order of 44 super-modern German Leopard 2 2A7s MBTs and 24 PzH 2000 self-propelled howitzers – for the total of 68 armored vehicles, backed by 12 training vehicles, with the value of around \$0.6 billion (Głowacki 2019). With deliveries starting in 2020, the Leopards and PzH are to equip a new heavy armored brigade, which, together with the planned near-doubling of the size of Hungarian active duty soldiers (from around 20,000 to 40,000), would mark a quantum leap in the increasing the country's conventional defense capacities. More is to follow, as the Hungarian army is to be rearmed with Hungarian (based on Czech license) built CZ Bren 2 assault rifles and Scorpio Evo 3 submachine guns. Likewise, Airbus is to work on Hungary's new air-defense system. Prior to 2020 not a single weapons system chosen by Orbán's government for procurement was of US origin, while the licensing and procurement contracts clearly locked Hungary into European-oriented defense networks and into the future. Perhaps to balance these decisions, Hungary announced a massive \$1 billion contract purchase of US-made air-to-air and land-to-air AMRAAM-ER missiles in August 2020 (Sprenger 2020). To finance these procurement programs Hungary must increase its defense spending to the promised 2% of GDP.

What is real and what is rhetoric remains a question when dealing with nationalist populist politicians like Orbán or Trump. Hungary hardly needs increased high-intensity warfare capacities to deal with terrorism or immigration – the threats emphasized by Orbán. Orbán, at least rhetorically, considers a Russian threat non-existent. Nevertheless, Hungary has continued to play the NATO "alliance game" through recent participation in NATO and V4 displays of defense readiness against Russia. Moreover, Hungary under Orbán started rebuilding Hungary's conventional defense capabilities after some 60 years of neglect, with Russia being one potential target of these efforts, and pro-Russian Serbia being the other. A whiff of Orbán's political schizophrenia, or, perhaps, shrewdness, is clearly on display here.

100   *Defending Eastern Europe*

The ultimate irony of Hungarian defense policy could be that the current government, dedicated to the cause of restoring Hungary's sovereignty, is actually illustrating the impossibility of full-on small country nationalism in a world enmeshed in international institutions. However, with the rise of Trump, Brexit, and wave after wave of populist nationalism across the globe, one wonders about the endurance of international institutions. If EU and NATO core states like the US, the UK, France, and Germany start destroying international institutions from within, the liberal internationalist model on which Hungarian defense doctrine is based might revert to a realist world of self-help and shifting alliances, as happened in the interwar period. Even Orbán would presumably not like a return to that world. If his actions as contrary to his rhetoric are an indication, he is betting on a Europe-oriented grand strategy for Hungary.

Perceptions of Slovak defense leaders after the 2014 crisis

Slovak defense interests after the Ukraine-Crimean challenge paralleled those of the Czechs in the double priority on both NATO and EU missions, while they also wrote a new agenda statement in 2015 that incorporated some of the changed themes. They had held the V4 presidency in 2014–15 and so helped move that organization toward an understanding of the new needs for the region in light of the spring 2014 threat from the east. Deployments often took on a different cast from those of the Czechs, and their capabilities in terms of personnel were lesser, due to the smaller size of their state and its population.

At the time of the 2014 crisis, the Slovak military possessed the experience of at least 30 deployments since 1993, and so they were prepared for any new commitments that might be necessary. In the previous two decades, the Slovak forces usually totaled about 600 in taking part in collective defensive activity in various locales. Supervision of their operations included NATO, the EU, the UN, and the Organization for Security and Cooperation in Europe (OSCE). The Western Balkans preoccupied much of their attention, but they also did what they could to support reform in Ukraine, Moldova, Georgia, and Armenia. Aspirations also included construction of an EU battlegroup with a total of 3,000 soldiers, and they ambitiously aimed at its commencement in early 2016. At the same time, there was a realism about the capabilities that they would employ in all of these commitments, for a full 70% of their military systems were at the end of their life cycle. There was a perception among all concerned that increased budgetary allocations to the defense sector were of paramount importance. Their main conclusion from the 2014 crisis was that "territorial defense" had increased in importance for the Slovak state and people. While regular troops and units were the heart of this task, they had learned from Russian actions in 2014 that a "hybrid war featuring irregular warfare tactics and procedures" would also be a future consideration of considerable importance (Pindják 2014, 81–6).

During the Slovak presidency of the V4, the organization committed to establishment of a V4-Ukrainian Conference/Forum that would establish a number of roundtables in which the participants would share knowledge about future needs and tasks that might make the situation in Ukraine more tolerable (mzv.cz 2018f).

When Slovak defense planners developed their new agenda for 2015, they highlighted the challenge of the Ukrainian crisis to their own security position. Importantly, the turmoil had created a transformation of the regional security situation from "stable conditions" to "low predictability." In other words, there was no guarantee of what the future would bring to Slovakia or its neighbors. Further, the controversy had damaged a general Slovak domestic consensus on foreign policy needs and future foreign policy decisions. Pressures for continued dialogue with Russia and the OSCE balanced the intense interest among many for heightened priorities with Western nations that were overwhelmed by the intensity of the new scene, with an outright Russian takeover of Crimea (mzv.sk 2018a).

There is no question but that NATO became more central in Slovak defense policy considerations after the tumultuous events of 2014. However, ISIS threats in North Africa, Iraq, and Syria also played a role in the heavier reliance on that Western security organization (mzv.sk 2018a). Slovakia made a purposeful effort to contribute to the missions outlined at NATO's Warsaw Summit in July 2016. The organization at that meeting decided overall to put four battalions in Estonia, Latvia, Lithuania, and Poland. In addition, they committed to develop a "tailored forward presence" in Southeast Europe. For its part, the Slovak defense community planned to send 152 troops to Latvia for three months in the middle of 2017, and those soldiers would be part of a V4 contingent. With regard to the Balkan area, they agreed to a mandate in which their embassy in Sarajevo became also a NATO contact point, and this fitted the pattern that they had earlier used in Kiev and Belgrade. They also made firm commitments that they would increase their defense budget to 1.6% of GDP by 2020, while they would earmark 20% of that defense budget to modernization and rearmament by 2016. Beyond those promises, the Slovaks continued to prioritize work in Afghanistan as they had in earlier years. For example, they deployed a contingent within a new NATO Training Mission in that nation, promised to continue financial aid of $200,000 to the Afghan Security Forces, and also put an emphasis there on the Official Development Assistance Fund.

102 *Defending Eastern Europe*

Further, their new emphasis on Ukraine included the training of Ukrainian demining specialists. They would locate some of those activities at three of their own centers in Slovakia and the rest of the work at the NATO Center of Excellence in Trenčín, Slovakia (mzv.sk 2018a).

For the Slovaks, EU defense commitments remained a vital supplement to NATO security operations. They envisioned activity within the EU framework of the CSDP to be a necessity in situations that had not engaged either NATO or the UN. They were particularly interested in contributing to CSDP centers that focused on security, human rights, and sustainable development. Specific EU missions that involved Slovak personnel thereby included the EU Advisory Mission Ukraine (EUAM) and the EU Border Assistance Mission (EUBAM) in Moldova-Ukraine. In the former project, Slovaks were part of a 260-person staff whose aim was strengthening of the civilian security sector in Kyiv, Kharkiv, Lviv, and Odessa. Work in the latter entailed efforts to harmonize border control on the 1,222-kilometer Moldova–Ukraine border as well as development and enforcement of customs and trade standards (mzv.sk 2018b).

In sum, the Ukrainian crisis did make a considerable difference in Slovak perceptions of their own defense needs and priorities. NATO activities for Ukraine were parallel to those that had preoccupied the Slovak defense sector in earlier years in the Balkans, Iraq, and Afghanistan. In addition, now the EU's Eastern Partnership Connections with Ukraine shone brightly for Slovak planners in light of that program's commitment to "democracy, reform, and stabilization." In the future, there would be meaningful work with Ukraine, Moldova, and Georgia on eventual EU economic and political integration. Russian sensitivities were very important too, as their reactions to Western activity in those three former Soviet republics would be strong and perhaps angry ones. In that light, Slovakia took a balanced view and hoped to maintain a dialogue with Russia on energy issues that were vital due to dependence on the pipeline that linked Russia with Slovakia and the Balkan nations. Slovak flexibility on the sanctions toward Russia would be likely, in light of their own national economic interests. However, any easing of sanctions would only be possible after a certain calm penetrated Ukraine (mzv.sk 2018a).

Conclusion

Overall, the Czech Republic took a more forthright stand in support of NATO goals than did Slovakia in the time before the 2014 Crimean crisis, while Hungary remained schizophrenic and ambiguous. The Czechs and Hungarians had entered the alliance five years before the Slovaks and had several years of experience in participating in NATO activities such as the liberation of Kosovo from the Serbian incursion of 1999. Slovakia valued the NATO presence but also valued equally the capacity of the EU defense capabilities to play a role in the equation of its own policy calculations. However, after the 2014 events in Ukraine, both the Czech Republic and Slovakia placed more emphasis on the commitments of the Western alliance to contain potential Russian military moves in the region – a policy that Hungary followed in its own idiosyncratic and self-contradictory way. Both committed in official security documents to send troops to the northeastern nations of Europe and followed through with "troops on the ground." It was not clear what the impact of the Trump presidency would be on such calculations. On the one hand, Trump's general unhappiness with the small NATO budgetary commitments to the alliance may have alienated Czech and Slovak political leaders and led them to resolve on a diminished security policy in the region. On the other hand, the vacuum left in the region by Trump's vacillation in policy may have strengthened their resolve to fill the gap themselves and do more. The perceptible Europeanist orientation of the three "secure" East-Central European countries seems to have crystallized by 2020 – if the United States is not to be relied upon, a modified security partnership centered perhaps on the Common Security and Defense Policy has to replace it, and even Eurosceptical Orbán's Hungary seems to have embraced this option.

What do these results portend for the five models of Russian foreign policy action that provide the frame for the activity and aftermath of the Ukrainian–Crimean crisis of 2014? Models 1, 4, and 5 of Russian behavior are unchanged. Imperial ambitions that are historical in origin continue to operate in a continuous way. Improvisation of policy by the Russian president and his inner circle look to be the better explanation of Russian moves than the organized step-by-step approach that characterizes the Rational Actor Model. Protection of the Russian base at Sevastopol was an enduring commitment that pervaded and outlasted the duration of the 2014 crisis that centered on Ukraine and its former republic in Crimea. At the same time, there is a real disconnect between Models 2 and 3 and Russian behavior in the Ukrainian/Crimean crisis. NATO interest in Ukraine greatly intensified in 2014, and both the Czech Republic and Slovakia (with Hungary, again, being ambiguous) made firm and concrete commitments to be part of future military tactics of the alliance in supporting that threatened PfP partner. Ukrainian membership in the alliance may not have been a realistic possibility, but extended connections with it have been an evolving reality. Finally, the answer to the concerns of Russian nationalists and populists about more alliance activity in the region led to the opposite of its intention, for NATO set up a new Rapid Response Force of 4,000 troops and

104   *Defending Eastern Europe*

transferred many troops from Southern Europe to the north of the continent. An enhanced and strengthened Western alliance was the result rather than its continental exit. Whether that strength will include increasing or decreasing participation of the United States is yet to be seen.

Notes

1 In the words of an anonymous Lieutenant Commander at the US European Command "working with Hungary is like watching a bad comedy set on auto repeat." See www.greekchat.com/gcforums/archive/index.php/t-54509.html, accessed August 13, 2017.

2 The hallmark of this rejection was Hungary's constitutional renunciation of war in its post-communist (amended 1949) Constitution, where article 6, paragraph (1) stated: "The Republic of Hungary renounces war as a means of solving disputes between nations and shall refrain from the use of force and the threat thereof against the independence or territorial integrity of other states." The subsequent paragraph (2) stated: "The Republic of Hungary shall endeavor to cooperate with all peoples and countries of the world." Significantly, similar provisions have long existed in post-World War II German, Japanese, and Italian constitutions. Among post-communist countries, we find a similar provision in the 1991 Slovenian Constitution. When Orbán come to power, paragraph (1) and its renunciation of war did not make it to the Hungarian Constitution of 2011.

3 See "Treaty on Good-neighbourly Relations and Friendly Co-operation between the Republic of Hungary and the Slovak Republic," www.kbdesign.sk/cla/projects/slovak_hungarian_treaty/related/treaty_sk_hu.htm, accessed June 20, 2018.

4 In particular, the 34th Bercsényi László Special Operations Battalion was designated as a special forces unit in September 2005 and gained new capabilities with heavy US training assistance and military hardware support. However, Maj. Szabolcz Péscsvarady in a monograph on the subject noted conceptual confusion, overlapping of responsibilities and waste of resources involved in the process of creation of Hungarian special forces (Pécsvarady 2010).

5 The paltry sum of 1.39% of GDP, one has to say, falls far short of the NATO recommended 2% of GDP. The whole notion that a country's defense spending is to be decided by an average of the proportion of what one's immediate allies spend certainly only makes sense under liberal internationalist premises – namely, based on a notion that "doing one's fair share" in a multilateral alliance framework should define a country's strategic needs.

6 Apparently, because of appalling service conditions (lack of winter gear and proper living accommodations) during the emergency border deployment, many soldiers and officers/NCOs quit the regular military, hence, the well-paid but poorly trained "Border Chasseurs" formation became a stop-gap measure to deal with the crisis. This information was given to the authors by Professor András Racz.

7 Increases in the military budget since 2015 have indeed been accompanied by increases (up to 50%) in military salaries (Hungarian Republic Ministry of Defence 2017). How these can be reconciled with the goal of rebalancing military spending toward procurement is not clear, but overall budget increases could address the problem.

7

Stable Balkan NATO/EU members: Albania and Bulgaria

Ivan P. Nikolov and James W. Peterson

Introduction: components of stability in the Balkans

Why is it the case that two Balkan states have weathered their historic crises and become valued members of the two alliances? After all, each was part of a region that conflict and controversy nearly tore apart in the period between 1914 and 1991. The catalytic events that led to the start of war in 1914 resulted from an attack from within the region, and by a Balkan assassin on a member of the Austrian royal family. World War II as well as the communist period created a situation in which the region was torn by both local and outside forces. The answer to the opening question about why stability has now set in is related to a variety of factors. Both Bulgaria and Albania entered NATO in part because of wars in Afghanistan and Iraq. Along with Romania, they offered a kind of buffer to the West as its forces moved into the neighborhood of those war-torn states, in light of the events of 9/11 and the subsequent rise of extreme Islamism in the Middle Eastern region. Thus, stability in the region emerged from a mix of political, geographical, and security factors of consequence.

Albania: membership in NATO in 2009 but not in the EU

It is clear that historical experiences serve as legacies that impact the defense strategy of Albania in certain respects. For example, it would have been difficult to predict that Albania would pursue alliance memberships after the maverick role that it played during much of the Cold War. The Enver Hoxha leadership had embraced alliance with the Soviet Union initially, but a flirtation with Chinese leadership eventually replaced that connection. Independence from any superpower in the communist world later became its hallmark policy. However, Ramiz Alia became the First Secretary of the Communist Party in 1986, and he both made overtures to and was accommodating with other states (Biberaj 1990, 1). This changed outlook on foreign policy may have paved the way for the pursuit of NATO membership after the collapse of communism in Southeast Europe in the 1990s.

Albania's huge Muslim majority makes it unique in the Balkans, as Kosovo has been the only state with similar ethno-religious characteristics since 2008. It may be that the special contributions its military was able to make in a number of peacemaking missions in predominantly Muslim states such as Afghanistan, Iraq, Kosovo, and Bosnia-Herzegovina are partly based on the expectation that its troops would work easily and smoothly with the local populations. However, this unusual feature of its potential contributions to NATO and EU missions is based on historical legacies that trace back many centuries. The Turks invaded its territory in the last part of the fourteenth century, and in 1468, Albanian geopolitical space formally became part of the Ottoman empire. They were under the control of the Ottomans for nearly 500 years and became technically independent in 1912. However, their ensuing experience was a stormy one, for the Great Powers immediately sliced off 40% of their territory, and then Albania succumbed to annexation by Italy in 1939. Thus, in addition to its Muslim character, a parallel legacy preceding the post-communist period was a "defensive nationalism" as part of their general state-based outlook (Biberaj 1990, 11–13). Protection by the Western military alliance in the early twenty-first century would have assisted in making up for these historical frustrations and defeats.

The current Minister of Defense of Albania is Olta Xhačka, and her career preparation is an interesting one for that position. She received her BA and MPA from Clark University in the state of Massachusetts in the United States. Her political allegiance in Albania is as a member of the Socialist Party, and she has also been a human rights activist. Perhaps her public administration education in the United States was based on the need to obtain an understanding of Western-based systems, as Albania planned for its accession to NATO that occurred in 2009. It is also true that the Ministry of Defense in Albania published a document in 2013, and its exclusive focus was on the role of women and on the need to increase their role in the defense area. Minister Xhačka thus sets an example at the very top of the organization of those values ("Olta Xhačka" 2019).

The ministry outlined its objectives for the future in its "Directive of Defense for 2017" under the leadership of former Minister of Defense Mimi Kodheli. Having been a member of the NATO for a full eight years, the document posited a goal of increasing the role of Albania in the Western alliance. Much of the planning for future defense projects centered on meeting NATO standards. For example, it aimed to obtain certification for its battalion group to participate in the alliance's NATO Response Force. In addition, it set a goal of increasing the readiness of its "Illyria" ship category

108 *Defending Eastern Europe*

so that its military vessels could participate in alliance naval operations. In terms of its air arm, the objective was making two Cougar helicopters ready for a role in NATO operations.

In more general terms and categories, it expressed the goals of contributing to three general alliance tasks. First, it would contribute to collective defense by linking its command structure to NATO forces. Second, it would continue to contribute to crisis management through its roles in Afghanistan, Kosovo, Bosnia-Herzegovina, Mali, and maritime activities in the Mediterranean. Third, it also put a priority on security cooperation that entailed contributions in the areas of arms control and disarmament. Clearly, the second of those objectives could provide a broad framework for the upgraded activities of its military units in land, sea, and air capacities.

The 2017 Defense Directive also established targets that would make Albania more secure by itself but also work more smoothly within the Western alliance. In the area of education, courses for officers and NCOs should in the future include modules in the English language, the tool of discourse within the alliance. Further, the Albanian military would play a heightened role in NATO military exercises but also be a host to more of its partners in Albanian national exercises. It stated forcefully and clearly that "gender prospects" should be pulled into its defense policies and established a target of both recruiting and promoting women to meet a 15% rate for them within the military. Thus, the membership in NATO had led to defense reforms that would interface the Albanian defense forces tightly with those of the larger military family ("Directive of Defense for 2017").

The engagement of Albania in NATO operations was a considerable one even before it became a full alliance partner. After the 9/11 attacks it sent 30 peacekeepers to Afghanistan with the principal task of providing protection to Kabul Airport. This unit was under the control of NATO member Turkey and part of a multinational unit that numbered 1,400 personnel. Five years after the Dayton Accord of 1995, Albania had 70 troops as part of a 4,200-member peacekeeping operation in Mostar, Bosnia-Herzegovina. It maintained that number of personnel through 2009, even after the transition in 2004 from a NATO to an EU operation. By 2009, Albania also had stationed 71 military persons in Iraq as part of a group that both provided security to Mosul Airport and served in escorting convoys (Peterson 2013, 56–7).

By 2019, the Albanian military had made considerable contributions in its first decade of NATO membership. Actually, between 1996 and 2017, it had involved 6,863 military personnel in peacekeeping missions. In 2019, it still maintained troops in Afghanistan, Bosnia-Herzegovina, Kosovo, Mali, the Aegean Sea, and South-Eastern Europe Brigade (SEEBRIG). Completed missions included those in Iraq, Chad, Georgia, and the ISAF mission in

Afghanistan that lasted until 2014 ("Engagement Policy and Evidence of AAF Participation in PK Missions" n.d.). Closer to home, it took part in the alliance's effort to take firm action in the area of mine countermeasures. The project was entitled the Standing Mine Countermeasures Group 2, and two of Albania's ships worked with a German flagship to complete the operation ("Butrinti and Oriku Exercise with SNMCM62 Flagship" n.d.).

Regional Balkan defense organizations were also an integral part of the defense plans and activities of the Albanian Ministry of Defense. In 1996, Tirana was the site of formation of the Southeastern European Defense Ministerial (SEDM), and it included all the Balkan players plus the United States as full members or as observer members. A vital part of this post-Bosnian War organization was SEEBRIG ("International and Regional Organization" n.d.). The official title of its peacekeeping force was Multinational Peacekeeping Force of Eastern Europe (MPFSEE), and in much of 2006, it maintained a mission in Afghanistan ("SEDM, Its Role, Dynamics, Engagement and Extension in South East Europe" 2019). That particular mission trained police officers, constructed checkpoints and patrols, taught police officers to respect human rights, and did training in vehicle control to ensure the security of Kabul. An Albanian Brigadier General Zuber Dushku headed SEEBRIG from 2009 until 2011, and its staff rotates from one country to another every four years. Ideally, it would contribute to "conflict prevention operations" under the auspices of the UN, OSCE, NATO, and the EU ("SEEBRIG" 2019).

Several additional regional defense organizations served the goal of broadening Albanian connections with nearby states that also were concerned about buttressing their security. In 2002, following the Prague NATO Summit, Albania joined with Croatia and Macedonia to constitute the Western Balkan Group. In a sense, it sought to emulate the success of the Vilnius Group that included the Baltic states of Estonia, Latvia, and Lithuania. In 2003 the Adriatic Charter was formed by the same three nations, and its purpose was getting them all into full NATO partnership. Albania and Croatia were successful in doing so in 2009, while Macedonia received a green light with conditions in 2018, and full membership as North Macedonia in 2020. At the OSCE meeting in Helsinki in 2008, both Montenegro and Bosnia-Herzegovina became members of the Adriatic Charter, and this may have helped the former become a full NATO member in 2017. For the latter, full alliance membership was still years away. There were substantive results that flowed from the formation of this group. They sent a joint medical team to Kabul Airport in Afghanistan, engaged in joint exercises, set up with the assistance of the Swiss a regional center for public relations and training in 2005, and established a Regional Defence College ("Adriatic Charter" n.d.). Such achievements were substantive and in part a response to Western criticism that these nations had done too little to prevent the damage that accompanied the Balkan wars of the 1990s.

In 2013, the Ministry of Defense published a report that evaluated the role of women in the Albanian military. In particular, it strove to work with the partner countries to share expertise on capacity building in this important arena. However, there was a sharp contrast between the proportion of women in its armed forces and the percentage in NATO operations. For instance, 11.2% of its military forces were women, with the Air Force doing the best at 14.7%. However, the proportions were only 0.14% in alliance operations and merely 1.2% in overall peacekeeping operations. It set goals to overcome this disparity and work toward a quota of 15% for women in the Albanian Armed Forces. It vowed to strengthen the role of women in joint exercises and peacekeeping operations as well as to try to promote more in rank ("The National Report 2013 Albania" n.d.). Many benefits could flow from success in this sector of defense development, and they would include strengthening the self-confidence of women in joining this sector of public activity as well as providing a broader perspective about the kinds of social and economic issues they would encounter in operations outside the nation.

Finally, what do the consequences of NATO membership look like in 2020? First, there is strong support by the public for this broadening of security protection, as opinion polls demonstrated that 89% of Albanians were positive about this partnership. Second, the alliance has had a profound impact on the strategic thinking of the state, for the ministry has set 49 force goals that will enable its troops better to interact with those of its alliance partners. Third, it has concentrated on developing a light infantry battalion of 1,000 troops that could contribute to alliance missions and projects. Fourth, its 330 troops continue to partner with others in Afghanistan. In Herat they work with Italian forces, in Kabul with the Turkish military, and in Kandahar with the Americans ("Relations with NATO" 2019). It is important that it continues to fulfill the promises made during the Partnership to Peace path that resulted in alliance membership in 2009.

While NATO is clearly its largest defense partner, the EU also plays a role in Albania's security considerations. It has a "Stabilisation and Association Agreement," and also produces progress reports for the European Commission. It has taken part in the EU's Common Security and Defense Policy (CSDP) that knit together the Albanian Ministries of Foreign Affairs and Defense. The EU will provide some funding assistance, and Albania has been willing to interlock its own defense spending process with theirs. Thereby, Albania buttresses its defense and security while hoping also to pave the way to eventual membership in the EU.

Bulgaria: membership in NATO in 2004 and in the EU in 2007

Background

Bulgaria has been a full-fledged member of NATO since 2004, however speculation about the loyalty of the country to the alliance is still discussed. The question "Is Bulgaria the Russian Trojan Horse in NATO?" still lingers (Maisel and DuVal 2017; Maison 2018; Grashkin 2020). It is probably a speculative question that still pays dividends, and a good illustration of the Russian political influence. It is often forgotten that the phrase was coined by Russian politicians and made public by the Russian representative to NATO, Dmitri Rogozin, back in 2008 as "Bulgaria is the Russian Trojan horse in Europe" – an expression of the Russian President Putin's aggressive designs for an Eurasian alliance under Russian hegemony (Shekovtsov 2014). Despite responses from Bulgarian officials, including the latest by the Bulgarian Prime Minister Boyko Borisov about the lack of evidence for such statements, but promoted by Russian-influenced sources in Bulgaria interested in cementing this idea amongst the NATO members, doubts still exist as to where Bulgarian loyalties really lie.

Myths and realities: Bulgaria and the gratitude to Russia

Interestingly enough, the majority of the discussions about the Bulgarian deference and special relations with Russia are based on rather superficial writings about the emergence of Bulgaria as an independent county as a result of the Russian–Turkish war of 1877–8 after over four centuries of subjugation within the Ottoman empire. Rarely do these go deep enough into the complicated relationships in the Balkans after this war. One of the major issues is related to the resistance of the Russian empire toward the unified Bulgarian state, and the preference for Serbia as the leader of Russian influence in the region. Moreover, the influence of Russia in Bulgarian politics suffered considerably as a result of the 1885 war between Bulgaria and Serbia and the unification of Bulgaria on September 6, 1885, recognized by the Bucharest Treaty of 1886.

Another historical event souring Russian–Bulgarian relations was the conflict between the armed forces of the two countries during World War I. Sometimes it is hard for analysts from outside to understand the fierce patriotism present in the young Bulgarian state in these early years. Probably the words of the Bulgarian general Ivan Kolev to his troops before the victorious attack of the Bulgarian cavalry against the Russian empire's Cossack troops in 1916 during the September campaign of World War I in the north of Bulgaria illustrate this spirit:

> Cavalry, God is my witness that I am grateful to Russia that liberated us. But what are their Cossacks doing here now in our Dobrudja? We will beat them and chase them away, like we will do with any enemy who is meddling with the unification of Bulgaria.

In other words, Bulgarians were grateful to Russia for the liberation from the Ottoman rule, however, they would firmly resist Russian intervention in their homeland.[1]

Discussing Bulgarian membership in NATO, it is somewhat surprising to find a lack of publications or comments on a rather important moment in these relations soon after the Soviet "liberation" of the country, namely the case of the NATO Company 4093.

The case of NATO Company 4093

After crushing the opposing political parties, and specifically the anti-communist wing of the Bulgarian Agrarian Peoples Union (BAPU)[2] in 1947, the anger of the democratic opposition in Bulgaria was palpable. The US government statement was that the "Communist-dominated Bulgarian Government is marching towards totalitarianism."[3] One of the reactions of the United States was the creation, on October 20, 1951, of Bulgarian Company 4093 as a NATO military unit by the American military command with Order #53 in Zeilsham, Germany.

The unit consisted of Bulgarian volunteers, in majority members of the Bulgarian Agrarian People's Union (BAPU) "Nikola Petkov" faction, who emigrated to the West. The first group of 49 soldiers was joined in the spring of 1952 by a second group of 38 volunteers, transported by the US Air Force from Turkey, Greece, and Italy and flown to Frankfurt. Gradually the company grew to 200 men, with four platoons and an administrative unit. They served at military storage facilities of the US Army in Germany. Polish, Czech, Russian and Baltic refugees also formed other companies of the guard service, and, eventually, a special guard battalion was formed.

During his visit to the unit in 1963, the leader of the Bulgarian anti-communist opposition abroad (and a member of Bulgarian Agrarian National Union (BANU)), Dr. G.M. Dimitrov, living in exile in Austria, stated that the Bulgarians from Company 4093 were not mercenaries, but NATO supporters and members. The company and the other units of the brigade were decommissioned on June 20, 1964 as a result of the Cold War détente with the USSR after the visit of Nikita Khrushchev to the United States. Remarkably, this episode of Bulgarian history remains virtually unknown in the West.

Stable Balkan NATO/EU members

Closer affiliations with NATO during 1992–4

After the visit of President Zhelev to the NATO Headquarters in 1991 and Bulgaria's joining the North Atlantic Cooperation Council, a reciprocal visit to Bulgaria by the Commander of the Southern NATO forces in Europe, Admiral Mike Buda, took place on February 20–22, 1992. After Luben Berov, President Zhelev's advisor, became prime minister in 1992, one of his first trips abroad was to visit the Secretary General of NATO Manfred Woerner at the NATO Headquarters on March 9, 1993.

The Bulgarian parliament moved on December 21 of the same year to approve the declaration in support of joining NATO and the European Security Zone. On February 14, 1994, President Zhelev visited the NATO Headquarters and signed the frame agreement with which Bulgaria joined the NATO program "Partnership for Peace." On November 28, 1994, Bulgaria, in a joint session of the North Atlantic Council in the format 16+1, accepted an Individual Partnership Program (IPP) with NATO, a program that had to be updated with specifics every year.

The main issue during this period remained the reduction within the Bulgarian armed forces and the liquidation of the eight batteries of IBM SS-23 Spider (Soviet designation OTR-23 Oka) with a range of over 500 kilometers. The Bulgarian military kept arguing that these batteries were of a modification that had a range of 400 kilometers, did not have nuclear warheads, and hence should be considered regular artillery units. The military brass argued these weapons were the only effective tools to deter a potential aggression from Turkey. The socialists managed to use this argument quite effectively both in the political discussions and in the media, often using the analogy of the conflict of the two neighboring NATO members, Turkey and Greece, around North Cyprus.

The government of Lyuben Berov could not carry out its promise. Berov resigned his post on October 17, 1994, and a "government of experts" of Renata Indjova was in place until January 15, 1995 when the socialist government of Zhan Videnov was approved by the parliament.

NATO developments during 1994–7

Active work toward both EU and NATO membership continued throughout the changing governments in Bulgaria, including the period of the rigid socialist government of Zhan Videnov, and despite the resistance of the conservatives in the Ministry of Foreign Affairs and those among the BSP majority in the 37th National Assembly (parliament). Joint American and Bulgarian teams of military and political experts worked on plans for transforming the national defense and security system, with rather limited results. Actually, at these meetings it was clear that the socialists were not united on the policies and the strategy of the country and there were at least three different fractions in the BSP. At the meetings with Xavier Solana, the Secretary General of NATO, they offered generally three different approaches, including security regulations through bilateral security agreements, an independent non-affiliated position with memoranda of understanding for cooperation with NATO on national security, and participation in all European organizational structures and full NATO membership (Capital 1996).

Generally, the opinion of the American expert Jeffrey Simon, whose report on the readiness of Bulgaria to join NATO was published and shared with the public, aptly reflected the situation at the end of 1997, especially his comment about "the seven lost years" (Simon 1998).

Frequent visits of NATO officials to Bulgaria kept the contacts alive. On May 2 and 3, 1996 the Secretary General of NATO Xavier Solana visited Sofia. Bulgaria was his last stop during his visits to the 11 countries from Central and Eastern Europe in the discussions for NATO membership. In Sofia he met with the Minister of Defense Dimitar Stoyanov and with the secretary general of the Bulgarian Atlantic Club, Simeon Passy (later foreign minister in the Simeon Sakskoburggotski government), as well as with members of the parliament from the ruling party. The visit was full of inconclusive discussions, and the position of the government was filled with obfuscation and generalities about cooperation with European organizational structures, with careful avoidance of the word NATO by the prime minister.

The newly elected President Peter Stoyanov had a quite different idea from the socialist government of this period. As an active Union of Democratic Forces member and ardent supporter of NATO membership for Bulgaria, on January 29, 1997, he visited NATO Headquarters and declared the desire of Bulgaria for full NATO membership. He argued that this desire was proven by the support for his presidential platform and his election. After the resignation of the Videnov government the transitional government of Stefan Sofianski (UDF) moved forward and on March 17, 1997, they accepted the National Program for Preparation and Joining NATO by Bulgaria. The decision involved the creation of an Intergovernmental Committee, chaired by the Minister of Foreign Affairs, the Minister of Defense, and included the Chief of Staff and Vice-Ministers from all government branches.

On May 8, 1997 the temporary "government of experts" approved a Declaration of National Agreement, where full NATO membership was listed as a strategic priority for Bulgaria. This Declaration was reconfirmed by the regular government of Ivan Kostov (ODS) on July 11, 1997.

The Bulgarian Army 2010 Vision and Plan 2004 controversy

The first step toward reorganization of the Bulgarian military, the "Plan for Organizational Development and Structure of the Bulgarian Army until 2010", approved with the Decision of the Council of Ministers (DCM) on February 18, 1998, rejected the previous "Conceptual Plan for Reform of the Bulgarian Army until 2019" from 1995 (see Kontsepstya za reformata v Blgarskata armiya do 2010, no 103, 1995). Soon after that, early in April 1999, the parliament accepted both the new "Military Doctrine of the Republic of Bulgaria" (Voennaya doktrina na Republika Bylgarya 04/08/1999) and on April 11, 1999, the plan for "Organizational Development of the Bulgarian Armed Forces until 2004," also known as the explosive "Plan 2004" (DMC 200 from 04/11/1999).

"Plan 2004" was met with anger by the military and by the political opposition, mainly because of the proposed drastic reduction of the 75,000 military service members in the approved "Concept 2010" from 1995 to a maximum of 45,000 due to the realities of the fiscal and demographic situation of the country. In addition, the document proposed further reduction of the purely military organizational elements through privatizing some of the paramilitary units. Until this moment the Bulgarian Armed Forces included the following units: Bulgarian Army, Border and Internal Troops, Ministry of Transportation Troops, Committee of Post and Communication Troops, Engineering Troops, National Security Service, National Intelligence Service, and National Guard Service. A year later, as result of the changes included in the new National Defense Doctrine and the Plan 2004, the number of units was reduced to only four branches.

Bulgarian military participation in NATO-EU operations in the Balkans (1997–2002)

On July 20, 1998, Bulgaria formally joined the Forces for Stabilization (SFOR) of Bosnia and Herzegovina and sent an engineering unit of 31 servicemen within the Dutch contingent. Later in 1998 a transportation platoon with ten trucks and 27 personnel was added to the logistics group "Beluga." This initial step was a small but decisive move toward proving adherence to the European and NATO policies and strategy and a demonstrated step away from Russia that was not met with the approval of all political forces and especially the "Russophile" segment of the society. In 2002–5 one Bulgarian infantry company was added as a security detail protecting the "Butmir" base in Sarajevo. Summarily, 1,134 Bulgarian military served at this location. Eventually the participation of Bulgarian forces increased after 2004 with additional units. Actually, this SFOR European NATO operation

116   *Defending Eastern Europe*

in 2012 was transformed into European Forces "Operation ALTHEA" and continues today, being the longest Bulgarian NATO-EU engagement (www.euforbih.org/eufor/index.php – accessed February 3, 2020).

The Bulgarian National Assembly and the government had several sessions related to the situation in Kosovo, beginning with a declaration from October 23, 1998. Another declaration related to the growing crisis in Kosovo was published on March 25, 1999, expressing the commitment of Bulgaria to NATO membership and a position for abstaining from military activities in Yugoslavia. With a decision of the 38th National Assembly from 1999, a small contingent of Bulgarian troops (an engineering platoon) was sent to Kosovo within the KFOR NATO forces as part of the Dutch Engineering Battalion, later from June 2001 transferred to the German Engineering Battalion.

Afghanistan 2002

In confirmation of its commitment to NATO membership, a Bulgarian military unit joined the NATO forces in Afghanistan in 2002 after signing on January 2002 the Memorandum on International Security of Afghanistan Forces (ISAF) in London. Quickly the National Assembly and the government approved the participation on January 21, 2002, and on February 16, 2002, a 32-member Bulgarian military medical team deployed at a British base close to Kabul. The mission of this team was over in 2003 due to the changing environment and a new team consisting of technical units and instructors was deployed there, beginning a period of expansion of NATO forces in the area.

Further steps toward civilian control of the Bulgarian Army, 1999–2000

An important step toward NATO-coordinated prevention of cross-border crime and national security was the visit of President Petar Stoyanov to Washington for a NATO high-level leadership meeting on April 24, 1999. At the meeting Bulgaria, as well as other aspiring non-members invited to the meeting, was offered a Membership Action Plan (MAP) for NATO membership. In addition, at this meeting the South-East Cooperative Initiative (SECI) was announced, a direct follow-up to implementation of the Dayton Accord from 1996. The countries within SECI included Albania, Bosnia and Herzegovina, Bulgaria, Croatia, Greece, Hungary, Moldova, Former Yugoslav Republic of Macedonia, Romania, Slovenia, Serbia, Turkey, and Montenegro. Later, a document called "Agreement on Cooperation to Prevent and Combat Trans-Border Crime" was signed in Bucharest on May 26, 1999, with the goal of trafficking control and collaboration in crime prevention (https://photius.com/seci/, accessed April 30, 2019). The coordinating role of SECI was charged to Austria. This initiative later developed as an important European Commission tool for cooperation in the region with focus on the Danube countries (2010 report at www.osce.org/cio/40625?download=true).

Later that year Bulgaria and NATO entered into an agreement for free transit of NATO air forces with operations "Joint Force" and "Joint Guardian." December 1999 was a month of intense meetings and discussions, including the meeting within the 19+1 format of the Political Committee of NATO (December 6, 1999). The Bulgarian Minister of Foreign Affairs participated in the meeting for approval of the Plan for Action for 2000–2002 of the SEEI and the Concept of Operational Capabilities on December 16, 1999. Prime Minister Ivan Kostov visited with the new NATO Secretary General Lord George Robertson on December 20, 1999.

Parallel to these high-level activities of the Bulgarian government, related to preparation for NATO membership, a joint Bulgarian–British team conducted a 1999–2000 study named "Review of the Organizational and Management Structure of the Ministry of Defense and the General Staff of the Bulgarian Army." This study was in implementation of the existing order of the Minister of Defense and actually an extension of the 1997–8 study by the team with a focus on democratic changes to reflect the increasing role of the civilian participation in the relationships with the military as well as elimination of policies from the Warsaw Pact past. While some US experts mentioned NATO membership as "the carrot" for Bulgaria, it was probably so for the politicians, but a lot less for the military, for whom the required changes and reductions were a rather bitter pill to swallow, even recognizing the realities on the ground, including the impossibly high financial burden on the national budget. For example, the military expenditures in 1999 represented 4.4% of the GDP even though these were hard times for the Bulgarian economy, burdened with a raging inflation.

Bulgaria in NATO military reorganization update: Plan 2015

The work for the further transformation of the Bulgarian military actually gained impetus with the country being officially in NATO. Based on the results from the Strategic Review Report of the national defense, accepted by the government with DMC # 465/05/31/2004, the National Assembly adopted the "Plan for the Organizational Development and Modernization of the Armed Forces until 2015" or simply "Plan 2015" (DMC # 301, 11/10/2004). Within this ten-year Plan 2015, conscription and a move to a fully professional army had to be completed by 2010, later changed to 2008. The size of the Bulgarian military had to be reduced by the end of the period

118   *Defending Eastern Europe*

from the 45,000, as stipulated in Plan 2004 to a planned force of 39,500, with a reduced number of tanks from 600 to 170. From the beginning Plan 2015 was unrealistic, considering the short term for its implementation (the original Kievnaar plan from 1999 was for a 20-year period for reforms). The ambitious plans on purchasing modern military equipment, "multi-role helicopters" (Eurocopter AS532 Cougar and AS565 Panther), transport aircraft (Alenia C-27J Spartan), communication equipment, new light and medium wheeled transport vehicles (Mercedes), second-hand frigates (Wielingen class), a minesweeper (Tripartite class), and other specialized equipment were partially implemented later in 2008 and 2009, spending over $2 billion.[4] This is why the plan was cancelled in 2010 and replaced with Plan 2020. The work continued in a new political environment by a new government led by the Socialist Party (BSP).

Bulgaria EU membership in 2007

Most of the work toward Bulgaria's EU membership was done during the Simeon Sakskoburggotski NDSV government, beginning with the declaration of the European Commission in 2002 on the three-year plan for the country to join the union after meeting the 31 requirements in the economic, political, and social spheres, with a special focus on the so-called "harmonization of the legal system" with the European democracies. On December 16–17, 2004, the EU in Brussels confirmed the end of the preliminary negotiations with Bulgaria on the accession and announced its desire to see Bulgaria as a full member in 2007. The European Parliament approved the invitation on April 13, 2005, and, on April 25, 2005, the agreement for Bulgarian membership in the EU was signed in Luxemburg. Bulgaria joined the EU on January 1, 2007.

Joining the EU was a very positive step forward for Bulgarian democracy. However, the workforce mobility introduced by this critically important step opened the doors for legal migration of the younger generations, especially the skilled professionals from Bulgaria to the West, thus limiting rather significantly military careers as a choice for many amongst the able-bodied men and women. According to several statistical studies in the next decade, over 1.8 million Bulgarians emigrated, significantly changing the demographic situation in the country negatively for both the economy and national security, something we will come to later in this chapter.

Further updates of the defense strategy and military plans in Bulgaria

With assistance from NATO, the Defense Plan 2015, adopted by the National Assembly in 2004, was updated in 2008 along the lines of Bulgarian Armed

Forces "deployability, usability, interoperability, and modernization of the entire military" with NATO (Le Jeune 2010, 11). The new plan emphasized civilian participation in and control of the military, ideas that have not been seen as appealing by the older military brass, still soaked in the Soviet-style spirit. A decision of the Council of Ministers #54 from March 21, 2008 adopted the "Updated Plan for organizational development and modernization of the armed forces based on Plan 2015" to address the growing NATO requirements. However, it was clear that a new review of the armed forces was needed. Such a review was conducted in 2010 during the term of the government of Boyko Borisov (2009–13).

As usual, the changing governments during political crises, rather typical for the process of transitions in Bulgaria, did slow down the process, halting solutions to main existing problems: corruption and lack of clear judicial process. The second Borisov government was no different. As a coalition of parties that included GERB, the Alternative for Bulgarian Revival (Alternativa za Bylgarsko Vyrazhanye, Алтернатива за Българско Възраждане, Bulgarian abbreviation ABV), and the Movement "Bulgaria for Citizens" (Dvizhenye na Grazhdanitye, Движение "България на Гражданите" – Bulgarian DBG, a party since 2014), this government was under a lot of pressure, both internal and external in many areas, from cancelling the hugely expensive contract with American-owned coal-fired power-generating facilities (Maritsa 1 and 2) to an unstable economy. There was also quite a political conflict with the change of the former anti-Russian President Rossen Plevnaliev and the election of a new, pro-Russian President Rumen Radev, supported strongly by the Socialist Party. These political changes partially explain why Bulgaria refused to join Romania and Turkey in the NATO navy exercises in the Black Sea (Naumescu 2017).

At the same time, the Borisov governments followed very closely the EU sanctions toward Russia, including refusing the Russian gas pipeline "South Stream" to be built across the country without EU consent. This created a lot of push-back by Russia and its Bulgarian sympathizers, including intensification of anti-European propaganda. Another anti-Russian act by the Borisov government, encouraged by the United States, was to refuse overflight by Russian airplanes to Syria in 2015.

The deepening of these conflicts led to the resignation of the second Borisov government on January 27, 2017, and a temporary government of Ognyan Gerdzhikov for approximately five months (January 27, 2017 to May 5, 2017). The new elections to both parliament and the new government returned Boyko Borisov and his party, the GERB, to power, however in a combination with three nationalistic and pro-Russian parties: "Ataka," the VMRO-Bulgarian National Movement, and NFSB, National Front for Saving Bulgaria party. Hence, the new "Borisov 3" government had to

120 *Defending Eastern Europe*

modify some of its initially strong anti-Russian positions with a more moderate tone to satisfy the electorate's expectations for seeking a compromise between NATO and EU sanctions and economic cooperation with Russia, on which Bulgaria depended exclusively for its energy. A compromise position was embodied in the following statement by the Ministry of Defense:

> Bulgaria supports the development of cooperation between NATO and Russia as essential for security in the Euro-Atlantic area in two interrelated aspects: that of the political dialogue and that of practical cooperation. (Ministry of Defense of Bulgaria 2017)

In 2019, in preparation for the meeting of Prime Minister Borisov with President Trump, the new American ambassador in Sofia, Hero Mustafa, emphasized two major areas of discussion: energy and purchase of more new weapons from the United States. On the first issue the topics for discussion were narrowed to two: gas independence of Bulgaria and nuclear energy modernization and safety (Paunovski 2019a).

The diversification of the energy delivery and independence will develop as a discussion on the way to eliminate the sole dependence of Bulgaria on Russian energy. The proposed solution was to be the construction of a new Bulgarian pipeline that connected to the Greek interconnector for gas supplies. The gas for this connector comes from Azerbaijan and Qatar, with the option for liquefied American gas deliveries. The idea for this Bulgarian connecting pipeline was to extend it further north to Hungary and west to the countries of the Balkans, opening the opportunity for Bulgaria to become a gas hub. US pressure on the Bulgarian government on this issue has increased recently with warning statements made by Secretary Mike Pompeo on July 15, 2020 about the "Turkish Stream" gas line to continue through Bulgaria as "Balkan Stream," characterizing the project as "an instrument for Russian influence" (Gardner and Humeyra 2020).

The second subject of the energy question related to a planned visit of representatives of the US Department of State and Department of Energy in Bulgaria, with the purpose of discussing the nuclear power complex "Kozloduy" and "Belene." The focus of the visit was to discuss its modernization and safety. Actually, this visit happened on December 10, 2019. Ann Ganzer, Deputy Assistant Secretary at the US State Department Bureau of International Security and Nonproliferation, spoke on behalf of the delegation about the November 16, 2019 visit during which her boss, Assistant Secretary of State Christopher Ford, spoke with Prime Minister Borisov (BTA 2019).

On military questions, the realities on the ground pushed the government of Bulgaria to contract the refurbishing of eight engines for its grounded Soviet MIG-29 until the new F-16 arrived. The plans of the

Ministry of Defense were to have at least 15 operating fighters instead of the current eight capable of flying. A contract with Poland to refurbish the engines, signed by Minister Nikolay Nenchev (Borisov 2 government), was attacked both by the opposition and by the Russians. The opposition demanded that Bulgaria get rid of all Russian planes and acquire new modern NATO-compatible airplanes. The Russian company, MIG, launched a protest that Poland had no actual license to rebuild these engines. The Air Force debacle was just another reason for the critique that "Bulgaria is the most dependent on Russian armament amongst the NATO members" (Deutsche Welle 2014). The Bulgarian military, however, seemingly accustomed through the years to the political theater in the country, continued to work on its alignment with NATO and EU operations.

The review of the Bulgarian armed forces in 2016 and the follow-up changes

The review of the status of the armed forces in April 2016, initiated by the government, indicated a sharp need for equipment modernization, especially in the Air Force where only eight functioning Soviet-era MIG-29 were left together with a dozen SU-25 bombers. The Commander of the Air Force, General Rumen Radev (later to become Bulgarian president), stated bitterly that Bulgarian fighter pilots have been learning to live with "dangerously low flying hours." The saga of the purchase of new fighter planes started with the search by the RFP for used and new planes from Italy, Portugal, Sweden, and the United States. The discussion had sharp political overtones: should Bulgaria buy EU machines or the more expensive American F-16 ones? Both the Swedish SAAB with its JAS-39 Gripen and the US Lockheed-Martin with its F-16 Block 70 engaged their lobbies in the country in a fierce battle, but in the end the United States' more aggressive diplomacy and in-country military and political liaisons prevailed.

The July 2016 meeting of NATO in Warsaw was a stimulus for lifting the limitations on NATO operations in the Black Sea region in preparation for vigorous defense against potential Russian aggressive acts. In the following years both US–Bulgarian and NATO and EU training military exercises have become regular elements of the programs of the Ministry of Defense and the branches of the armed forces.

In 2016, the Council of Ministers approved three important legal documents: the Law on the Military Reserve, the Law on Military Police, and, most importantly, the Law of Defense. In doing so, they expanded the functions of the Ministry of Defense to provide security and to allow integration of partnering military formations in the process.[5]

After the turmoil with the resignation of the Borisov government (Borisov 2) on January 2017 and the election of the new Borisov government (Borisov 3) on May 4, 2017, the prime minister and his government felt strengthened to make some unpopular moves. The new Minister of Defense Krasimir Karakachanov was from the nationalistic party VMRO (Movement for Bulgaria), and he had to prove that he was a strong and decisive supporter of the armed forces.

In the strategic review of the changing political environment, the escalation of the crisis in Eastern Ukraine, and the naval conflict between Ukraine and Russia in the Sea of Azov have brought an urgency to modernize the military and strengthen the alignment with NATO and the EU. Within the management plan of the government for 2017–21 a review of the status of the armed forces and the implementation of Plan 2020 was conducted by the Ministry of Defense in 2018.

Part of this urgency was addressed with the rotation of the location of troop exercises (like the "Black Sea Rotational Force" exercises) between Bulgaria and Romania, as well as with other countries within the Task Force that involved both NATO and EU troops, including US National Guard units, better intelligence, coordination, and sharing have been stepped up within the alliances. Increased cyber security and training in prevention of and dealing with large-scale military cyber-attacks and hybrid warfare, more attention to the educational institutions of the Ministry of Defense, and closer cooperation with civilian branches and citizens have been positive changes toward building a modern military.

The concept for a strategic "Road Map 2032" was presented by the Minister of Defense at the Council of Ministers on June 21, 2018. It was decided to move forward with a deeper review of the defense capabilities and a long-term strategic plan until 2032, allowing for a longer-term planning and modernization of the armed forces. Part of this preliminary document was the decision of the government in January 2018 to implement within a shorter horizon until 2024, the commitment of Bulgaria at the Wales Summit in 2014 to fund its military at 2% of GDP, and to seek a distribution of this funding within the formula "60–20–20": 60% for personnel, 20% for maintenance, and 20% for investment in new equipment and technologies.[6] The decision of the minister on the new defense review was published on February 7, 2019, as a guide for the process within the 2019–20 time frame for the development of a new "Program for the Development of the Defence Capabilities of the Armed Forces of the Republic of Bulgaria till 2032 (Program 2032)," based on the decision of the Council of Ministers from January 18, 2019 (Bulgarian Ministry of Defense 2019a).

National defense and security updates: missions abroad, border- and cyber-security

An important element of Bulgaria's security is the country's military missions abroad, both with NATO (ten operations) and with the EU (three operations). Improving the in-country coordination of all units of the Bulgarian military forces on military missions has been the recent focus of attention of the Bulgarian government. The changes made in the military continued to be with a focus on alignment with the NATO standards, mission, and structures for cooperation. It was reported that 760 military personnel participated in missions of NATO, the EU, and UN, including a company as part of the EU "ALTHEA" operation in Bosnia and Herzegovina, and the "Decisive Support" NATO operation in Afghanistan with 139 Bulgarian soldiers.[7]

The mission "National Security Support in Peace Time" includes "Border Control Assistance," "Antiterrorist Operations," and "Disaster Relief Assistance for the Populations."

In the area of "Border Control Assistance" the Ministry of Defense supports the police forces from the Ministry of the Interior in controlling the borders and prevention of illegal immigration. While in 2016 over 2,700 troops participated in this mission, the changes in the migration patterns later in 2018 allowed reduction of the troop numbers to around 700, mostly in logistical support for the border police forces. "Antiterrorist Operations," within the Plan 2017–21, is a task where the military dedicated mainly its Military Police and the "Special Forces" brigade 68 units, plus some military medical units with a total of up to 1,100 involved operationally when needed. "The Disaster Relief Assistance" is probably the most extensive involvement of troops with over 100 units, with approximately 700 personnel and specialists additionally trained for this purpose, and with two units dedicated to assistance in case of a disaster at the nuclear power station "Kozlodui" in the north. This group of forces provides also evacuation capabilities from difficult to access areas and conditions.

In reaction to the increasing weaponization of the cyber activities of Russia a new strategic program, "Cyber-resistant Bulgaria 2020," has been initiated in 2016.

Areas of concern for the Bulgarian military

Personnel

The report of 2016 raised one of the most important issues for the Bulgarian military – the growing lack of people willing to sign up as professional

124   *Defending Eastern Europe*

soldiers and as reservists. The vacancy rate has grown from 10% in 2014 to 20% in 2016 for the Land Forces, which have been the most active units used in all NATO joint operations abroad. Only 71% of the positions for regular soldiers and 80% for officers were filled (Bulgarian Council of Ministers 2016). Amongst the reasons for this situation, the report listed low pay, lack of legal stability and social support for the military, unclear career perspectives, and worsening demographics, with candidates not being able to cover the minimum requirements for the profession. It did not help that, according to the survey carried out by the Ministry of Defense in March 2016, 28% of Bulgarians held negative opinions about the armed forces. The personnel situation did not improve during the following years. Quite naturally the low aspirations among the appropriate age cohorts for a military career led to a decline in the total number of the military personnel to 31,300 in 2016 and 2017 and 31,000 in 2018, well below the stipulated expectations of a minimum of 37,000.

In 2018, despite modest increases in pay and benefits for the military, only 743 individuals applied for 1,183 job vacancies, of which 411 were selected as eligible for hiring. If in 2013 there were 5–6 candidates for one spot, in 2017 and 2018 there was less than one candidate. It was even worse for the Reserve forces, where in 2018, only 11 candidates qualified for 2,023 announced positions. In 2018, the deficit of personnel was 19% for the officers, 17% for officer-candidates, 9% for sergeants, and a total of 27% for the soldier ranks in all services (Bulgarian Council of Ministers 2018, 2019).

Equipment

The situation with military equipment remains at a critical stage, despite some slight increases in funding. As stated in the 2018 report, even with sufficient funding some of the systems are so obsolete that they cannot be repaired to function effectively. Even more, they endanger the lives of the people using them (Bulgarian Council of Ministers 2018, 30). According to the data provided by the ministry, technically defunct are 48% of the tanks, 40% of the infantry transporters, 80% of the aviation, and 10% of the ships (Bulgarian Council of Ministers 2018, 30). The situation has become especially critical in the Air Force where, due to equipment failures, people died in 2017–18.

The Board of Portfolio Management at the Ministry of Defense has selected the following three national priorities within the National Defense Plan update until 2024, with the premise of reaching 2% of the GDP funding for defense: "Purchase of New Type Military Planes," "Acquisition of a Multifunctional Patrol Navy Ship," and "Acquisition of Basic Military Equipment for the Formation of Battalion Fighting Groups within a Motorized Brigade."

The Air Force, Navy, and Land Forces upgrades

The new versatile airplane discussion has been ever-present in the media during the last decade as well as a point of hot political discussion. The political tensions during the Borisov 2 government around corruption and low economic performance in the poorest EU country provided reasons for not going ahead with this investment, despite pressures from diplomats and political figures from some major NATO member countries. However, the third Borisov government was based on a parliamentary coalition which included the nationalistic party VMRO, and counted a VMRO civilian Minister of Defense Krasimir Karakachanov in its ranks. Moreover a strong lobbying from both the US embassy in Sofia and Ambassador Rubin pushed for a US-sourced procurement program. As a result, the decisions in the selection process were made in rather quick succession. In June 2018, an RFP for the fighter planes was sent to seven countries. Four companies from three countries – the United States, Sweden, and Italy – were selected in October 2018 by a working group appointed by Prime Minister Borisov. At the end of 2018 the opinion of the evaluation was reviewed and a proposal to work with the United States on the purchase of eight F-16 block 70s was introduced in the National Assembly by the Council of Ministers. Among the negatives of this purchase were the fact that the United States required an upfront payment, initially over $1.6 billion, while the Bulgarian side was looking for a purchase within the amount of $1 billion. Eventually, after negotiations that included limiting the equipment options and the armament, it was agreed to pay upfront approximately $1.2 billion. This purchase created a deficit of over 2.1% in the national budget for the year. Another criticized element of the deal was the fact that the plant to make these machines has not yet been built, and initial delivery was to start in 2024. However, Borisov and his team pushed the deal through. A quote from an article in the Bloomberg News from January 9, 2019, aptly reflects the political situation:

> The cabinet's choice pitted Bulgarian President Rumen Radev against Borisov. Radev, a former Air Force chief supported by the opposition Socialists, said in a statement "the tender was fouled up" and accused the government of picking the winner in contradiction with rules approved by it and parliament. The cabinet has also agreed "to overpay a huge amount," according to President Radev. The U.S. is working on fitting Bulgaria's budget and operational needs, Secretary of State Mike Pompeo said in a statement on January 19, 2019.

126   *Defending Eastern Europe*

In the meantime, an agreement was reached in the National Assembly to refurbish 15 planes from the aging MIG-29 fleet with new engines. A contract with MIG-Russia for over 45 million BNL was made for spare parts, with the actual rebuilding to be done in Bulgaria. Eight rebuilt engines were coming along according to the contract with Poland. The funding for a total of approximately 150 million BNL for 15 fighter planes within six years, and a separate 100 million BNL for eight SU-25, to be refurbished in Belarus within four years, has been criticized by the opposition both from the left and from the right, but it went through the approval process with the National Assembly dominated by GERB (Paunovski 2019b).

The growing tensions along the Black Sea region indicated the need for two more multifunctional patrol ships to add to the existing five. The failure to sign a contract in 2017 forced another start-up of the process, and after approval by the National Assembly in 2018, an RFP went in November 2018 to seven providers. While waiting for the process on negotiations and contracting for these new vessels, a proposal to update the current frigates class E-71 has been put in motion with foreign firms within EU/NATO. Another planned update was related to the upgrading of the radar system with new tri-coordinated systems. Recently the Italian defense company "Fincantieri" blocked the RFP for two patrol ships (corvettes) with a complaint before the Supreme Administrative Court. The Bulgarian Ministry of Defense, however, decided to continue with the German company Lurssen the project for building two modular ships at the cost approximating 1 billion BNL (580 million euro) based on unofficial information that the Italian company complaint will be rejected by the court (TOC 2020).

With regard to the modernization of infantry carriers, the plan is to purchase 150 modern new vehicles for three battalions. The plan is still in a development stage with the RFP. There were four applicants to this RFP: ARTEC GmbH (Germany), Patria (Finland), NEXTER Group (France), and General Dynamics Land System – MOWAG (Switzerland). The US offer did not meet the price criteria and was not considered). The recent information is that the RFP process could be restarted, since the Ministry of Defense extended the time for applications by the German company (Nikolov 2020).

Many of the projects are coordinated with funds and commitments within NATO, EU, and bilateral agreements. Some examples include those with the US military such as the Strategic Airlift Capability (SAC) for training air force crews, United States Central Command (USCENTCOM) for transportation of troops to and from Afghanistan, NATO Alliance Ground Surveillance (ASG) for the radars and other surveillance equipment, NATO Security Investment Program (NSIP) – a strategic program to upgrade the air control and management within the unified NATO system, support for NATO air force operations and land-based naval communications systems for command and support of military vessels, the US Foreign Military Financing (FMF), the Foreign Military Sales (FMS), and the Capacity Building Programs (CBP). According to the opinion of an expert, Professor Todor Tagarev, former Minister of Defense, on March 17, 2020, some of the large projects, like the navy ships or infantry transporters will be delayed due to the COVID-19 crisis (Bloomberg News 2020).

Funding

The increase of GDP during the period 2015–18 resulted in an overall increase of the absolute amount of the funding for defense within the 1.2–1.4% that the Ministry of Finance set aside for defense. For example, in 2018 the funding for defense approximated in absolute values the volume of funds from 2008. However, in 2008 this 1.55 billion BNL was 2.25% of the GDP, while in 2018 the 1.59 billion was only 1.48% of GDP (without correction for inflation since BNL is pegged to the euro and remains fairly stable). In addition, the type of equipment and infrastructure of the new weapon system is in a different class of much higher expenditures compared to the traditional ones.

Another persistent problem for Bulgaria is corruption and resulting low economic performance, making it the poorest EU country. Hence in comparison with Belgium, for example, with its 2019 GDP per capita of $42,000 dollars as compared to Bulgaria's $8,200, 0.98% of GDP for the Belgian military is in a different category of funding than the same percentage for Belgium. Even with the last three years averaging an annual growth of 3.7% in GDP, the government budget in Bulgaria, approximately 44% of the GDP at 44.1 billion BNL, is being planned by the Ministry of Finance at a 0.5% deficit of 600 million BNL (Denizova 2018).

While defense is listed among the three government priorities of education, defense, and social services, the political support at the moment is prioritizing the other two with planned increases of the salaries of teachers at 20% and higher level of the payments for health benefits, including medicine and social services. The simple truth is that defense has suffered very seriously through the years of transition, being pictured as an unnecessary burden on Bulgarian society, with lazy and incompetent personnel and obsolete Soviet technology. The number of persons over 65 among 7 million Bulgarians has reached over 2.1 million in 2017 or 23% of the population, higher than the average 19.1% for the EU. Hence, the pressure on the government in the election 2019 was to increase the low pensions as part of the Code for Social Security novelization ongoing since 2018 (Krysteva 2019).

128   *Defending Eastern Europe*

A growing problem and a high priority for the government is also the spreading poverty in the country, especially in the northwest region.[8] The budget in 2019–20 attempted to address this issue with both national and EU fund transfers to the local communities. However, it will be a hard issue to deal with, especially with the entrenched regional and ethnic problems left to develop for decades.

Another major issue is the emigration of over 3.5 million Bulgarian citizens by 2017 (two million in 2011), a process that is growing and involves the most able-bodied and qualified people, including the potential recruits for the military. According to *Darik News* (September 20, 2016) between 2010 and 2016, some 26–27% of highly educated Bulgarians with university education emigrated on an annual basis (Ivanova 2016).

According to military reports, insufficient financing was listed as one of the main problems that not only lowered the efficiency but also the morale of the forces. A strong warning signal is the fact that the level of enlistment for the Reserve Forces is barely at 20% of the planned personnel. Realistically, the modernization of the Bulgarian defense system should be addressed as a NATO and EU funding issue. The understanding of this reality is gaining ground with the sharpened crisis in the Black Sea and in the Western Balkans today, and it is reflected with multiple joint projects within the alliances, evident below.

Joint military exercises within NATO and the EU: a positive change

A new moment in these exercises was the addition of the "Platinum" element of combining the older practices with new, more complex training and with more inclusion of non-NATO or EU member countries. Here are some examples of the 2018 training exercises:

- "Platinum Lion 18" was conducted at the "Novo Selo," Bulgaria tank polygon. Over 700 troops and 100 machines participated in the training with teams from Bulgaria, the United States, Romania, Moldova, Albania, Serbia, Republic of Georgia, and Montenegro with the main goal to improve the tactical operational coordination of the troops.
- "Platinum Wolf 18" exercise had a goal of training for engagement abroad. The interesting part of this exercise was that it was conducted in Serbia, at the base "South" in Boenovac, with 500 troops from the United States, Serbia, Bulgaria, Hungary, Montenegro, Romania, Slovenia, the United Kingdom, and the United Arab Emirates.
- "Black Sea Rotational Force 18.1" was combined with "Platinum Eagle 18" in Romania at the "Babadag" base with troops from Romania, Bulgaria, US marines, Ukraine, Moldova, and Republic of Georgia.

Stable Balkan NATO/EU members   129

- "Thracian Eagle 2018" involved the aviation, air defense units, and ground troops from Bulgaria, the United States, and the United Kingdom; "Thracian Star 2018" was with Bulgarian, US, UK, and Greek troops (Bulgarian Ministry of Defense, 2019b).

Final thoughts

In conclusion, it is clear that the Republic of Bulgaria has made its choice for its national security and economic future. The country was acutely aware of the crisis in Eastern Ukraine and the growing Russian military potential in Crimea, as well as in other parts of the world related to the national energy dependency. This situation has made Bulgaria look for closer ties and better relations with the Turkish government, a major economic partner with a lot of influence with the Bulgarian Turkish minority. Bulgarian military hospitals opened their doors for wounded Ukrainian soldiers from the conflict, having 29 of them in 2018. Continued military participation in NATO and EU operations currently includes Kosovo (KFOR, UNMIK), Bosnia and Herzegovina (EU "ALTHEA"), Afghanistan (Resolute Support), Republic of Georgia (EUMM), Somalia (EU NAVFOR ATALANTA), Liberia (UNMIL), Mali (EU TM-Mali), NATO "Active Fence," and numerous NATO/EU operations. Participation in the past has made it clear that the choice of the country has been made! It is not with Russia, there is no nostalgia for the Warsaw Pact. The choice is with NATO and the EU.

Conclusion: application of alliance politics theory to the two stable Balkan NATO/EU members

First, both NATO and EU membership for the two stable Balkan states has helped to close the geographic distance they each possess from each other. In a sense, those alliances have benefited each state. They substituted for the partnership of Bulgaria with the communist-led Soviet Union during the Cold War. Albania was a very independent state in the communist era and broke its ties with first Moscow and then Beijing. Membership in NATO seemed to offer it a modicum of widely based security that had been missing during the Cold War.

Second, the political differences that existed in the region prior to 1991 began to change in more common directions after the fall of regional communism. Both NATO and the EU posited democratic norms and institutions as a condition of membership, and both Albania and Bulgaria made intentional progress in that direction. The pace of change differed between them, and the legacies of the communist past differently affected their plans for the future. However, the targeted norms and values were similar and held in common.

Third, the profound ethnic differences between them remained and did not disappear, for Bulgaria was a proud Slavic Christian Orthodox culture while a contrast to Ilyrian and Muslim Albanians. However, their connections with NATO and the EU gave them a sense of common purpose within which the ethnic differences somewhat receded into the background. Further, they took part together in military missions in Afghanistan and Iraq as well as in NATO and EU-sponsored projects that aimed at establishing human-service and educational institutions that would help navigate the passage of those two Balkan nations into a more promising future.

With the assistance of and participation in these three components of alliance theory, there was a strong possibility that, for Albania and Bulgaria, the concept of neighborhood could replace that of "shatter-belt."

Notes

1 See http://epicenter.bg/article/archive/45944/11/61, accessed September 5, 2019.

2 The BAPU leader Nikola Petkov was executed on September 23, 1947 after the approval of the Soviet authorities.

3 See https://trove.nla.gov.au/newspaper/article/18037886, accessed September 5, 2019.

4 In Bulgarian Leva (BNL). However, it was a very heavy burden on the weak national finances (Tzvetkov 2014).

5 See Закон за изменение и допълнение на Закона за отбраната и Въоръжените сили, обн. ДВ, бр. 98 от 9.12.2016 г., изм. и доп. бр. 103 от 27.12.2016 г.; Закон за изменение и допълнение на Закона за резерва, обн. в ДВ, бр. 103 от 27.12. 2016 г.; Закон за изменение и допълнение на Закона за военната полиция, обн. в ДВ, бр. 86 от 01.11.2016 г., accessed November 6, 2019.

6 See "Национален план за повишаване на разходите за отбрана на 2% от БВП на Република България до 2024 г. [National Plan for Increased Spending for Defense to 2% GDP of the Republic of Bulgaria to 2024]."

7 For a list of the Bulgarian engagement in NATO and EU operations with a brief summary see the site of the Bulgarian Ministry of Defense at www.mod.bg/en/tema_MissionsOperations.html, accessed September 12, 2020.

8 See the publication of the National Insurance Institute, Sofia 2018, "КАРТОГРАФИРАНЕ НА БЕДНОСТТА В РЕПУБЛИКА БЪЛГАРИЯ [Mapping the Poverty in the Republic of Bulgaria]," accessed September 8, 2019.

8

Vulnerability of former Yugoslav NATO (Slovenia, Croatia, Montenegro, and North Macedonia) and non-NATO (Bosnia-Herzegovina, Kosovo, and Serbia) states

James W. Peterson

Alliance politics theory and the post-Yugoslav states

Alliances face many challenges, and among them are "gravitational distance," "typological distance," and "attributional distance." The first pertains to a situation in which a strong power is located too far from states that it might want to support and protect, and its "gravitational" pull is thereby weak. In the second challenge, new "types" of states have emerged from a formerly unified geopolitical entity that may have disappeared, and there results a vacuum of commonality among them. Third, the assumption and "attribution" of common state values may disappear, as a "shatter-belt" replaces a buffer zone that may have kept different cultures working together (Hendrickson 2002, 461–2).

In effect, all three of these issues emerged after the break-up of Yugoslavia in 1991. Both the United States and Russia had an interest in supporting and even protecting some of the new states that were born, but both were a geographic distance from them and unable to offer continuous assistance. The "gravity" was very weak between the global powers and the new nations that had come to life. For instance, this was true of American sympathy for Slovenia and Russia's long-standing support for Serbia. Similarly, the Yugoslav federation was a kind of artifice throughout its history, and it was no surprise that different political patterns or "types" developed within the various states. For example, Slovenia and eventually Croatia adopted democratic patterns, while the Serb-dominated remnant of Yugoslavia turned in a highly centralist direction that also included Montenegro for some years. There was a real fragility or "shatter-belt" effect in terms of "attributed" cultural characteristics. Christian Orthodoxy, Islam, and Roman Catholicism all emerged as strong ideological forces that were in conflict through their political leaders. This was especially true during the Balkan wars of the 1990s.

132   *Defending Eastern Europe*

In coping with the three distance challenges noted above, there are a number of steps that states take. One answer is to work together in the former geographic space of the fallen empire or federation. This often occurs if there is an outside enemy putting pressure on the new countries or if one of them becomes a threat to the rest (Kelley 2007). Another possibility is membership in a "larger common space" that might be an alliance. Often, the regional organization will nurture the growth of democracy within the individual states, and a certain level of democratic developments may even be a precondition for alliance membership or even candidate status (Hendrickson 2002, 455–66). An additional positive feature of democratic development within an alliance framework is the increase in international acceptance of the new state and its policies. Further, economic development may proceed apace, as the alliance provides more resources, and this benefits security if those new assets are part of the growing military infrastructure (Peverhous 2002, 614–21).

At the same time, new democracies can have endemic problems based on their lack of the growth of a participant political culture in the past. Alliance prodding to develop effective administrative bureaucracies can help to offset the instabilities that often accompany the injection of democratic patterns into unfamiliar settings (Pye 1966, 37–9). Alliances can reinforce this need for administrative strength in order to counter ethno-federalism (Haftel and Thompson 2006, 254). Striking a balance between establishment of democratic practices within a framework of central administrative power is no easy task, but new states that lacked both of these features within their previous centralized state or even empire need to take steps in that direction. Alliance membership that results would make such efforts worthwhile, while the experience of working with allies can result in new insights, techniques, and resources.

A number of these assumptions help clarify the post-1991 experience of the seven states that had emerged from the previous Yugoslav space by 2008. Serbian nationalistic aggression surely drove Slovenia, Croatia, and Bosnia-Herzegovina toward the West and its alliance structures. Within Yugoslavia, Serbia had the upper-hand in terms of leadership of the military and political arenas, but it lacked that kind of gravitational pull after the break-up. Efforts to restore control created war, suffering, and continuous instability for three intense years from 1992 to 1995. It was not a surprise that outside intervention by NATO was a significant factor in the end of the wars with the final, forced Serbian retreat. The 1999 struggle in Kosovo was very different as it involved Serbian intervention into its own republic that was 90% Albanian. However, the results were similar with NATO Air Force units and negotiations forcing the Serbian retreat. Importantly, both NATO and eventually the EU sent peacekeeping forces that remained for an indeterminate time in order to prevent a renewal of hostilities.

Vulnerability of former Yugoslav states 133

Thus, alliance politics theory helps explain a number of the key developments within and between the seven successor states to the old Yugoslavia. Partnership for Peace (PfP) status within NATO as well as the hope of eventual membership in it assisted in overcoming "gravitational distance," for it brought the United States and its partners into the region in restoring a balance against the pull of both Serbia and Russia. Alliance-nurtured growth of democratic as well as bureaucratic institutions created common forms that counteracted the "typological distance" that had emerged after the collapse of the Yugoslav brand of communism. Perhaps "attributional distance" was the key challenge in the region of the seven states, for ethnic and religious differences were so powerful. Under the leadership of Tito, they had simmered under the surface but never broken out into raw conflict very often. However, the end of the Cold War unleashed powerful centrifugal forces. NATO maintained peacekeeping forces in Bosnia-Herzegovina from 1995 until the end of 2004, and then the EU took over the process. It would be fair to conclude that alliances provided a buffer zone that helped to prevent the fractures that could have generated a new "shatter-belt" after 1995.

Overall, alliance politics theory, with its three assumptions, helps explain the trauma that characterized previous Yugoslav space after the death of the federation that had existed since 1918. At the same time, the theory is useful in pointing to and highlighting the particulars of the restoration of balance and stability in the region. At the same time the fact that Yugoslavia was a federal state prior to 1991, regardless of its failure, must have simultaneously prepared the successor elites to run their own independent states, and to work within a framework of (con)federated multilateral structures flowing from the West.

In this chapter, in the initial sections, the emphasis will first be on the four successor states that became part of NATO and/or the EU. They include Croatia, Montenegro, North Macedonia, and Slovenia. Second, coverage will spotlight the three states that have not yet become part of either alliance, The three states that will receive attention at that point are thus Bosnia-Herezegovina, Kosovo, and Serbia. In both sections, alliance theory is a useful way of evaluating both the predicaments and possibilities of all seven states that receive attention in the chapter.

Slovenia: membership in NATO and in the EU in 2004

Prior to the outbreak of the Ukrainian crisis in 2014, Slovenia was making steady progress as a NATO member. It had been a full part of the alliance for an entire decade, and participation in its operations had become a part of its security and defense "life." For example, its 2010 National Security

134   *Defending Eastern Europe*

Strategy put an emphasis on the importance of interoperability between its defense goals and those of NATO and the EU. Activities in Afghanistan had been important, for its Air Force emplaced troops in both Herat and Kabul, while both Army personnel and civilians worked on a Provincial Reconstruction Team (PRT) in that country. Its troops were also part of the NATO operation in Kosovo from 2000 to 2007, and it had sent an air squadron to Bosnia. Importantly, Slovenia's defense planners set up a PfP language training center in the western part of the country, and this served the needs for understanding the local languages in the countries in which they served as well as the need for all to have some understanding of English that was the common method for communications in NATO (Peterson 2013, 45–8).

In 2016, two years after the Russian takeover of Crimea, Slovene defense leaders put together a new Strategic Defense Review. In it they highlighted the instability in their southern and eastern neighborhoods and also lamented the rise of extremists in all part of the surrounding European continent (Strategic Defense Review of Slovenia 2016, 1, 9). Partly in response to those challenges, they decided to add a new medium battalion group. In 2018–23, they planned on construction of two medium battalion groups to support NATO's potential use of its Article 5 and also to assist in building an alliance "rapid response" force (Strategic Defense Review of Slovenia 2016, 6–7). The Review also spoke about national defense as incorporating and protecting alliance members, as well as the expected security of their own state. Assistance from the Alliance was also vital, for it added components "that the Republic of Slovenia does not develop." Unfortunately, Slovenia had not really modernized its armed forces after 2009, although it had switched to an entirely professional army (Strategic Defense Review of Slovenia 2016, 4–5).[1] In return, Slovenia had contributed to alliance missions in the Mediterranean and Africa. Its plan for achieving the NATO goal of committing 2% of GDP to defense spending was surely a long-range one, for the target year was 2027 (Strategic Defense Review of Slovenia 2016, 7–8). In sum, Slovenia and the Western military alliance engaged in mutual support efforts with one another and built on what they had begun just after admission of the state in 2004.

Croatia: membership in NATO in 2009 and in the EU in 2013

In the pre-2014 period, Croatia was able to contribute in substantial ways to alliance missions. It even hosted a NATO military exercise in 2008, one year prior to its formal admission to NATO. At the peak of the Afghan War, it contributed 200 troops in 2006–7 and then upped it by 100 for 2007–8, which was a large commitment in proportion to its military capacity. In particular, its personnel work in the north as part of the effort to protect Mazar-e-Sharif, as well as helicopter training for Afghan pilots. In nearby Kosovo, it provided 20 soldiers in 2009. In order to mesh more effectively with its new allies, it changed its military education to meet NATO standards, established a multimedia unit to study English, and built a new radar operations headquarters (Peterson 2013, 58–9).

Croatia's most recent defense review was done in 2013, and so it has not upgraded plans yet since the Crimean crisis. In that document, it was pointed out that the membership achieved in 2009 had provided the state with "political recognition" and was proof that it then had put in place the democratic standards that had been missing in the late 1990s. In fact, the authoritarianism of the Tudjman presidency had postponed its admission for a full five years, as Slovenia and Croatia had both been at a similar level of economic development during the Tito regime. Attaining EU membership in 2013, the year of the publication of the defense review, was another step in strengthening its defense position (Strategic Defense Review of Croatia 2013, 2). At that time, Croatian leaders did not detect any direct threats to their security, but there was still a fear that there might be legacies from the bitter conflicts of the 1990s or from the emergence of additional "open issues in the region" (Strategic Defense Review of Croatia 2013, 13). The document noted an increase in contributions to peacekeeping forces between 2006 and 2012. It doubled its military presence in Afghanistan from 150 to 300, increased the numbers in Kosovo from 150–200 to 400–450, accelerated its presence in EU operations from 150–200 to 400–450, and multiplied UN forces from 150–200 to 400–425. New goals for the next five years included the creation of a deployable battlegroup by 2018. In addition, that five-year plan included committing at least 50% of its land forces for peacekeeping operations, with 10% "sustainable in operations" (Strategic Defense Review of Croatia 2013, 21–4). This ambitious agenda was backed by relatively high levels of defense spending, which, after some decline in 2010–14, featured a robust steady pattern of 1.85% to 1.75% of GDP between 2015 and 2019, which amounted to around $1 billion as of 2019 (NATO Public Diplomacy Division 2020).

Concrete projects and contributions included extension of the MIG-21 lifespan, accelerated recruitment of volunteers into the military, transformation of the Croatian Defense Academy into a higher education institution, and greater utilization of civilian experts in peacekeeping operations. In light of their political experiences in the 1990s, Croatian defense planners agreed to work with nearby non-NATO states on the process of their own democratization. They also agreed to contribute in a concrete way to one NATO project, and the one they chose was a Military Police School in Afghanistan

136   *Defending Eastern Europe*

(Strategic Defense Review of Croatia 2013, 26–52). Most recently, in the fall of 2018, they sent one of their ships to the Mediterranean to participate in the Operation Active Endeavour, and this was their first such NATO defense contribution. They had 33 military personnel on the missile boat Vukovar, and that ship would be part of the Italian Navy in the operation. Such a presence would help improve "situational awareness" to rebuff threats to the Western alliance (Press Release, September 7, 2018). As late as August 2018, they were the biggest part of the 9th HRVCON that the alliance dispatched to Afghanistan on August 31, 2018. Croatians made up 67 of the unit's 106 members, and all the other contributing participants represented four other nations that had been part of the former Yugoslavia ("News", September 6, 2018). Such efforts extended the commitments made in the previous decade but were fleshed out in a much broader way.

Montenegro: membership in NATO in 2017 but not in the EU

Montenegro became an independent state in 2006 and a NATO member more than a decade later in 2017. However, in the first year of its formal independence from the old Serb-dominated Yugoslavia, it did deploy 33 soldiers to Afghanistan to help secure the base in Panonia in Pol e Khomri Province. Mutual defense visits took place with Norwegian defense specialists whose nation had been part of NATO for a long time (Peterson 2013, 78–9). Montenegro's most recent review of defense policy occurred in 2013, only three years after the previous one in 2010. The document noted that there were at that time no threats to Montenegro's territorial borders, but problems with the defense infrastructure were ongoing. Their percentage of GDP devoted to defense had sunk from 1.3% in 2009 to 1.15% in 2012, and that item needed considerable attention (Strategic Defense Review of Montenegro 2013, 2–8). The military budget started increasing as of 2016, and as of 2019, the tiny Montenegro spends a respectable 1.65% of its GDP on defense, which amounts to $92 million (as compared to $57 million and 1.4% of GDP in 2015) (NATO Public Diplomacy Division 2020). This pays for approximately 1,600 military personnel.

Future goals for Montenegro included the creation of two companies in an infantry battalion by 2017 that would be in conformance with NATO PfP standards. It would also accept the alliance recommendation that it locate a military radar station to monitor space at its Vrsuta site. However, it decided not to pursue purchase of its own combat aircraft, so dependence on its partners would continue to be the reality in that arena. A general goal in 2013 was to increase the percentage of GDP devoted to defense in a marginal way to 1.4%, a goal that was exceeded by 2018. Despite its small

Vulnerability of former Yugoslav states 137

size, the Montenegro plans were compatible with alliance standards and a meaningful contribution of its own.

North Macedonia

In the period leading up to the 2008 NATO Summit, North Macedonia/ Macedonia held PfP status and was very interested in becoming a full alliance partner. At that meeting, Georgia and Ukraine held similar positions about the desirability of immediate admission to NATO, but the organization turned all three down in light of their need to make more progress on meeting the alliance's criteria. For North Macedonia, long-standing Greek concerns were a huge barrier to its hopes of admission. Prior to that 2008 Summit, North Macedonian leaders had done all possible to demonstrate their solidarity with alliance projects and missions. For example, they sent 790 troops to Afghanistan as part of a British unit after 2002 and retained 142 there as late as 2011. In addition, their troops assisted in the training of the Afghan police and army. After the EU took over the peacekeeping force in Bosnia at the end of 2004, North Macedonia deployed a medical team to Butmir in 2006. It also sent a helicopter unit to assist with other EU units in Bosnia. North Macedonia also provided 11 rotations of troops to Iraq in the important task of training the security forces there. In the period between 2003 and 2008, Macedonian troops in Iraq numbered 490. Finally, it sent officers to assist in Kosovo in 2005–6. During the following year, they took over management of the Host Nation Support Coordination Center in Kosovo and provided medical assistance to KFOR troops (Peterson 2013, 74–6). Symbolically, the country also officially became a candidate country for EU accession in 2005.

North Macedonian security leaders wrote a Strategic Defense Review in 2018 that headlined their goal of achieving full membership in the Western security alliance. In fact, they were proud to report that NATO had already labelled their support operations as "combat ready" ("Strategic Defense Review 2018 of the Republic of Macedonia," 4). Specifically, they anticipated that the Army of Macedonia's (ARM) main contribution to the alliance would be a Motorized Infantry Brigade. They projected attainment of the goal of earmarking 2% of GDP to defense by 2024, although their 2018 level was very low at 0.95% (approximately $120 million) (Macrotrends 2020b). In light of the fact that they had a sizable Albanian minority of 40% in the population, they also indicated an objective of improving the "representation of smaller ethnic communities" ("Strategic Defense Review 2018 of the Republic of Macedonia," 5–6). Contributions to the NATO effort in Afghanistan continued after ISAF ended on the last day of 2014.

138   *Defending Eastern Europe*

Under the new Resolute Support Mission, North Macedonia continued its involvement and even increased the size of its force by 20% in 2018. In 2017, it chaired the U.S.-Adriatic Charter, an important organization that originated in 2003 in an effort to prepare West Balkan states for eventual NATO admission ("Strategic Defense Review 2018 of the Republic of Macedonia," 18–19).

In spite of those important alliance contributions, North Macedonia still experienced challenges that required the attention of its security officers. For example, the 2004 Ohrid Framework Agreement that ended the conflict between the Macedonian and Albanian populations called for inclusion of more of the minority populations within military units. By the year 2018, minority groups represented 20% of the officer corps, 27% of NCOs, and 30% of enlisted personnel. Females made up 12% of officers and NCOs as well as 35% of civil servants who worked within the Ministry of Defense. In the spring of 2018, for the first time, a woman received an appointment to command a combat unit in the infantry ("Strategic Defense Review 2018 of the Republic of Macedonia," 25). It is also true that the "name issue" continued to prod the Greeks into opposition to Macedonia's admission. In spite of that problem, North Macedonia received an invitation to join NATO at its 2018 Brussels Summit. However, there were still further tests that it had to meet before that would become a reality ("Strategic Defense Review 2018 of the Republic of Macedonia," 49). In principle, alliance planners designated that North Macedonia complete the name change agreement prior to official admission ("Relations with the former Yugoslav Republic of Macedonia", 2018). In effect it was changing its name from "The former Yugoslav Republic of Macedonia" to "North Macedonia." With this issue out of the way, North Macedonia formally joined NATO on March 27, 2020.

Bosnia-Herzegovina

Bosnia-Herzegovina was the site of a strong NATO peacekeeping force from the end of its 1993–5 war until the end of 2004, at which time the EU took over administration of the mission. At the same time, the state hoped for eventual admission to the Western alliance and took part in several key operations. An important one included dispatch of a rotation of troops to ISAF in Afghanistan in 2010. The operation lasted six months in Helmand Province, and they worked under a Danish command. In addition, Bosnia-Herzegovina sent 288 troops to Iraq in the period 2005–10. In the fall of 2010, it had sent a combat unit to Tuzla. Interestingly, some of its troops had been trained by the EUFOR peacekeeping force located in

Vulnerability of former Yugoslav states   139

Bosnia, so that was a success for the EU in a double set of defense missions. Further, they accompanied representatives from many other states on a trip to Brussels to prepare Afghan training missions that assist in the transition from ISAF to the Afghan National Army (ANA) (Peterson 2013, 64–6).

Bosnian defense managers understood the need for upgrade to their military and security capabilities in light of the hope for enhanced links with the Western alliances. Reforms of their defense system and reorganization of their armed forces were a top priority in the near future, and PfP status, attained in 2006, made that a necessity ("Path to Partnership for Peace," 2016). Democratic development was also a necessity after that admission, and the leaders began to make plans in that direction ("Relations with Bosnia and Herzegovina," 2018). More specifically, demining in their own countries was an immediate necessity in light of the horrendous residue from the war in 1992–5. In late 2018, the 3rd Demining Battalion handed over responsibility for the demolition sites to the affected communities of Bosanska Krupa and Brod ("Responsibility for Demining Workshops," 2018). Another specific step beyond attainment of PfP status was an invitation by NATO to join the Membership Action Plan (MAP), the path to official membership. However, the alliance first required that Bosnia-Herzegovina initially switch all immovable defense properties from private hands to the state. At the same time, NATO assisted the state, as they helped after a flood in 2014 ("Relations with Bosnia and Herzegovina," 2018). Clearly, the NATO link was an important one but complicated, for the affected state had been a creature of NATO and EU concern but also a provider of assistance that proved to be more than symbolic.

Kosovo

Kosovo is the most recent newcomer to the category of states that emerged from the destroyed twentieth-century Yugoslavia. After its declaration of independence in 2008, Serbia, Russia, and many other states refused to grant diplomatic recognition to Kosovo. In the early years after independence, there were conflicts with Serbia over location of the border between them, as its minority Serb population was located along its border with the Serbian Republic. NATO had located its Kosovo Force (KFOR) there after the brief war in 1999, and so it sometimes happened that those international troops were caught up in the middle of the post-2008 border conflicts. Its security as a questioned new state received support during a conference in 2011. Kosovo's strategic partnership with both NATO and the EU was a topic of discussion, while Kosovo's leaders affirmed that PfP status would become an official future goal (Peterson 2013, 68–72).

140   *Defending Eastern Europe*

Recently, the Kosovo Security Force (KSF) made important contributions in a number of settings, and some of those reached out to their Serbian minority. For instance, in early October 2017, some of the force's medical personnel visited elderly persons in the Serb community. Their Liaison Unit for Crisis Response (LUCR) performed additional humanitarian work that supplemented the medical assistance ("Kosovo Security Force Conducted Medical Visits to the Communities," 2017). Several months later, the president of Kosovo took part in a ceremony in which the Security Force publicly promoted five minority members. In part, this was part of an effort to make the KSF approximate the NATO level of activity and professionalism ("Kosovo's President Promoted KSF Minority Members," 2017). Finally, in mid-2018, the KSF minister offered best wishes on the tenth anniversary of the state's independence. He pointedly offered his regards to all Kosovo citizens, regardless of ethnicity, religion, and race ("The Wishes of KSF Minister Rrustem Berisha on the 10th Anniversary of Kosovo's Independence," 2018). Thus, Kosovo's leaders were pointing the population in the direction of a tolerant set of policies that would ease any existing tensions with outside nations, NATO, and the EU.

The Serbian Republic

Serbia received PfP status in 2006, at the alliance's Riga Summit, but it did not receive permission to participate in NATO discussions until April 2011. Intervening in that five-year period was the declaration of independence by Kosovo in 2008. Serbia was very hostile to that move as well as the alliance's support of it. In fact, Serbia began to refer in its security document more often to its EU connections than to the NATO linkages. Discussions between the military alliance and Serbia centered on topics such as the need for its Ministry of Defense to play a role both in the democratization of the state and the representation of women in the military. One positive outcome of the 2011 discussions with the leaders of the military alliance was an agreement to let KFOR control two contested border sites between Serbia and Kosovo (Peterson 2013, 80–3). It is also the case that the history of Serb aggression against its neighbors in the 1990s played a role in the partial stand-off between the state and NATO.

In the wake of the tensions between the two that accompanied the creation of Kosovo, Serbia decided that full membership of the alliance would no longer be a goal, although it did not abandon its PfP status. In January 2015, the two agreed on an "Individual Partnership Plan" as a kind of midway relationship between PfP and membership ("Relations with Serbia," 2017). During 2018, Serb leaders followed through on their desire to move

Vulnerability of former Yugoslav states 141

more directly toward the EU for meaningful alliance dialogue. As a result, both the Serb President Vucic and Defense Minister Vulin agreed to work toward a "lasting solution" to the tensions between Serbs and Albanians in Kosovo. All parties agreed that EU stability was impossible without dependable security relationships in the Balkans ("Minister Vulin: The EU to Support Brave Efforts of President Vucic (Serbia)," 2018). Discussions between Serb and EU leaders also centered on responses to the refugee crisis of 2015 and after. The Serbian Defense Minister made the attention-grabbing statement that Serbia would not be a "parking lot for immigrants." He called upon the EU to distinguish more clearly and forcefully between legitimate refugees and mere "economic migrants" ("Minister Vulin: EU to Take a Clear Position on Migration (Serbia)," 2018). Serbian security would still entail a balance between its NATO and EU connections, but the former was receding in importance and the latter increasing.

Comparative concluding analysis about the former Yugoslav states: are the NATO alliance partners in a stronger defense/security position than the non-alliance states?

One way of answering that question is review of the findings on defense preparedness and peacekeeping mission contributions of the two sets of states. A second approach to an answer is linkage of those conclusions to the three alliance politics models. For the purposes of this discussion, consideration of North Macedonia will be part of the second set of states, for all of its defense activities considered here took place prior to its NATO admission in 2020.

First, the three alliance members all contributed to NATO missions in Afghanistan as well as the NATO/EU peacekeeping operation in Kosovo. They performed formal defense reviews, as Slovenia completed its most recent one in 2016 and the other two in 2013. None achieved the desired objective of committing 2% of GDP to the defense sector, but each set a target year for attaining it. All aimed at improvement in military capabilities, and that commitment became more pressing after the 2014 Crimean crisis. Slovenia was the furthest along in defense integration, for it had been a formal alliance partner since 2004. Croatia had a larger defense potential due to its size and level of budgetary commitment to defense. Montenegro was just beginning its move in the direction of meeting alliance standards, for it was a small state and just recently admitted to the military alliance.

The four non-alliance partners had a more diversified experience in regard to NATO, for their political experiences had been so different from one another and from the three that became partners. NATO had maintained

142   *Defending Eastern Europe*

a peacekeeping presence in both Bosnia-Herzegovina and Kosovo, while Serbia had been the provocative state in regard to the wars of the 1990s. North Macedonia was unique in its side conflict with Greece, a situation that had frozen its alliance partnership prospects. In addition, Kosovo still lacked NATO's PfP status, while Serbia had given up its desire to join the alliance after the creation of Kosovo in 2008. The international community still had a concern about the long-standing fragility of Bosnia-Herzegovina with its three ethnic groups, while Macedonia had the challenge of coming up with a name change that would be acceptable to its own population as well as its neighbor to the south.

At the same time, each of the four had perspectives about security that spilled over beyond their own borders. Not surprisingly Bosnia and Macedonia were the states that offered the most troops to international missions. Both contributed troops to operations in Afghanistan, Iraq, and Bosnia, while Macedonia also played a role in the Kosovo peacekeeping force. Kosovo defense planners as well as those in Serbia needed to resolve local issues such as the instability along their border with one another. Macedonia was unique in its careful preparation of a defense review in 2018 and in its stated commitment to achieve 2% of GDP in the defense sector by a certain date. Such diversity prevents a unified conclusion about the defense preparedness of the group of four, for their security situation depended on their individual size, capabilities, and intentions regarding alliance membership.

In general, it is possible to conclude that Slovenia, Croatia, and Macedonia were in the strongest security situation in the region. All had consistently contributed to NATO missions in the neighborhood and were making plans that dovetailed with alliance objectives. In that sense, the fate of NATO member Montenegro was similar to that of Bosnia, Kosovo, and Serbia. Its small size and recent admission even led to White House Oval Office speculation that it might not merit NATO protection. However, its past history was free of the ethnic and border tensions that afflicted the other three, troubled non-alliance states. Thus, there was a promise that they could mesh with alliance standards and make a small but substantive contribution to regional security. From this perspective, it was not possible to conclude that the alliance partners were in a stronger security situation than the non-alliance partners, but the short-range future would no doubt strengthen the case for such a clear-cut conclusion.

Second, how do the three alliance theory models assist in formulating conclusions about the security of the two sets of states? The first assumption highlights the power of "gravity" in underpinning state security. A powerful force such as the former Soviet Union can hold dissimilar states together even in spite of their individual differences. In the 1990s, Serbia made moves that suggested they wanted to replace Moscow as that center of gravity. However, Serbia's defeat left a vacuum but also a problematic situation in relation to regional stability. In effect, NATO and the EU have become the replacement gravity forces in light of the collapse of the Soviet Union and the weakness of Serbian military force. Three states are part of that alliance, while North Macedonia joined it in 2020. NATO peacekeeping forces have played a role in preserving the stability of Bosnia and Kosovo, and so that alliance anchor has been vital in their defense prospects. In that sense, Serbia is an outlier to that gravitational force, and yet its dialogue with NATO and hopes for a stronger connection to the EU make its geographical position part of the nexus of alliance gravity among two organizations more stable.

A common "type" of state can also be a force for stability, and that is important in light of the communist past of all the countries that were formerly part of Yugoslavia. In the 1990s, there was an assumption that the "democratic peace" would replace previous Cold War hostilities. Slovenia was the foremost illustration of that phenomena. However, there was a sense that the Balkans were more reluctant to move quickly to democratic patterns and forms than the East Central European states or the Eastern Balkans. However, Croatia threw off its authoritarian leadership in 1998 and made steady progress toward democratic norms. Later declarations of independence by Montenegro and Kosovo in the early twenty-first century provided them with the opportunity to transition their political systems to the democratic model. The dedication of Kosovo leaders to extension of military leadership roles to minority groups attests to that type of progress. Despite the independence of Serbia from NATO guidance and supervision, their political leaders were committed to election stability and the regular rotation of existing political parties in office. Bosnia's commitment to democracy was inextricably tied to the values of the NATO/EU missions that played a role in its governance and protection, while North Macedonia worked to incorporate minorities as well as women in its military structure of power. Thus, alliance connections in the mid-range future were a force that would ease the region from its authoritarian past to a more open and pluralistic future. In conclusion, the membership issue in the two alliances did not offer meaningful member/non-member distinctions in terms of common movement toward democratic values and structures.

Common "attributions" have traditionally been missing in this Balkan region of new states that emerged from the broken Yugoslavia. Does a "shatter-belt" of ethnic tensions prevent the achievement of regional stability that might evolve from the pull of "gravity" of the two alliances as well as the common moves to a democratic "typology" of political systems? Slavic-Muslim differences have paralyzed Bosnia, Kosovo, North Macedonia, and in an indirect way Serbia. Serbian efforts in the 1990s

144 *Defending Eastern Europe*

to push back Muslim influence in Bosnia and Kosovo created enormous stress for the region as well as the international community. However, both NATO and the EU have offered scenarios that included members of the key minority communities in the structures of the troubled states. In the end, stability based on the other two components of alliance politics theory has overridden the deeply rooted ethnic tensions connected with the profoundly different group "attributions." In a cautious way, it is possible to predict that the clouds of alliance gravitational pull and democratic developments have contained ethnic tensions among the seven states and paved the road for enhanced security for this important component of the Balkan region.

Note

1 This reflects the fact that Slovenian military spending has systematically shrunk, both as a percentage of GDP and in total spending between 2010 and 2015, to reach the nadir of 0.93% of GDP and $0.4 billion in 2015. Since 2015 the defense spending has increased, albeit slowly, both in real and proportional terms, to reach 1.04% of GDP and $0.65 billion in 2019 (Macrotrends 2020a; NATO Public Diplomacy Division 2020).

9

States with significant security issues: Poland, Romania, and Moldova

Jacek Lubecki and James W. Peterson

Alliance politics theory

Alliances face many challenges, and among them are "gravitational distance," "typological distance," and "attributional distance." The first pertains to a situation in which a strong power is located too far from states that it might want to support and protect, and its "gravitational" pull is thereby weak, but still a function of power-size. In the second challenge, new "types" of states have emerged from a formerly unified geopolitical entity that may have disappeared, and there results a vacuum of commonality among them. Third, the assumption and "attribution" of common state values may disappear, as a "shatter-belt" replaces a buffer zone that may have kept different cultures working together (Hendrickson 2002, 461–2).

In coping with the three distance challenges noted above, there are a number of steps that states take. One answer is to work together in the former geographic space of the fallen empire or federation. This often occurs if there is an outside enemy putting pressure on the new countries or if one of them becomes a threat to the rest (Kelley 2007). Another possibility is a membership in a "larger common space" that might be an alliance. Often, the regional organization will nurture the growth of a common ideology and a social system, for instance, liberal democracy within the individual states, and a certain level of domestic ideological and structural commonality/developments may even be a precondition for alliance membership or even candidate status (Hendrickson 2002, 455–66). An additional positive feature of ideological and structural domestic commonalities within an alliance framework is the increase in consensual acceptance of a new member state and its policies. Specifically, with respect to capitalist liberal democratic order, economic development may proceed apace, as the alliance provides more resources, and this benefits security if those new assets are in part of the growing military infrastructure (Peverhous 2002, 614–21).

146 *Defending Eastern Europe*

At the same time, new liberal democracies can have endemic problems based on their lack of the growth of a participant political culture in the past. Alliance prodding to develop effective administrative bureaucracies can help to offset the instabilities that often accompany the injection of democratic patterns into unfamiliar settings (Pye 1966, 37–9). Alliances can reinforce this need for administrative strength in order to counter ethno-federalism (Haftel and Thompson 2006, 254). Striking a balance between establishment of democratic practices within a framework of central administrative power is no easy task, but new states that lacked both of these features within their previous centralized state or even empire need to take steps in that direction. Alliance membership that results would make such efforts worthwhile, while the experience of working with allies can result in new insights techniques, and resources.

Both Poland and Romania have an accentuated need for alliance-based security in light of relatively recent developments. The Russian threat to the Baltics and Poland has been greater since the 2014 takeover of Crimea, and this challenge to Poland is understandable in light of many centuries of Polish–Russian hostility. Romania has taken steps to cooperate with American policy initiatives such as missile defense, and those initiatives have recalled in Russian leaders past challenges in communist times from Bucharest. Gravitational distance from the United States/the West has decreased for Poland and Romania states as a result, and they have welcomed closer relations with both NATO and the EU, with an emphasis on the former in its Atlanticist/pro-US version. Moreover, both Poland and Romania became liberal democracies, thus diminishing typological distance between them, given that that during the communist period the two countries embraced very different types of communism. Attributionally, besides the ideological commonality, Romania and Poland could now draw on traditional links of alliances from the interwar period, when Poland and Romania were the two most closely linked anti-Soviet allies in the *cordon sanitaire* dividing Europe from the Soviet Union.

Poland: perceptions of Polish defense leaders prior to the 2014 crisis

While Poland joined NATO against Russia's strenuous opposition, Russia could do little to prevent its erstwhile "ally's" membership in the Western security organization (Całka 1998). Russia of the 1990s was famously weak and chaotic with its military disintegrating and humiliated in Chechnya. The Polish national security strategy of 1992 therefore rightly pointed out that instability in the post-Soviet space rather than a direct military aggression by any country of the region was a serious security risk to Poland.

Moreover, a prevalent notion in Poland was that Russia "understands" language of power and that Polish membership in NATO would be followed by a détente and thaw in the Polish–Russian relationship based on mutual respect (Magdziak-Miszewska 1998). This is precisely what happened after 1999. Punctuated by President Kwaśniewski's visit to Moscow in July 2000 and President Putin's visit to Warsaw in January 2002, an era of good feeling and economic cooperation between Poland and Russia seemed to be dawning, even though little specific in terms of solving potentially conflictual issue was achieved (Autorzy Rzeczpospolitej 2002a, 2002b). This positive trend was not to last – by 2005 the Polish–Russian conflict flared again over the direction of Ukraine's democratic development, as Poland pursued the "Eastern policy" of supporting Ukrainian democracy and independence from Russia, and Russia saw these Polish actions as an infringement into its legitimate sphere of influence (Burant 1999; Strzelczyk 2005).

Still, there was a sense of an almost absolute absence of a conventional military threat upon Poland's entrance into NATO, and the nation's new (2000) National Security Strategy duly took this into consideration, stating that "in the foreseeable future Poland's independent existence is not threatened, our country is not threatened by a direct military aggression."[1] Instead of focusing on a traditional military-threat-oriented defense strategy, the new comprehensive formula of Poland's security strategy took into account a whole range of "fashionable" non-conventional threats, including terrorism, and international organized crime. Poland saw NATO and its Atlanticism as the cornerstones of its defense policy, but was also looking forward to upcoming (2004) membership in the EU as reinforcing both military defense and non-military aspects of Poland's security.

A reformulation of Polish strategic defense documents in 2003 put even more emphasis on non-conventional threats and a US-oriented coalitional and global strategy of dealing with these threats. Accompanying these developments was Poland's increasing reliance on NATO and on the US within NATO (Atlanticism) as the true guarantee of Poland's security.[2] That framework of thinking seemed to require a greater emphasis on Poland's compatibility with NATO and the US security and globalized defense strategies and actions, rather than on Poland's indigenous and autonomous defensive capabilities in the local and regional contexts. This was a dangerous course of action for Poland to follow, given fissures in the Western security community that appeared in 2003 over Iraq, and the fact that Russian power was growing, fueled by authoritarian stability achieved under Putin, and high global energy (oil and natural gas) prices.

The events of 9/11 shook up the world of global security, and led to the US and NATO operations in Afghanistan, and to the US-led invasion and occupation of Iraq. These events shattered the safe premises of Poland's

148 *Defending Eastern Europe*

newly found sense of security, most importantly, by fracturing the Western alliance in the run-up to the war in Iraq. Given the firmly Atlanticist foundation of Poland's defense strategy and policy, Poland, like all East-Central European, and, indeed, most peripheral European countries (the UK, Spain, Portugal, Italy, Denmark, the Netherlands) took a firmly pro-US course. The overall European political pattern is explained by a pattern of balancing within the Western alliance against the Franco-German tandem opposing the United States. Thus, both in Western and Eastern Europe the weaker or peripheral countries chose to preserve their freedom of action by supporting the United States in the "war on terror."[3]

For East-Central Europeans/former Soviet countries, the fear of Russia's neo-imperial revival and reliance on the United States as the only reliable ally against Russia was clearly the motivator of the respective countries' support of the United States in the War on Terror (see Table 9.1). Poland was within a group of high-contributing countries, sending by far the highest number of troops among all East-Central European/former Soviet countries in absolute terms and second largest number in relative terms, after Georgia. In that group of high-contributing countries were also Georgia, Estonia, Croatia, and Romania. Among Visegrád countries, Slovakia, Hungary, and the Czech Republic were all moderate contributors. Polish exceptionalism was thus clearly visible in the regional East-Central European context, making the country more akin to Baltic countries, Georgia and Romania – countries with a traditional security concern about Russia.

Besides realist considerations Poland's exceptionally high level of willingness to deploy troops on multilateral missions or in support of the allies was a function of the country's conceptualization of its security in terms of "alliance loyalty," which reflected the strategic culture steeped in a fear of being abandoned by allies. Indeed, Polish President Kwaśniewski, in his farewell speech to units deployed as part of a stabilization force in Iraq, invoked lessons of September 1939, when "Poland was abandoned by its allies" while "We will not be allies who abandon our friends in need, as this will guarantee that we, when in need, will not be abandoned in turn and can count on US support" (Kwaśniewski 2003).

Significantly, Polish commitment to missions in Iraq and Afghanistan, and, then, commitment to EU missions in Europe and Africa was maintained by three different governments representing the three normally bitterly opposed factions of Polish politics – the post-communist "left" (mostly SLD party in power 2001–4), the conservative "right" (mostly PiS, Law and Justice party, in power 2005–7, and since 2015), and the liberal "right" (PO, Citizens Platform party in power 2007–15). Also, when political commitment to the criticized mission in Iraq crumbled in 2006–8, even greater commitment of Polish mission to Afghanistan followed. That happened regardless of the fact

States with significant security issues 149

that the Polish public opinion clearly opposed these deployments,[4] which also received fairly negative media coverage[5] and were criticized by a substantial portion, if not the majority, of the country's intellectual elite. Indeed, the deployments and their fallout generated a vehement elite debate about the future direction of Poland's security and defense policy.

The decade of the peak of Polish foreign missions between 2001 and 2011 was indeed marked by substantial Polish efforts at military modernization. The steady and accelerating shrinkage of large Warsaw-Pact style conscript-based forces and steadily increasing military budgets (in real terms) freed up resources for this effort regardless of the relative high and persistent (but shrinking) cost of military "social security" (pensions) which in the 2001–17 period held steady at around 20% of the total military budget. Pursuant to the May 25, 2001 "Program of Restructuring and Technical Modernization of the Armed Forces of Poland for 2001–2006," renewed and adjusted in 2004,[6] and after the country's economic crisis passed in 2004, successive Polish governments launched substantially funded procurement programs, that, for the first time since the fall of communism, modernized the equipment of the Polish military (Bursztyński 2009).

The particular element of the Polish procurement effort which was so costly (estimated at $7.5 billion total cost) that it had to be financed separately from the normal Ministry of Defense budget was the purchase of a new generation of fighter-bombers for the Polish Air Force. The decision to buy 60 multipurpose airplanes was made by the Polish parliament (Sejm) in June 2001 in a statute that also set up a separate financing mechanism for the purchase. The decision to buy 36 F-16Cs and 12 F-16Ds, over the competing Mirage 2000 and Saab Gripen offers, was made in June 2002, and the airplanes were purchased and fully paid for by 2015. The decision to procure 690 Rosomak (Wolverine) APCs, a licensed variant of Finnish Patria's Armored Modular Vehicle, in turn, was made in December 2002 and the vehicles delivered by 2013. Many other programs followed, involving mostly land and air (transport airplanes and helicopters, for instance) equipment most useful for expeditionary warfare that Poland was waging in the 2000s. In the meantime, the Polish Navy remained largely neglected.

With the Polish forces' material modernization they also underwent a decisive structural reform, becoming by 2010 an all-volunteer, fairly small professional force suitable for NATO- or EU-led expeditionary warfare. Indeed, the thrust of doctrinal and structural changes were predicated on a Polish defense policy based on the premise that Poland is safe from conventional or nuclear attack, that expeditionary warfare waged by relatively small professional forces and not territorial defenses are the future of the Polish armed forces. These premises were becoming increasingly unsustainable as Poland's neighborhood heated up in the East.

150 *Defending Eastern Europe*

Romania: perception of Romanian defense leaders prior to the 2014 crisis and afterwards

Shortly after obtaining NATO membership in 2004, Romania endeavored to spell out its principal security objectives in its 2007 National Military Strategy. Interestingly, Romania defined security in a multi-organizational way that included the key importance of membership in both NATO and the EU. However, Romania also included the significance of bilateral ties to the United States, "Black Sea Dynamics," and the job of building bridges to the East European democracies. Romanian decision-makers also made mention of their interest in the Black Sea Forum for Dialogue and Cooperation (Peterson 2013, 44–5). Topics of concern were quite different after the Crimean crisis of 2014, and the "White Paper on Defence Bucharest 2017" reflected those alterations. Heightened concern about defense needs resulted from the Russian takeover of Crimea, the rise of the Islamic State, the huge refugee flow, and the accompanying humanitarian crisis. Romania also announced the unusual decision to devote 2% of its GDP to the defense sector for that year and for a decade through 2026 ("White Paper on Defence Bucharest 2017" n.d.). This made Romania part of a distinct minority, which, unsurprisingly, includes Poland, Estonia, and Latvia, among the alliance partners that satisfied the demands of American leaders such as former Secretary of Defense Robert Gates and President Donald Trump.

For Romania, concern about future Russian intentions was a guiding star for its foreign policy. The White Paper ticked off a number of issues that included Russia's potentially aggressive future intentions toward Georgia, Ukraine, and Moldova. Instability in the entire Black Sea region became a top worry, as Romanian leaders portrayed their state as a "riverine" into that water body. In a related matter, to them the Western Balkans appeared to be very unstable, and so a top security objective was clearly to work with NATO to make more muscular their defense posture in the Black Sea region. They expressed the hope and desire to take on more top positions in the NATO command structure in order to broaden their defense outreach and expand their security umbrella ("White Paper on Defence Bucharest 2017" n.d.).

Additionally, cooperation on security issues with alliance partners was very important for self-perceptions about an expanded role for defense protection. Romania had partnered with German troops in Afghanistan and Kosovo, and it also viewed work with the Polish military and Turkish forces as significant. Such linkages within NATO added to the "credibility of the Romanian Armed Forces." Work within the alliance also entailed the preparedness of its forces in terms of deployability. As such, its target was to make deployable in the next two years 50% of its land forces, 40% of its air

States with significant security issues 151

forces, and 80% of the naval forces. It was also important that such units be able to sustain operations for a defined length of time, and lower targets were set for each service in that respect. Another side of that issue was preparedness to host the military forces of NATO members and partners, and Romania vowed to accomplish that as well. Clearly, it was very proud of setting the objective of devoting 2% of GDP to defense as early as 2017. A number of other NATO members had established goals that would hit 2% in the early 2020s. In addition, the Romanian defense planners vowed that they would make sure that defense equipment constituted a high proportion of that defense budget plan. They noted that equipment made up 46.61% of their budget, whereas the NATO Wales Summit of 2014 had set a goal of only 20% for equipment ("White Paper on Defense Bucharest 2017," n.d.). Romania was committed to becoming an effective alliance partner, more than a decade after joining the Western alliance, but it also strove to meet and exceed NATO expectations in a number of significant regards.

Deployment of troops within the NATO framework was a consistent part of the Romanian alliance commitment. Even before joining the alliance, it sent troops to Kosovo after the air strikes of 1999 pushed the Serbs back out of that republic. Romania was willing to keep about 70 troops there after Kosovo declared independence in 2008, a contribution to Balkan stability (Peterson 2013, 148, 167). In addition, it contributed to both regular missions and training operations in Bosnia-Herzegovina and Iraq (Peterson 2013, 145). The number of troops in the former numbered 67, and they served first under NATO and after 2004, in EUFOR. In the latter, they located two military personnel to assist in training the military and police, in preparation for the allied departure in 2011 (Peterson 2013, 50). In the same year, Romania sent an additional 36 soldiers to Zabul in Afghanistan. In addition, 70 of their military personnel took on the assignment of being in charge of security at Kabul Airport, after Hungary ended its one-year parallel mission. Those troops had the responsibility for coordinating 450–500 flights per day and also keeping an eye out for IEDs that might be located anywhere nearby. In light of the dual American-led operations in Afghanistan and Iraq, Romanian defense officials provided use of a Black Sea air base for the American military to move troops to those two locations (Peterson 2013, 47). These multiple commitments reflected serious NATO membership obligations but also Romania's desire to contribute to regional security. Overall, when compared to other East-Central European and Balkan new members of NATO and EU, Romania, together with Poland, the Baltic countries and Croatia was one of the outstanding contributors to NATO-, EU-, and US- led military operations.

After joining NATO in 2004, Romania also underlined its commitment to broader Balkan and Black Sea projects. The country developed a new

152   *Defending Eastern Europe*

National Security Strategy that described the possibility of transforming the tension-filled borders of that area into bridges to the new eastern democracies. The Romanian perception of the Black Sea was that it could be a center of dynamism instead of perpetual conflict. As such, Romania noted its intention to participate in the Black Sea Forum for Dialogue and Cooperation (Peterson 2013, 44–5). The 2017 White Paper stressed the significance of SEDM and its many projects. Romania also took part in Operation Black Sea Harmony and stitched together a Peacekeeping Battalion with its traditional historical enemy, Hungary ("White Paper on Defense Bucharest 2017" n.d.). The 2016 Warsaw Summit of NATO set additional goals that involved Romanian geographic space. NATO decided to set up a more "tailored forward presence" in the Multinational Brigade South-East and located additional troops in Romania. In 2019, the fourth Polish contingent replaced its third contingent and established a presence in Romania for the next six months. Polish capabilities in this mission included 225 soldiers as well as 47 pieces of equipment ("Transfer of Authority between the Polish Contingents at Craiova" 2019). In light of the Russian takeover of Crimea in 2014, there was thus a much closer interface between NATO objectives and those of Southeast Europe and the Balkans. It is important to mention that Romania, Poland, and the Baltic countries increasingly see each other as strategic allies, and this reproduces a pattern of pre-World War II military alliances (when Poland's closest allies were Latvia and Romania, especially the latter).

The White Paper also emphasized the importance of links to the EU that Romania had joined also in 2004. The document did all possible to emphasize the linkages between NATO and the EU in terms of their implications for Romanian defense planning. For example, it noted that some Romanian troops were assigned to the NATO Response Force as well as to the EU battlegroups. Specifically, Romania also needed to develop equipment purchase plans as well as communication systems that were compatible with the infrastructure of both alliances. It also needed to link its own research centers to those of the EU and NATO. It was also the case that the NATO Security Investment Program (NSIP) could assist in acquiring those additional capabilities, while allied military equipment itself would be welcome on Romanian territory. Military education was also important, and Romanian military personnel would be welcome at institutions of both alliances ("White Paper on Defense Bucharest 2017" n.d.).

Romania took on an important EU assignment in the first half of 2019, as it assumed the presidency of the EU Council. Thus, it had a heightened sense of responsibility for the EU Rapid Response Force, its battlegroups, and the Permanent Structured Cooperation known as PESCO. Romania's leadership role was also an outgrowth of the EU-NATO Joint Declaration

States with significant security issues   153

at the Warsaw Summit of 2016. In the language of the summit, Romania bore the potential to become a "vector of stability and security in the South-East of Europe" ("White Paper on Defense Bucharest 2017" n.d.). All EU defense ministers came to Bucharest at the end of January 2019. Their host was the Minister of Defense of Romania Gabriel Les and the meeting chair was Frederica Mogherini, the High Representative of the EU for Foreign Affairs and Security Policy ("Informal Meeting of the EU Defence Ministers in Bucharest" n.d.). All 28 defense ministers were in attendance, and they cast a spotlight on PESCO. After discussing the success of 18 PACE crisis management exercises performed in 2018, they called upon the PESCO personnel to identify future projects of importance ("EU Defence Policy Directors Meeting in Bucharest" n.d.). Clearly, the enhancement of EU interest in security matters for Eastern Europe was resulting in new plans that were important to the region.

It is also worthy of note that women's issues in the defense sector played a role, at least during the January 2019 EU Defense Ministers conference in Bucharest. The topic for their kick-off dinner was "Women, Peace and Security," and discussion centered on the fact that this was a "shared priority" among the EU, NATO, and the UN. In practical terms, the group agreed to utilize this perspective in "peace operations and crisis management" ("Informal Meeting of the EU Defence Ministers in Bucharest" n.d.). Such a vital topic highlighted the practical links between the two alliances and the ways in which their objectives could dovetail on such matters.

In 2008, both the Czech Republic and Poland agreed to take part in a US project of the Bush administration that was known as the missile shield proposal. Essentially, there would be ten anti-missile interceptors located in Poland, and the radar to detect the incoming missiles would be based in the Czech Republic. The target was essentially Iran, one of the three countries listed by the American president on the "Axis of Evil" in his 2002 State of the Union message. However, there was controversy over the proposal. Scientists raised questions about whether it would really be able to detect any incoming missile, and there were many public demonstrations in the Czech Republic against it. As a result, President Obama cancelled the project unilaterally in 2009, and so it was temporarily on hold. Eventually, he made an agreement with Poland and Romania to build a scaled-down version of the project that would be a joint US–NATO undertaking. A result was the signing of the US–Romania Ballistic Missile Defence Agreement (BMDA) ("White Paper on Defence Bucharest 2017" n.d.). In 2011, the Romanian Supreme Defense Council approved participation in this new missile shield proposal. Plans included location of an interceptor site at the Deveselu former air base in Romania, and 200 soldiers would defend the site against a possible attack by Iranian missiles. In 2020, the infrastructure

154 *Defending Eastern Europe*

would be ungraded, as Poland would provide more advanced interceptors (Peterson 2013, 47). Location of these interceptors in Romania underlined the value of having included Balkan nations in NATO, in light of their role as a kind of geographic stepping stone in the direction of troubled Middle East states such as Iran, Iraq, and Afghanistan.

Romanian historical legacies have also played a partial role in its pursuit of defensive alliances in the post-Cold War decades. Its twentieth-century nationalist approach during much of the communist era was in part a function of a "group defense mechanism" that flowed from the country's ethnic pride. The state had inherited its language from the Romans who settled Dacia as early as the second century AD. Thus, Romania's links to Latin culture made it unique in the Balkans as well as within the East European entire orbit (Gilberg 1990, 5). Perhaps, this special ethnic and cultural background prepared the country for adopting a National Communist approach under the communist leader Nicolae Ceauşescu. It may have generated a state self-perception of its potential contributions in the region as a "bridge" or "mediator" among quite different states from the Slavic family (Gilberg 1990, 224–5). Its defensiveness in historical terms might have paved the way for the priority that it placed on both NATO and EU membership only a decade and a half after the collapse of the Ceauşescu regime.

Further, Romania possessed a special orientation toward the Balkan region in the communist era, and that commitment carried over into the time of membership in the NATO alliance. During its years under communist control, it perceived its Balkan partners as part of a southern Comecon region that consisted of Romania, Bulgaria, Yugoslavia, and Albania (Gilberg 1990, 214). Given their limited level of industrialization, that set of nations was quite different from the more advanced economies such as Czechoslovakia and the Baltic states. Perhaps, this regional self-image was a strong root of their participation later on in the twenty-first century in the Black Sea Forum as well as in SEDM. The regional leadership, under NATO and EU membership, that Romania displayed in those later years in the Balkans was therefore deeply rooted in the historical uniqueness of the state but also future driven by the eastern defense challenges that included wars in Iraq and Afghanistan, Russian expansionism in Ukraine, and contributions requested of them in the US–NATO missile shield program.

Polish defense policies after the 2014 crisis

By 2010/11 Polish defense policies, military doctrine, force structure, and even equipment were largely adjusted to the realities of NATO and EU alliance politics and policies. Poland had a fairly small and decently equipped

States with significant security issues 155

(for its limited goals) professional military force which participated at unusually high rates in NATO, EU, and US-led expeditionary operations across the world. Behind the reality was the notion that Poland does not face conventional regional military threats, but rather unconventional "new" and "global" threats and whatever residual security concern the country had (chiefly, the threat of Russian neo-imperialism) it could safely face them down as a member of the most powerful military and political community/ alliances in the world – NATO, and, within it, the Polish–US "special" alliance developed through unflinching Polish loyalty in Iraq and Afghanistan.

The shock of 2013/14 Ukrainian events forced the then ruling PO (liberal center-right) Polish government to acknowledge the insufficiency of Polish forces and limitations of defense policies pursued between 2001 and 2011. The adjustments both in terms of doctrine and policies were created and enacted between 2010 and 2015. These included a comprehensive Strategic National Security Review (2010–12) with the resulting *White Book of National Security* (2013) divided into classified and unclassified sections (Koziej and Brzozowski 2015). On September 17, 2013 a Council of Ministers resolution established and consolidated a list of 14 priority military modernization programs, confirmed and expanded in June 2014 (Omitruk 2015). Finally, in 2014 a new *National Security Strategy of the Polish Republic* was created (Rzeczpospolita Polska 2014). All these programs, taken together, represented a major adjustment in Polish defense policies, strategy, military doctrine, and the direction of Polish military modernization. Still, these programs found themselves criticized by the PiS party, which found itself in power in 2015, and, since, conducted its own Strategic Defense Review and created a *National Defense Concept for the Republic of Poland* (2017) and *National Security Strategy of the Republic of Poland* (2020). The consensus, clash, and debate between these two visions and sets of programs has defined the Polish defense policies of the 2010s, and will define it for the next decades (Sutowski 2016).

The PO program, on the grand strategy level, represented an incremental, rather than radical, adjustment to the previous policies. The 2014 *National Security Strategy* repeated the key premises of all previous strategies from 1992 on: the central goals of peaceful internal and external liberal developments as the principal goals, and reliance on key institutions; NATO and EU/CSDP and their strength as guarantees of Poland's secure development. Polish professional, well modernized armed forces were to be the key elements of the military defense sub-system of Polish national security structures. These elements of continuity with the previous strategies, however, hid rather important changes.

For the first time in Polish post-communist formulations of its threat perception, Russia was mentioned several times implicitly and explicitly

156   *Defending Eastern Europe*

as a threat; as a country that does not respect international principles of sovereignty and a country with a potentially offensive military potential whose revival as a great power comes at "the expense of its neighbors," and therefore has "negative influence on regional security" (Rzeczpospolita Polska 2014, 10, 19–21). In terms of specific threats, the strategy pointed out hybrid warfare ("armed operations below the threshold of classical war") as a possible threat, with an all-out conventional war being less likely (Rzeczpospolita Polska 2014, 20).

Answers to this new heightened perception of threats was to be multiple, and included strengthening of both NATO and EU and their respective policies and response mechanisms. Most importantly, both NATO and Common Security and Defense Policies were to be reconsolidated around territorial defense functions, seen as primary, with expeditionary global capacities seen as important but secondary (Rzeczpospolita Polska 2014, 29). Polish armed forces, especially, were to create a "full spectrum capacity" focused on territorial defense and deterrence capacities – a genuine ability to impose pain on any potential enemy contemplating aggression (Rzeczpospolita Polska 2014, 30–1). In concrete terms, the *Strategy* called for continuous and stepped up modernization of Polish armed forces. The priority in terms of defensive technologies was to air and anti-missile defense systems, as well as information and cyberwarfare capacity. Importantly, the *Strategy* called for a recreation of territorial defense troops and a military reserve system – both totally neglected with the professionalization of armed force in the 2010s (Rzeczpospolita Polska 2014, 45–6). Otherwise, Polish troops were to invest in greater mobility and C3 (command, control, and communication) capacity, and upgrade their mobility – all to prevent strategic and tactical surprise. The deterrent capabilities were to be centered around programs that Prime Minister Tusk announced in June 2014, under the moniker "Polish fangs": these included up to 400 US-produced medium range (to 370 km) Lockheed AMG-158 JSSM air-launched self-guiding cruise missiles to be installed on Polish F-16s, and new submarines to be equipped with underwater guided ballistic missiles, as well as new medium-range (to 300 km) HOMAR multiple-launch rocket system (Omitruk 2015). Financial capacity for these new programs was immediately created, and the programs started to be implemented forthwith with visible adjustments to Polish procurement defense budgets.

PO's program of reform of Polish military and defense policies did not calm down PiS predictable criticisms, with the latter accusing PO of leaving Poland vulnerable to Russian threat (Sutowski 2016). With the PiS victory in presidential and parliamentary elections in 2015, the conservative right-wing government could create its own policy and strategy, based on a presumption of a radical break from the past 25 years of Polish policy.

States with significant security issues 157

In 2017 the new, controversial PiS Minister of Defense Antoni Macierewicz presented a new *Defense Concept of the Polish Republic* authored by a team led by Deputy Minister of Defense, Tomasz Szatkowski (Ministry of National Defense 2017).

Right away, the document stated that:

> Over recent years, those forces have been developed based on erroneous assumptions. There was a lack of both an accurate assessment of Poland's geo-political situation, and of a sound strategic diagnosis supported by the careful observation of trends in our neighbourhood. This resulted in a wrong conviction that the risk of an armed conflict in our part of Europe was marginal, and that any potential threats would be attributed mainly to non-state actors.

The document went on to say that "the scale of threats resulting from the Russian aggressive policy had not been adequately assessed in the past." This diagnosis, according to the document, creates a need for a radical change in Polish defense policies, based on the creation of defenses adequate to the existing level of threat, which includes a possibility of not just "actions below the threshold of war" but might also include an open inter-state armed conflict (Ministerstwo Obrony Narodowej 2017, 19–20). In this potential conflict, Polish autonomous defensive capacity is crucial, in concert and alliance with NATO and EU, which still remain the pillars of Polish security, but might be objects of Russian institutional aggression aimed at disintegration of Western structures. The *Concept* then engages in a speculative, opaque, and abstract discussion of the EU and NATO as subject to future and unspecified "changes" – perhaps a code word for weakening or disintegration. In this threat environment "real capacities and actions" matter first and foremost, and, as based on other PiS statements, Poland's bilateral alliance with the United States is to be prioritized.

The *Concept* went on to state that Poland aims at spending 2.5% of its GDP on defense, which would make the country (based on 2016 figures) the third relatively largest NATO spender after the United States and Greece (NATO Public Diplomacy Division 2017). These substantial new sums are to be put into force enlargement and armaments programs. In terms of operational land forces, a new division is to be added to the existing force structures, while a new/old (as communist governments had them and they were later abolished) Territorial Defense Forces, modeled on the British system of reserves (or US Army-National Guard), are to be created. The Territorial Forces are to be 53,000 strong, and be attached to particular provinces, where they would train, among others, to conduct guerrilla operations in case the area is overran by an enemy's regular troops (Likowski 2017).[7] Overall, by 2025 Polish armed forces are to be 200,000 strong and superbly equipped, with substantial deterrent capacities. They are also to be led by a

158 *Defending Eastern Europe*

new command structure with a Commander in Chief in times of war being also the Head of General Staff in times of peace.

What dominated Polish defense policies between 2017 and 2020 was the realization of ideas stated in the *Concept* as well as the prioritization of bilateral alliance with the US and stepping up of unilateral and multilateral (NATO- and EU-oriented) military readiness measures aimed against a potential Russian aggression. These efforts were far from smooth. Until January 2018 Minister Antoni Macierewicz's erratic leadership led to massive purges and a wave of resignations among military officers, thus undermining Polish military professionalism and standing in NATO (Ćwieluch and Rzeczkowski 2017). Similarly, the disarray in the Ministry of Defense created problems in military procurement efforts. However, since January 2018 and takeover of the ministry by Mariusz Błaszczak, presumed to be PiS leader Jarosław Kaczyński's closest political ally, the efforts accelerated, resulting in the signing of several procurement contracts. By early 2019, these included, most significantly, a $0.5 billion contract to acquire 20 medium and short range US multiple rocket and missile systems (HIMARS – Polish name HOMAR), and a $2.5 billion contract to acquire Lockheed Martin's "Patriot" air defense systems (Polish name of the program *Wisła* – Vistula), as well as a contract for Poland's acquisition of some 30 F-35 fighter bombers (Polish name of the program *Harpia*), for the total of $3–5 billion. All of these contracts amounted to a huge proportion of Poland's future defense budget, and were conspicuously US-oriented, whereas, for instance, a contract to buy French Airbus Caracal helicopters was cancelled, infuriating the French. With Polish territorial defense forces being built at a furious pace, and NATO (US) troops' presence on the Polish soil, Poland clearly became, together with Romania and the Baltics, among the most militaristically-minded and militantly Russian-averse country-member of NATO. Given Poland's strategic culture and history of mutual hostilities and geopolitical rivalries with Russia, which go back 400 years to the sixteenth century and current geopolitical and ideological realities, Poland's role in this respect is unsurprising.

Still, the newest formulation of Poland's national security strategy, issued on May 12, 2020 reasserted continuities rather than fractures in the country's post-communist defense policies. While repeating the 2014 identification of Russia as the chief foreign security threat to Poland, the strategy was firmly Atlanticist, seeing in NATO and the EU the chief pillars of Poland's military security, backed by a domestic military buildup – again, the pledge of 2.5% of GDP to be spent on national defense was repeated in the document. At the same time, the bilateral security relationship with the United States, while mentioned, was not overly emphasized, instead, the thrust of the document was firmly liberal-internationalist and institutionalist, with no hint of Poland's intent to weaken rather than strengthen NATO and the EU. Moreover, areas of "soft" security: cyber-defenses, information space defense, economic and financial security, human security and environmental protection (including a fight against climate change) occupied the majority of the document, with purely military security relegated to no more than 5–6 pages in a 35-page policy statement. It is clear that the EU rather than NATO will be Poland's chief institutional platform for its pursuit of soft security interests (Rzeczpospolita Polska 2020).

Moldova: non-member of both NATO and the EU

Moldova's inclusion in this chapter, even though the country does not belong to NATO and the EU, is motivated by the country's special status vis-à-vis Romania and Russia. As discussed in Chapter 3, the country features the oldest "frozen" military conflict of the post-Soviet space in Europe, and is suspended between its cultural belonging to the Romanian nation, and its special status vis-à-vis Russia and Transnistria. Moldova's transition to market economy and democracy has been far from successful – the country is the poorest in Europe. Moldova's prospects for joining NATO are murky at best, as Moldova lacks a domestic consensus on such a membership (see Chapter 3) while the country's poverty and corruption makes prospects for EU membership remote.

Defense-wise, Moldova went through short, brutal, and violent conflict with Transnistrian separatists, and temporarily had to build up its military forces, maintaining substantial (for a small country) military assets until 1994. By all indicators, battered by Moldova's economic and political decay, these forces have almost totally withered away and today Moldova has around 4000-strong land forces with no armor heavier than 1960s/1970s style APCs – fairly weak for a country of some 2.6 million people with a potential security challenge.[8] Moldova's mechanized infantry include mostly residual and obsolete ex-Soviet or ex-Romania armored assets, no real air forces, and obsolete air defense equipment (IISS 2019, 170). Moldova's is thus rather defense-less against any serious military conventional military threat, with its security and military forces barely able to maintain internal controls. The US, NATO, EU, and PfP therefore undertook several efforts to engage Moldovan military and security structures in political and military activities aimed at bringing the country closer to Western-led networks of security all with mixed results, as the country's domestic political realities feature a high level of Russian influence and ambiguity on Moldova's long-term political alignment.[9]

160 *Defending Eastern Europe*

Clearly, Moldova's weakness points to a potential serious crisis, which might break out, again, over Transnistria and entangle Romania, and perhaps NATO. The country thus forms of part of Europe's insecurity zone in the borderlands of the former Soviet Union.

Conclusion

The mix of "gravitational," typological," and "attributional" distances noted in the introduction has certainly played a role in the political and defense development of both Poland and Romania.

Perhaps both have not suffered as much from gravitational distance from a formerly strong and protective power, for both were quite independent from Moscow during most of the Cold War. Poland moved away from the Soviet tug in the 1950s and challenged the leadership of Moscow for several decades. Although Romanian domestic practices were unchanged from those established with the formation of the communist bloc in the 1940s, their foreign policy was really one of neutrality between the West and East in the last two decades of the Cold War. In spite of those unique situations in relation to the communist bloc, leaders in both nations have welcomed the opportunity to play a role in both NATO and the EU. Poland and Romania have both joined the military alliance, and Romania entered the EU a few years after joining NATO. Thus, the constant interaction with both alliances after the end of the Balkan wars of the 1990s had provided them with a connectedness that has replaced any "gravitational distance" that existed.

"Typological distance" has been a different kind of challenge for Romania, as its leaders clung to authoritarian patterns, after the end of the Cold War, to a greater extent than did the East Central states further north in the region. Elections took place after 1989, but the centralist streak was hard to suppress. However, the membership plan that both NATO and the EU presented to Romania called for steps to ensure the growth of genuine democracy as well as a participant political culture with a meaningful role for the public. Thus, they needed to check off key required points in those regards, as they moved toward embrace by the two alliances. Overcoming "typological distance" has taken time but has been accomplished within the framework of liberal institutions and organizations.

In Poland, in turn, this distance from the West seems to have actually increased recently, with the election of the populist-nationalist PiS to power in 2015, reaffirmed by 2019 elections. However, given the bilateral US–Polish orientation of Polish security and defense policy, the distance, simultaneously, decreased in Polish–US relations, where Poland's current leadership sees a special affinity with President Trump's administration.

States with significant security issues 161

Table 9.1 Contribution of the former Soviet bloc/East-Central European and Balkan countries to the "War on Terror"*

#	Country	ISAF peak deployment	Operation Iraqi Freedom-peak deployment	Total in Afghanistan and Iraq	Populations (c. 2008)	Total troop commitment as a percentage of population (from highest to lowest)
1	Georgia	1,600	2,000	3,600	3,720000	0.0968%
2	Poland	2,600	2,500	5,100	38,116,000	0.0134%
3	Estonia	120	40	160	1,340,602	0.0119%
4	Croatia	450	60	510	4,453,500	0.0115%
5	Romania	1,600	730	2,330	21,680,974	0.0107%
6	Macedonia	135	80	215	2,061,315	0.0104%
7	Lithuania	200	120	320	3,369,600	0.0095%
8	Latvia	70	136	206	2,270,700	0.0091%
9	Hungary	540	300	840	10,041,000	0.0084%
10	Bulgaria	767	485	1,252	15,217,711	0.0082%
11	Slovakia	293	110	403	5,379,455	0.0075%
12	Albania	140	120	260	3,619,778	0.0072%
13	Czech Republic	415	300	715	10,424,926	0.0069%
14	Azerbaijan	100	250	350	8676000	0.0040%
15	Slovenia	70	0	70	2,039,399	0.0034%
16	Ukraine	3	1,650	1,653	48,457,102	0.0034%
17	Armenia	40	46	86	3,231,900	0.0027%
18	Bosnia	0	36	36	3981239	0.0009%
19	Moldova	0	24	24	3,383,332	0.0007%
20	Kazakhstan	0	29	29	15,217,711	0.0002%

Note: *This table is the clearest metric indicating the respective countries' desire to show their loyalty to the US/NATO-based security system, mostly in function of their perception of the magnitude of Russian or Serbian threats.

Source: Compiled from ISAF and Multinational Assistance Force-Iraq websites.

162 *Defending Eastern Europe*

At the same time, let us remember that Poland's orientation toward US–Polish bilateralism long pre-dates the PiS government, and was practiced assiduously by Poland's post-communist left during President Bush's tenure in office. Clearly, realism and geopolitical realities, not ideological affinities, are far more important in explaining Poland's and Romania's actions. Moreover, Poland's most recent formulation of its national security strategy points to a reassertion of Atlanticism and European orientation – not a bilateral relationship with the United States – as centerpieces of the country's defense strategy.

"Attributional distance" with its emphasis on the growth of common values has also been a challenge, for culturally Romania is not part of the larger Slavic family that characterizes so much of the rest of the region. Romania has thus become part of the Black Sea community and its different cultural and defense organizations, and so it may have compensated for the distance generated by its location in a Slavic neighborhood. Embedded in Southeast Europe, they share with Bulgaria strong roles in Black Sea-based organizations. Therefore, Romania has partially overcome "attributional distance" through activities and missions that offer a sense of cultural closeness to communities that differ from their Slavic surroundings. In this last respect, the growing Polish–Romanian security relationship, which clearly reproduces pre-World War II patterns of anti-Soviet alliances, points, again, to the prevalence of common threat perceptions, geopolitics, and realist considerations over cultural considerations in explaining Polish and Romanian defense cooperation.

Notes

1 Government of Poland, in "Strategia Bezpieczeństwa Narodowego Rzeczypospolitej Polskiej [National Security Strategy of the Republic of Poland or SBRP 2000]" and "Strategia Obronna Rzeczypospolitej Polskiej [Defense Strategy of the Polish Republic]," in *Zbiór dokumentów – Dokumenty z zakresu polityki zagranicznej Polski i stosunków międzynarodowych* No. 1 (2000). In the conclusion of this latter document we find the following statement: "The safety of the Republic is not under threat for the first time in a few centuries. Poland is safer than in any time of its modern and early modern history ... However, indivisibility of security means that efforts to improve Poland's security must start far away from the borders of the Republic. We firmly strive to assure that in the 21st century Poland will be not only a consumer, but also creator of security." These last two sentences were to prove prophetic.

2 Changes that the doctrine has undergone between 2000 and 2003 are telling. Thus, Section 3.2.1 of Poland's 2000 Defense Strategy stated: "The Atlantic

Alliance is the main factor of political and military stability of our continent. For Poland it constitutes a real base for security and defence [*sic*]." The 2003 Strategy had a different formula: "Poland is a part of an allied defense system. NATO and bilateral political and military cooperation with the USA and other main states-members of the alliance constitute the most important guarantee of external security and peaceful development of our country. Our bilateral relationship with the USA is a crucial chain of the transatlantic link." See Rzeczpospolita Polska, "Strategia Bezpieczenstwa Narodowego Rzeczpospolitej Polskie [National Security Strategy of the Polish Republic]," Biuro Bezpieczenstwa Narodowego, www.bbn.ogv.pl/pl/dokument/strategia_bezpieczenstwa.html, 2003.

3 The realist "internal" balancing logic within NATO has been noticed by scholars, most notably James Thompson and Andrew Michta. See James Thompson, "History's Rhyme," paper presented at Mid-Western Political Science Association Annual Conference, 15/04 Chicago, 2004 and Michta (2006). The dictum that NATO's function is to "Keep Americans in, the Russians out and the Germans down" still held in this respect.

4 See various CBOS (Center for the Study of Public Opinion) surveys of Polish public opinion 2003–17, www.cbos.pl. For instance, Centrum Badania Opinii Spolecznej, "O Udziale Polskich Zolnierzy w Operacjach Za Granica, Tarczy Antyrakietowej i Zagrozeniu Terroryzmem," February 2008. Center for the Study of Public Opinion (CBOS). www.Cbos.Pl. www.cbos.pl, accessed October 3, 2008. Also, while Poland remains one of the most pro-American countries in the world, the 2003–17 period was characterized by a substantial growth in negative views of the United States and its policies, clearly as the result of the Polish deployments on NATO or US-allied missions.

5 For instance, an incident in the Afghan village of Nanghar Khel (actually, Sha Mardan close to Nanghar Khel) called the "Polish My Lai" was widely reported and shook the country. Briefly, the story involved the Polish troops deployed to the Pakitka province, who, after a Taliban attack against a US convoy, deliberately mortared a neighboring village, killing six and severely injuring three civilians, mostly women and children. See Górka and Zadworny (2007) and Kulisha (2007).

6 The 2004 novelization of the 2001 statute required, among others, that procurement spending has to represent at least 16% of the military budget, and has to grow to reach at last 20% of the budget by 2006. Indeed, by 2006 this goal was reached and then exceeded in 2007 and 2008.

7 These forces are being created at a furious pace and their four brigades are already in place. The cadre officers tend to come from Polish special forces, which gives the new formation a specific ethos and character. Polish partisan and media controversies around these forces tend to be ideological and focused on whether PiS are not building a "private army" for internal repression. Experts are more concerned about the cost of these forces taking away and diluting modernization efforts of regular operational forces.

8 Lithuania has a comparable population of 2.7 million and 30,000 strong standing military – six times bigger than Moldova. Moldova appears to be the weakest country of post-communist Europe militarily, except for Kosovo and Montenegro.
9 For instance, a substantial plurality of Moldovans oppose the country's potential NATO membership, with 48% against and 23% for the membership (Baltic Surveys/Gallup Organization for Republican National Institute 2018).

10

Challenged Baltic states: Estonia, Latvia, and Lithuania

Olavi Arens

The Baltic states reappeared on the world maps as independent entities in the aftermath of the failed August 1991 putsch in Moscow. While the total population of the Baltic countries is small (six million), their total land area (175,728 sq. km. or 67,643 sq. miles) is not insignificant (over one half of Poland). From the Baltic perspective this was a "restoration" of independence and a return to Europe that had been achieved in the aftermath of World War I and the Russian Revolution of 1917–20. Independence had been lost in July 1940 as a result of the Molotov-Ribbentrop Pact, World War II, the Soviet occupation, and the resulting annexation of the Baltic states in July 1940.[1] Throughout the 51-year period that followed, the United States maintained a policy of non-recognition of the annexation. Indeed, during the last phase of the Cold War, while not one of the major topics of discussion like arms control and German unification, President George H.W. Bush and Secretary of State James Baker brought up the Baltic question at every meeting with Soviet President Mikhail Gorbachev and the Soviet Foreign Minister, Eduard Shevardnadze (Bush and Scowcroft 1998, 15–29, 525–6, 533–4; Arens 2016). The independence of the Baltic states was recognized by the Soviet Union on September 6, 1991 after the failed putsch, but before the disintegration of the USSR. The rest of the international community accorded recognition that began with Iceland on August 22 and included the United States ten days later on September 2. The Baltic states, which had been members of the League of Nations from 1921 to 1940, were admitted to the United Nations on September 17, 1991.

In the three major crisis periods of twentieth-century Europe: World War I and the Russian Revolutions and Civil War, World War II, and the collapse of communism and the end of the Cold War (1989–91), the Baltic peoples managed to assert themselves in two of the three. In fact, we may view 1939–40 as the exception, because the Baltic states were completely isolated from the rest of the world, and Stalin was able to deal with each one in separate one-on-one negotiations in the fall of 1939 to secure military

166 *Defending Eastern Europe*

bases that gave the Soviets military control that later turned into an occupation in June 1940 and an annexation one month later. In 1918–20 and 1989–91, the striving for independence by the Baltic peoples was one of many problems and issues that a Russia in turmoil needed to resolve. The Russian solution in both cases was to recognize the separation of the Baltic states from Russia.[2] Indeed, for President George H.W. Bush the Baltic states were the exception, as until December 1991 he opposed the dissolution of the rest of the Soviet Union. The USSR dissolved on December 25, 1991, four months after the Baltic states had successfully reasserted their independence.

The most important part of the early security agenda of the Baltic governments was the removal of Russian troops from their territories. This was achieved first by Lithuania in 1993 and by Estonia and Latvia in 1994. The establishment of Baltic armed forces began at ground zero (Luik 2019).[3] While the Baltic populations had been subject to Soviet conscription, and thus had served scattered throughout the Soviet military, the military had not been an attractive career option for them. Hence there was a dearth of officers for the newly established militaries. That actually may have been a good thing, since it contributed from the beginning to a rejection of Soviet military culture. Initially, each maintained a "conscription" military. However, the percentage of a given age cohort actually serving was rather low – well below 50%.

What argued against neutrality as a long-term option was a memory of the historical experience of the 1930s when neutrality failed to prevent the Baltic states losing their independence. During the early 1990s aspirations to membership in the EU or NATO were considered far-fetched and at best a distant perspective even though both organizations had declared their openness to membership by other European states.[4] However, the Baltic elites wished to use the moment to move as rapidly as possible toward adopting Western political and economic institutions and shedding the Soviet past before the international situation changed.

Once the initial political decisions had been made – new constitutions adopted, basic administrative structures established and elections held, attention was focused on how the Baltic countries should change a Soviet "command" economic system to a functioning market system. The Baltic states adopted what was called the "shock therapy" approach of radical change that inflicted initial pain in the hope that an economic downturn would be followed by a rapid rebound. The ruble was discarded, new currencies were introduced, a free trade policy was introduced, and privatization of industry, commercial enterprises, and property took place. The political leaderships were willing to take the risk, and the Baltic peoples were willing to make the short-term sacrifices for the long-term gain – shoring up

Challenged Baltic states

independence and some degree of economic well-being that would resemble what they saw in the West (Laar 2014).

In 1995 association agreements were signed with the European Union and in 1998 all three were accorded "candidate" status for EU membership. The Baltic states were accepted into EU membership on May 1, 2004 along with seven other states. Since then, the Baltic states have emerged in economic terms on par with the states of East-Central Europe – the Visegrád group (Poland, Czech Republic, Slovakia, and Hungary) and Slovenia – as the success stories of the post-communist economic transformation in East-Central Europe.[5]

In 1994 all three joined NATO's Partnership for Peace program that was established for the former communist-dominated countries. The Partnership for Peace program proved to be the right program at the right time for them. Each Baltic state was able to partner with the National Guard of a US state – Lithuania with Pennsylvania, Latvia with Michigan, and Estonia with Maryland – that provided valuable advice and training opportunities in the United States during the initial phase of establishing defense forces (NATO 1994). Shortly afterward, a special relationship between the Baltic states and the United States was cemented by the signing of the "Baltic Charter" in 1998. According to the Charter:

> The United States of America welcomes the aspirations and supports the efforts of Estonia, Latvia and Lithuania to join NATO ... Sharing a common vision of a peaceful and increasingly integrated Europe, free of divisions, dedicated to democracy, the rule of law, free markets, and respect for the human rights and fundamental freedoms of all people. (Charter 1998)

Indeed in 1999 the Baltic states were accepted into the Membership Action Plan (MAP) that was to be a way station to NATO. Among the MAP conditions were:

> Demonstrate commitment to the rule of law and human rights;
>
> Establish appropriate democratic and civilian control of their armed forces;
>
> Provide forces and capabilities for collective defense and other Alliance missions;
>
> Allocate sufficient budget resources for the implementation of alliance commitments. (NATO 1999)

On the basis of the above documents it could be argued that the expansion of the NATO alliance into East-Central Europe most closely followed the liberal theory of international relations that argues that alliances are constructed on the basis of value systems, in this case the values of liberal democratic societies.[6] Yet the issue was never one of only values. Many in

168 *Defending Eastern Europe*

the Baltic states valued the security guarantee of Article 5 above all else. On the US side some American foreign policy experts were hesitant about expanding NATO eastward and in particular granting membership to "former Soviet republics." Certainly the Russian foreign policy elite had objected to the 1999 NATO enlargement that gave membership to Poland, the Czech Republic, and Hungary. In a study prepared for the US air force that was published in 2001, Thomas S. Szayma expressed the view, that had some currency in the US military, that because of past Russian objections to NATO expansion: "Conceivably Estonia, Latvia, and Lithuania could be in their current stage well into the next decade" (Szayna 2020, 106).

NATO at the time was trying to integrate Russia into the Western vision of a new European security order. In 1997 a "Founding Act on Mutual Relations, Cooperation and Security" was signed by Russia and NATO that declared:

> NATO and Russia do not consider each other as adversaries ... respect for sovereignty, independence and territorial integrity of all states and their inherent right to choose the means to ensure their own security ... the alliance will carry out its collective defence by ensuring ... capability for reinforcement rather than by additional permanent stationing of substantial combat forces. (NATO 1997)

Furthermore, 9/11 intervened and led Russian President Putin to briefly explore the possibility of alignment with the United States against Islamic extremism. As a result, Russian opposition to NATO expansion to the Baltic states became somewhat muted. In 2002, in a new spirit of optimism a NATO–Russia Council was established in Rome. Vladimir Putin declared at the meeting:

> As realists, we recall that the history of relations between Russia and North Atlantic Alliance has not been easy. We have come a long way – from opposition to dialogue, from confrontation to cooperation ... For Russia its geopolitical position, the enhancement of cooperation with NATO as an equal partners is one of the real embodiments of the multiple approach, to which there is no alternative and which we intend to pursue resolutely ... twenty influential world States have realized that they have common vital security interests. First and foremost – the threat of international terrorism. (Putin 2002)

President George W. Bush stated his support for NATO enlargement in a speech in June 2001. Invitations for NATO membership for the Baltic states were issued at the Prague Summit of 2002, alongside four other former communist countries – Romania, Bulgaria, Slovenia, and Slovakia. The Baltic states were officially accepted into membership on March 29, 2004. Official US acceptance had been preceded by Hearings (four sessions) before the Senate Committee on Foreign Relations in March–April 2003. The

Challenged Baltic states 169

dominant theme at the Hearings was expressed by Nicholas Burns, the US ambassador to NATO, who noted:

> [The] greatest strategic goal of the United States and European allies has been the construction of Europe that would be whole, free, peaceful and secure … That is what President George H. W. Bush believed … President Clinton believed … hallmark of President Bush's European policy. (Burns 2003)

The vision was one of the spread of democratic values to the countries of Eastern Europe and establishing a common rule-based world order based on democratic values. When asked about Russia's attitude, in particular to the Baltic states joining NATO, the answer given by the witnesses (among them: Nicholas Burns; Gen. Wesley Clark, former NATO commander; Ronald Asmus, RAND; and Marc Grossman, State Department) was that Russia no longer objected since it was being drawn into a cooperative relationship with NATO.

However, Stephen Larrabee (RAND), in his written statement noted that in "March 1997 Russian President Yeltsin tried to get a private oral agreement from President Clinton – 'a gentleman's agreement' – that would not be made public, not to admit the Baltic States into the Alliance. President Clinton flatly refused to make such a commitment" (Larrabee 2003, 5). Yet, now President Putin no longer voiced opposition.

A number of other reasons were advanced in favor of admitting the candidate countries to NATO. It was noted that all of the candidate countries had sent peacekeeping forces to the Balkans – Bosnia and Kosovo. All were sending peacekeeping forces to Afghanistan and were ready to do the same in Iraq. Furthermore, it was noted that all had joined in the Vilnius-10 declaration of support for the US invasion of Iraq. The Vilnius-10 declaration was not advanced as a major reason for supporting membership, but the willingness to participate in the missions was important. It indicated that the countries accepted the NATO view that since the Cold War had ended, the major field for NATO activity in the foreseeable future was out-of-area missions. In addition it was noted that each country pledged to maintain or reach the 2% of GDP level for defense spending.[7]

Retrospectively, the optimism expressed by the witnesses that, now that the Baltic states were on their way to being admitted, their relations with Russia would actually improve proved to be overly optimistic. Also the promises of the applicant states to meet the 2% of GDP standard in defense spending were not kept in the decade that followed.

The Baltic states had begun contributing to peacekeeping operations first under the UN umbrella in Croatia in 1994 (Lithuania) and 1995 (Estonia). By 1996 they were contributing platoon-sized units embedded in the forces of NATO countries like Denmark to Bosnia-Herzegovina and then from

170 *Defending Eastern Europe*

1999 to 2009 to Kosovo. Baltic contributions for each operation exceeded in rotations to more than 2,000 soldiers. All three Baltic states participated in the operation in Iraq from 2003 onwards and likewise in rotations their contribution totaled over 2000 (Paljak 2013, 234–9).

Afghanistan, however, proved to be the most important area of involvement for the Baltic militaries. Lithuania came to be the framework country in the Provincial Reconstruction Team of an Afghanistan province (Ghowr). Well over 7,000 Baltic soldiers in rotation have served in Afghanistan. The casualties have been larger than for any other mission. Total fatalities have been: Estonia 12 (two in Iraq, nine in Afghanistan, and one in Kosovo); Latvia 7 (three in Iraq and four in Afghanistan); Lithuania 2 (one in Bosnia and one in Afghanistan) (Paljak 2013, 224–5).

While the monetary cost of participation has not been huge, at their high point in 2007–9 the costs did take up 5–9% of the defense budgets of the three states (Paljak 2013, 221–3). Besides contributing to NATO security missions and gaining visibility, the missions and the partnering with more experienced militaries like that of the United States, United Kingdom, etc. provided valuable training and learning opportunities. The present leadership of the Baltic land forces is made up of veterans of these NATO deployments (Alauskas and Anglickis 2010; Hovi 2010).

The most tangible NATO action on behalf of the Baltic states has been air policing. None of the Baltic states possessed, nor was planning to acquire, an air force of jet-fighters to police their air space. NATO also provides air policing for Albania, Slovenia, and Montenegro, its members in the Balkans. The flights over the Baltic states began in March 2004, a day following the official acceptance of the Baltic states into membership, from the Šiauliai air base in Lithuania. Russian aircraft that had violated the airspace of one of the Baltic states were intercepted and escorted until they left Baltic airspace. In 2014, following Russian aggression against Ukraine, a second deployment of a four jet fighter squadron was added to Šiauliai and a second base at Ämari, Estonia was opened up for a third deployment. For a brief period a fourth squadron operated from an air base in Poland. This meant the existence of four NATO deployments in the Baltic states at the same time until late 2015. As the immediate crisis eased, the flights were cut back to one deployment from Šiauliai and a second from Ämari. During the Ukrainian crisis period the United States, besides participating in a deployment with extra aircraft, also provided a rotating company of soldiers on the ground for each Baltic state (Jakstaite 2019, 34–5). President Barack Obama declared in Tallinn, Estonia on September 3, 2014: "The defense of Tallinn, and Riga and Vilnius is just as important as the defense of Berlin, and Paris and London" (Obama 2014). The show of American force was important politically in the Baltic states and provided psychological reassurance of support. To August 2020 Germany has provided for 12 air deployments and Poland, France and Belgium for eight each. Besides Poland, three other states in East-Central Europe have contributed (Czech Republic – three; Hungary – two; Romania – one). In all, 18 members of the 30-member NATO have contributed at least one air deployment during the 15-year period ("Baltic Air Policing" 2020).

The financial crisis of 2008–10 hit the Baltic states hard. Real GDP decreased at the lowest point by 22% for Latvia, 19.5% for Estonia, and 14.8% for Lithuania. The ensuing recession was far deeper than elsewhere in Europe. It led to a substantial loss of population through emigration to Western Europe; Latvia had to resort to borrowing from the IMF (Pataccini et al. 2019, 403–8; Ozoliņa 2019, 515–31). During this period, as part of austerity measures, defense budgets were slashed, and the previous promises of 2% GDP defense expenditures were pushed into the future. However, continuation of support for NATO missions was regarded as important, because it showed that the Baltic countries were contributing to NATO and hence deserved the NATO collective security guarantee. It took Lithuania until 2014 and Estonia to 2015 and Latvia to 2017 to recover to the pre-recession levels (Eurostat 2020b).

Meanwhile, Russia began a major military modernization program in 2008, the year of the Russian-Georgian war. The generally accepted figure for Russian defense expenditures for 2018 is $61.4 billion (3.9% of GDP), which seemingly placed Russian expenditures in the same category as France and the UK. A more realistic set of figures that highlights better the Russian military challenge to NATO is provided by the military analyst, Michael Kofman, who argues that instead the calculation should be made using PPP statistics and not the standard GDP ones (Kofman 2019). Kofman points out that the Russian military procurement is largely autarkic, and hence arms purchases are not dependent on international market prices and using the ruble–dollar exchange rate is misleading. Besides that, the personnel costs of the Russian military are considerably lower than in Western militaries. Kofman suggests that it is more realistic to view Russia's military spending to be between $150 and 180 billion and its expenditure on defense procurement and research and development at approximately 50% of the defense budget as opposed to the 30% figure for typical Western defense budgets.

An added worry for the Baltic states has been the implications of the large *Zapad* military exercises that Russia has conducted on its Western border areas. *Zapad 1999*, conducted ostensibly to deter a NATO attack on Russia, ended with the use of nuclear weapons on Poland and even the United States (Kofman 2017, 5).[8] Subsequent *Zapad* military exercises have been conducted in 2009, 2013, and 2017. They have been interpreted in the West as simulating attacks against the Baltic states and Poland. The one conducted in 2013 involved an estimated 76,300 troops (not the announced 22,250) and included an amphibious landing of troops exercising with two landing craft (Peterson and Myers 2018, 224–5). The exercises have all involved the supposed defense of Belarus and the Kaliningrad region against attacks from Poland and Lithuania.

NATO also recognized that the challenge from Russia was not just a military one. Already in 2008 a NATO Cyber Security Center in Estonia had been opened in the aftermath of the Russian cyber-attack on Estonian computers in 2007. In 2014 a NATO sponsored Energy Security Center was opened in Lithuania and then in 2016 a Strategic Communications Center in Latvia. At its Wales Summit in 2014 NATO decided to establish a Very High Readiness Joint Task Force (VJTF) that would be able to act very rapidly to events "at the periphery of NATO territory" (NATO 2014). At the Warsaw Summit of 2016 NATO went a step further from the Wales Summit by authorizing the deployment of four NATO combined armor battalions to Poland and the Baltic states as a trip-wire measure.[9] Care has been exercised to avoid "additional permanent stationing of substantial combat forces" that was stipulated in the NATO–Russia Founding Act. Indeed Russian military observers have been allowed periodic visits to the bases at which NATO forces are housed to verify that no "substantial combat forces" have been introduced (NATO 2019). At the Brussels summit of 2018 the commitment for readiness came to be phrased as 30X30X30X30: 30 battalions, 30 ships, and 30 air squadrons were to be ready to move within a 30-day period (NATO Public Diplomacy Division 2018). Baltic defense needs have become one of the driving forces to rebuilding NATO's military capability which had eroded badly in Europe. The United States reversed its troop drawdowns in Europe in 2014 when President Obama set up the European Reassurance Initiative and received Congressional approval for up to $1 billion of support funds. The Trump administration requested and received Congressional approval to raise the ERI spending to $5.9 billion in 2019.

While there has been some cooperation among the Baltic states on matters of defense, most of it occurred in the early years following the recovery of independence. BALTBAT (Baltic Battalion) was initiated in 1993/4 with the goal of participating in peacekeeping missions. Each Baltic country was to provide a company of soldiers, plus supporting units to the battalion. BALTBAT units served in a number of missions abroad including in Bosnia-Herzegovina and Lebanon in the late 1990s (Sapronas 1999). The BALTRON (Baltic Naval Squadron) received its initial impetus in 1995. The basic idea was to provide three ships for mine sweeping activity in international operations. BALTNET (Baltic Air Surveillance Network), a radar network that covers Baltic airspace, received its impetus also in 1994.

It was recognized right from the beginning that Baltic airspace needed to be regarded as one unified area placed under joint allied protection (Ministry of Foreign Affairs of Latvia 2014). The fourth major project in cooperation came to be BALTEFCOL (Baltic Defence College) that was housed in the Estonian university city of Tartu. The Defence College provides military education for Baltic as well as officers from other NATO countries in particular for staff positions. The College also began publication of a journal, *The Baltic Defence Review*. The initial director of the college was a Danish officer, Gen. Michael H. Clemmesen, and the faculty has represented a total of 12 states, most of them NATO members.

By-and-large each state has pursued its own vision of defense that, while sharing common aims with the others, has been largely determined by internal politics. Decisions to purchase certain weapons were made by the defense ministries of each state at different times and have reflected the budget realities of those years. Very few arms purchases have been joint. The downside is obvious: the different weapons systems – infantry fighting vehicles, anti-tank weapons, self-propelled artillery, automatic rifles, etc. – are of different make and require different handling and ammunition. In a recent welcome change the defense ministers of Finland, Estonia, and Latvia signed an agreement of intent to purchase light armored vehicles jointly to provide greater mobility for their infantry (*Baltic Times* 2020).

While there was general agreement on moving toward a 2% of GDP before accession to NATO, the goal was reached only by Estonia in 2007, 2008, and 2009 before the devastating financial crisis of 2008–10. While Estonia was able to reach the 2% benchmark by 2015, Latvia and Lithuania reached the goal in 2018. Currently all three have cleared the 2% hurdle and are among the eight NATO members (besides the United States) which meet the 2% test (NATO Public Diplomacy Division 2020).

Estonia's strategic concept has been heavily influenced by Finland. The concept calls for comprehensive security to include civil defense and psychological defense to combat disinformation. The Scandinavian defense model is structured by a relatively small professional force that is buttressed by conscription, reserves, and a home guard system (Davis 2008, 2016; Szymański 2018, 2020). Conscription, as it actually works in Estonia, has meant that about one-third of an age cohort has been called up for either nine or 11 months of service. Following military service, unless they make the military their career, the conscripts go into the reserves. The territorial defense system is dependent on reserves, who have been trained to perform specific military tasks during conscription, responding rapidly to a mobilization order. Reserves continue to participate in snap exercises and are permanently liable to be called back into service in case of a mobilization.[10] The reservists may also belong to *Kaitseliit* (Defense League) and thus continue their training with that organization. Currently the Estonian standing military consists of 3,400 professional military and about 3,200 conscripts – hence a standing force of 6,600 that includes a small navy and air force. The land forces consist of two brigades, the first one includes a partly mechanized battalion of professional soldiers with the other battalion largely filled by conscripts. The second infantry brigade is based on a standing battalion that consists of professionals and conscripts. The rest of the brigade consists of framework units that will be filled by reservists. The plan is to be able to mobilize an army of 18–20,000 that would be trained and fully equipped with weapons and ammunition. The *Kaitseliit*, minus the reservists, would provide some extra combat units, but its major function is to fulfill civil defense needs. The long-range plan to 2026 calls for increasing the number of the mobilized force to 25,000 and be in a position to field a third brigade. The emphasis in recent purchases has been on ammunition and the purchase of new automatic rifles (18,000 from a US firm), the acquisition of infantry fighting vehicles, self-propelled artillery and anti-tank weaponry (Javelins and longer-range Spike LRs).

Latvia, upon entering NATO, opted to end conscription in 2004 and follow the recommended policy of post-Cold-War NATO to rely on a professional military (Szymański 2016). The policy stressed participation in peacekeeping operations for which mobile professional soldiers were desired. In the aftermath of Ukraine and 2014 Latvia made a major change in its conceptual thinking on defense by shifting to the need for territorial defense (Rostoks and Vanga 2016; Veebel and Ploom 2017).[11] The center-piece for Latvian defense forces has come to be a brigade with two battalions and other support units. At present the Latvian military consists of about 6,500 professionals, with the largest number serving in the army brigade; a smaller number serve in a small navy and air force. A robust volunteer *Zemessardze* (National Guard) of 8,000 exists that is trained by the professional military. In wartime planning the *Zemessardze* has a more important combat role to play than the Estonian *Kaitseliit* or the Lithuanian Rifleman's Union (Šaulių Sajungu). How well it could perform in a wartime situation has been a question (Szymański 2020, 14–15). Since conscription remains unpopular in Latvia, and the need to supplement the regular forces was recognized in 2016, an additional reserve force of volunteers for the army numbering 3,000 is being organized. Accordingly, at present in a crisis situation a force of around 17,500 could be mobilized. Recently, NATO has set up a divisional staff under Danish leadership that is to create a divisional headquarters for an Estonian-Latvian division. As is the case with Estonia and Lithuania, Latvia has also adopted the concept of comprehensive societal defense that in Latvia includes the introduction of civil defense courses in high school with encouragement to enlist in the *Zemessardze*

Challenged Baltic states

or the reserves.[12] Recent equipment purchases have included ammunition, infantry fighting vehicles, anti-tank weaponry, and self-propelled artillery.

The 2017 Lithuanian national security strategy states that all citizens are expected to resist an invasion and references this to the history of the guerilla war waged by Lithuanians against the Soviets following World War II (Ministry of Defense of the Republic of Lithuania 2017, 2018). The Lithuanian population and economy are almost the size of Estonia's and Latvia's combined. This is reflected also in the size of its military force. In 2019 Lithuania's military consisted of 11,000 professional soldiers, sailors, and airmen. In addition there are about 4,000 conscripts (25% of the age cohort). Hence a standing force of 15,000. Lithuania had suspended conscription in 2010 but then reintroduced it in 2015 as a way to build reserves. Conscription has helped to create a volunteer reserve of 5,000 that can be mobilized into the regular military, adding up to a total force of 20,000. In addition *KASP* (National Defense Volunteer Forces) is expected to provide six infantry battalions that are regarded as part of the defense of the country. A mobilization would provide for a military approaching 30,000. Finally an 11,000 member voluntary paramilitary Riflemen's Union (*Šaulių Sajunga*) exists to support the civil defense of the country. In case of occupation, all of the forces that still remain are supposed to continue a guerilla war against the occupiers. The main forces are organized into two brigades – one mechanized, the other a motorized infantry brigade. A third brigade would be formed from reservists in case of mobilization. Recently, Lithuania has requested advice from the Pennsylvania National Guard on forming the staff for a division. Divisions formed in the Baltics would come under the command of the NATO Multi-National Corps Northeast based in Szczecin, Poland. Like the Estonian and Latvian forces the Lithuanian military has recently purchased ammunition, infantry fighting vehicles, self-propelled artillery, anti-tank weaponry, and has even contracted for two NAMSAMA medium-range anti-aircraft batteries, something that neither Estonia nor Latvia has yet to do. Lithuania has also purchased 200 light tactical armored vehicles from a US firm (*Defense Post* 2019).

Since 2014 we see greater cooperation among the militaries and defense ministers of the region and regular exchanges of information. NATO has increased its military exercises in the region that draw on the resources of a number of NATO countries outside the region including non-NATO Finland and Sweden (Szymański 2019). The planned Spring 2020 *Defender Europe* exercise was to have included 20,000 US troops transported across the Atlantic. In preparation a US battalion has been stationed in Lithuania since 2019. Unfortunately, COVID-19 interrupted the exercise, but another one has been planned for Spring 2021. Mobility of troops across Europe to the east – Poland, Baltic states, and Romania – has become a major NATO

176 *Defending Eastern Europe*

task. Fortunately, NATO has partnered with the EU to provide solutions. Removal of legal restrictions for crossing state borders and a need to upgrade infrastructure (roads and bridges) have been identified. In preparation for *Defender Europe* extensive consultation between NATO planners and EU officials were held on these issues, and indeed the EU has allocated some funds (less than what was requested) toward infrastructure improvements in its next seven-year budget (Hodges et al. 2020; Scaparrotti and Bell 2020).

As the Baltic Air Mission has demonstrated, Baltic airspace is one. This is further underlined by the unified BALTNET radar network that provides an air picture over the Baltic states and forwards it to Ueden, Germany (Harper et al. 2018). Recently, the single Baltic Control and Reporting Post that relayed the Recognized Air Picture to Ueden and in turn to the NATO air base at Ramstein, Germany has been supplemented by two additional reporting posts, a welcome upgrading of the system (*Baltic Times* 2019a). Baltic air defense exists at the present time with only short-range Stinger and Mistral missiles. The installation of medium range anti-aircraft missile batteries, however, needs a NATO coordinated common approach.[13]

From NATO's point of view the naval balance in the Baltic Sea is also something that needs upgrading. The Russian Baltic Sea fleet, two-thirds of which is stationed at Kaliningrad (the remainder is at St. Petersburg) needs to be checked to prevent any amphibious operation on one of the Estonian islands or even the Swedish island of Gotland in the middle of the Baltic Sea. The task that the small Baltic navies undertook to fill in the context of NATO out of area operations was mine-clearing. Any new acquisitions of ships are expensive and in the future the defensive needs of the Baltic states themselves should be prioritized (Lange et al. 2019; Young 2019).

What the above summary shows is that despite the different defense policies pursued by the three, the outcome has been broadly similar. All three states have now committed themselves to total territorial defense. This means that the relatively small professional force in each state has to be supplemented by conscription or by volunteers. In addition, all have some version of a home guard to help organize civilian society in case of emergencies and provide host nation support for additional NATO forces. Small military units continue to be sent on peacekeeping missions, for example, to Afghanistan or to Mali (part of the French-led effort to stabilize North Africa), to gain military experience, but this is now regarded as secondary to the main goal of territorial defense.

For a time, especially when Lithuania suspended conscription in 2010, the Estonians were regarded as out of step with NATO concepts which called for the training of mobile professional militaries that could be used for out-of-area operations. Indeed a number of authors accused the Estonians, who retained conscription and the idea of territorial defense, of harboring doubts

Challenged Baltic states 177

about NATO's ability to defend them, since collective defense was part of the mission statement of NATO (Young 2018, 178–9). Yet subsequent to Ukraine in 2014, the RAND Corporation played out a series of game simulations which tested the defensibility of the Baltic States and concluded that in case of a Russian attack they would be vulnerable (Shlapak and Johnson 2016). The outcome was, bluntly, a disaster for NATO. In other words, in 2014–15, and we can assume earlier, NATO was in no position to defend the Baltic states. The model for NATO defense that is being currently worked out assumes that the Baltic states will take on a considerable part of the burden of initial defense upon themselves.

Much of the discussion on the defensibility of the Baltic states began with the above important RAND Corporation study, sponsored by the Office of the US Under-Secretary of the Army that was conducted in 2014–15. RAND conducted a series of board war games that involved a Russian attack on the Baltic States with an initial force of 22 armored battalions that could be assembled in five days to attack Estonia and Latvia with the objective of seizing control before NATO could react. The conclusion reached by the RAND war games was that within 35–50 hours the Russian forces would reach Tallinn and Riga, and despite the emergency airlift of five lightly armed US battalions to the scene, NATO would suffer a catastrophic defeat. The Baltic states have come to be regarded as the most vulnerable NATO area for Russian aggression. The authors of the study were dismissive of Estonian and Latvian battalions: "seven of NATO's (12) are those of Estonia and Latvia, which are extremely light, lack tactical mobility, and are poorly equipped for fighting against an armored opponent." The RAND study concluded that to avoid losing quickly what was needed was:

> A total force of six or seven brigades including at least three heavy brigades backed by NATO's superior air and naval power and supported by adequate artillery, air defenses, and logistics capabilities, on the ground and ready to fight at the onset of hostilities appears able to avoid losing the war within the first few days. (Shlapak and Johnson 2016, 5–8)

David Shlapak of the RAND Corporation presented the RAND scenario in testimony before a subcommittee of the House Armed Services Committee on March 1, 2017 (Shlapak 2017). He downplayed any difficulty terrain would cause for the Russian advance. Rivers were mentioned in terms of establishing front lines, not in terms of difficulty for armored vehicles, both tracked and wheeled, in crossing them once the bridges had been destroyed. Shlapak repeated his argument that an initial defense of about 28 days could be sustained only by a minimum of seven NATO brigades (Shlapak 2017, 5).

There is some room to question the RAND assessment as it stood in 2016. For one, the study did not take sufficient account of the terrain of the Baltic area. Furthermore, the RAND authors' assertion that NATO's light forces "lack of maneuverability meant that they could be pinned and bypassed if the Russian players so desired," seems to suggest that the Russian forces had better knowledge of the terrain than the largely native Estonian and Latvian defending forces. Yes, it is true that there are highways, but there are also sections where the roads are flanked by lakes, marshes, and forests, giving limited opportunities for heavy armored vehicles to maneuver and by-pass narrow corridors.

Four years have passed since the analysis, and improvements in the Baltic forces can be noted. Perhaps most importantly there has been a substantial investment in anti-tank weaponry, including Javelin and Spike missiles; there is also greater mobility with an increase in the number of motor vehicles; some armored vehicles and self-propelled artillery have been acquired. A number of places exist along the roads to Tallinn, Riga, and Vilnius where tank maneuverability is limited and mobile infantry with anti-tank weaponry would be quite effective.

The RAND analysis should be compared to another conducted in 2016 by the Potomac Foundation and the Baltic Defense College located in Tartu, Estonia (Peterson and Myers 2018, 203).[14] A sophisticated computer program was developed that took into account the nature of the terrain in the Baltic countries that after all is not very tank-friendly and took into account the ability of the defending forces to use natural features in defense. The Hegemon computer simulation factored in terrain, simultaneous movement of forces, logistics, and degraded intelligence. Furthermore, in the simulations Baltic defense experts were asked to participate as well as experts on the Russian military. The Russian attacking forces were set at 150,000 or 20% of the current Russian army with 400 tanks. The Baltic militaries were expected to be able to mobilize 72,000 which is considerably larger than the figure used by RAND, but more in line with actual realities. No airlifted American units were involved. It was concluded that with doable modifications: continuation of force modernization, use of special force tactics at various attack corridors, and most importantly coordination of defensive forces and planning among the Baltic militaries, the Baltic defense could stretch to two weeks. At that point much depended on holding open the Suwałki corridor between Lithuania and Poland. Polish and American forces stationed in Poland needed to cooperate with Lithuanian forces to hold open the Suwałki corridor to allow the passage of NATO reinforcing troops to move into the Baltics. The conclusion:[15] "Even with little NATO reinforcement two weeks of combat required to defeat forces defending Baltic States ... Baltic States are very defensible." Crucial throughout was NATO control of the Baltic airspace that only the US air force could provide (Hooker 2019).

Challenged Baltic states 179

Following the 2016 Warsaw summit NATO committed a multinational battalion to each of the Baltic states and to Poland on a rotational basis. The United Kingdom became the framework country in Estonia, Canada in Latvia, Germany in Lithuania, and the United States in Poland. Each framework country was to provide the staff and some heavy armored equipment, while other countries provided additional troops. Among the participating countries of East-Central Europe we can list Poland, Czech Republic, Hungary, Romania, Slovenia, Slovakia, Croatia, Montenegro, and Albania. Among West European countries France, Italy, Spain, Denmark, Norway, Belgium, Netherlands, and Iceland have been contributors (NATO Public Diplomacy Division 2017, 2019). In addition the United States has been rotating a battalion to Lithuania to participate in field exercises.

While it may be true that from a purely military perspective it made more sense to have the three NATO battalions in the Baltics combine into a fighting unit as a brigade and to have a unified single country brigade, this was, after all, largely a political gesture – a trip-wire. It was meant to show that in case of a Russian attack, NATO would be involved. Besides, each Baltic country needed to be assured – the arrival of NATO troops and their activity was reported in the local press and proved to the population of each state that NATO was involved and that the Baltic countries were not alone. The NATO troops could also regularly interact with Estonian, Latvian, and Lithuanian troops in local field exercises and Baltic troops would get training in dealing with tanks and armored military units.

The alternate scenario to a Russian full-scale attack would be a Russian attempt to create a situation in the Baltics analogous to what exists in Transnistria, Abkhasia, Ossetia, and the Donbas – that is the creation of a contested border strip area that would destabilize one of the Baltic states. It is something that did not happen during the disintegration of the Soviet Union in 1989–91. However, we should keep in mind that Russian aggression against Ukraine occurred during a period of uncertain authority at the center. As has been argued by a number of authors, the conditions in the Baltics are different (Kasekamp 2018). Stable, democratic governments exist; the Baltic states are members of the EU; living standards, minimum wages, pensions, health-care systems are a grade above those in Russia, something that the Russian-speaking populations of the border areas are aware of. As against this, it needs to be recognized that most of the Russian-speaking population in the Baltics lives inside a Russian news media and information bubble. After all, it is easy to access Russian radio and TV channels. Still, knowledge of conditions in the Donbas has spread and does not serve to encourage a similar attempt being made in the Baltics. This does not preclude the possibility of the Russian military attempting to create a breakaway zone, let us say in Lettgallia, in southeastern Latvia, without

180   *Defending Eastern Europe*

much local support (Pridham 2018). What would Latvia do? Presumably Latvia would declare a state of war with Russia. What would NATO do? If Russia had to weigh the possibility of NATO becoming involved, it may be enough to deter it.

While it is true that in the present circumstances, Russian forces would prevail in a conventional war, this need not be the case in the future, provided NATO and in particular the states in the Baltic Sea region – the Baltic states, Poland, Germany, and Denmark with the United Kingdom and the United States, and non-NATO countries Sweden and Finland take appropriate action in the immediate future. A security balance can be created in the Baltic Sea region that would be strong enough to act as a deterrent and be in the security interest of the states in the region. The irony for Russia is that even if by some stretch of imagination it succeeded in upsetting the present reality, it would still be faced with the fact that access out of the Baltic Sea is controlled ultimately by Denmark and NATO. Denmark as a NATO member can move to deny Russian access to the North Sea and the wider world by blockading Russian shipping from entering or leaving the Baltic Sea. Currently approximately one-third of Russian trade moves through the Baltic Sea. Furthermore, the Russian oil pipelines in the Baltic Sea can be interdicted.

A central element in creating a military balance in the Baltic Sea region would involve the Baltic states developing the capability of preventing a Russian military victory in less than two weeks. As long as the Suwałki corridor remains in Polish and Lithuanian hands, NATO would be in a position to transport its forces to the Baltic area by land, since sea transport has been blocked by anti-area denial rockets stationed in Kaliningrad. Air control will depend on the United States. Would Russian missiles stationed in Kaliningrad be attacked? A danger of escalation into a wider war exists (Shirreff 2016).[16] At present it is hard to imagine Russia undertaking anything major in the region without full control of Belarus and without major military bases located on Belarus territory (Howard 2019). As the Baltic peoples and governments, in their declarations, have expressed sympathy and support for the 2020 striving of the Belarussian population to establish a democratic government in Belarus, they also realize the crucial importance of a reasonably independent Belarus to their security.

New advances in air surveillance by drones make it difficult to envisage a sudden massive Russian attack on the Baltic states without forewarning. Forces called together for a snap exercise may be capable of beginning an aggressive act, but are hardly in a position to complete it. For that, a major logistic build-up is necessary. The units participating in *ZAPAD 2017* were insufficient by themselves to launch a major military campaign in the Baltics (Kofman 2017). War, the conclusion of which cannot be predicted, places much greater demands on logistics. Once a quick victory scenario has been denied to Russia, does Russia have the economic resiliency to wage a longer campaign? Does Russia have the economic capacity to enable it to occupy hostile territory?

Massive placement of NATO troops in the Baltic states is not the solution. It would lead to another escalatory measure on the part of Russia. Instead, a response is needed that will bring into question the scenario of a quick, cheap Russian victory. What may help are new methods of warfare that use new technology like drones that can be produced cheaply and are programmed to detonate on reaching their targeted vehicles. These devices could be utilized by reserve soldiers with some technical expertise (Flanagan et al. 2019; Hammes 2019).

Vladimir Trenin, an astute Russian observer of Russia's foreign policy in the context of world politics, noted in 2019:

> The fundamental error of Russian foreign policy since the mid-1990's has been the fixation on the problem of NATO expansion. The roots of this mistake can be found in an outdated mode of strategic thinking that assigns excessive importance to the factor of geography and strategic depth ... In today's circumstances it is difficult to imagine the creation of a bridgehead along Russia's borders for launching a mass assault on it, as in 1941. (Trenin 2019)

There is no need to introduce massive NATO forces in the Baltic states. The present NATO plan for Baltic defense is sufficient. Mobility of NATO forces has emerged as a major NATO requirement – the ability to move NATO (US, UK, French, etc.) forces eastward rapidly. The plan needs to be made operational. Baltic forces need to be upgraded, NATO forces need to be on rapid response status and surveillance needs to be upgraded to avoid surprise. What needs to be understood by the Kremlin is that a massive strike against the Baltic states or an attempt to unite Kaliningrad by land to Russia or Belarus will lead to a disastrous war against NATO. In addition, an attempt to gain some local advantage by seizing control of strips of Baltic territory will not contribute to any major improvement in Russia's strategic position in the world. It will instead deepen the wedge between the EU and Russia.

NATO for the Baltic states represents security, membership in a club that would guarantee them the security that had eluded them in the interwar period. By remaining stable the Baltic states help maintain stability in Northeast Europe. In fact, it may be that the possibility of a Russian threat to the Baltic states has helped revitalize NATO in its core mission. Two of the framework nations in the Baltics for the Forward Deployment Battalions after all, are non-EU members – the UK and Canada. NATO's actions in the Baltics show that the organization is still able to react quickly and head

Defending Eastern Europe

off a possible crisis and thus provide for the collective security of its members for which it was designed. The United States has increased its defense expenditures for Europe as well as increased its troop presence. There has been a NATO solution; from a realist perspective a balance can be created in Northern Europe that can act to deter a possible Russian attack.

The EU has partnered with NATO in some of its PESCO initiatives. The key provisions are the removal of legal impediments for a rapid deployment of NATO forces through European states to the eastern border and improving the infrastructure to make it possible. In event of a crisis NATO forces (US, British, French, German, etc.) could thus move rapidly to reinforce the existing Forward Presence units in place. The premise behind this cooperation is that the United States is still the partner of choice for European countries and the EU. NATO is the proven organization in which cooperation with the United States, and now also with the United Kingdom, can take place. Defense of the Baltic states resides in the guarantee of collective security provided by NATO. A strengthening of the European components of NATO have to include both the EU and non-EU states like the United Kingdom in cooperation with the United States and Canada across the Atlantic.

Notes

1 Histories of the Baltic nations differ significantly from Russian and Soviet historical views on their relations in the twentieth century (Kasekamp 2010; Plakans 2011; Putin 2020).

2 According to Jack Matlock (US ambassador to the Soviet Union): "Many of Gorbachev's associates feel he could have preserved the Soviet Union, at least in truncated form, without the Baltic States but with most of the others, if in 1989 or early 1990, he had offered a confederation of the sort he was willing to accept in the summer of 1991" (Matlock 1995, 659). See also Hutchings (1997, 26–128, 132–3, 325–6) and Plokhi (2014, 403).

3 Luik, the Estonian Minister of Defense, noted: "Estonian defensive forces began their build-up not from point zero, but from a minus point; the clean-up." See also Laaneots (2017).

4 NATO, Washington Treaty, April 4, 1949, Article 10: "The parties may, by unanimous agreement invite any other European State ... to accede to this treaty," www.nato.int/cps/ic/natohq/official_texts_17120.htm/, accessed August 16, 2020. Treaty of Rome, March 25, 1957, Article 237: "Any European State may apply to become a member of the Community." http://data.europa.eu/eli/treaty/teec/sign, accessed August 16, 2020.

5 Eurostat, "PPP/per capita, average of EU28 in 2019": Estonia 84%; Lithuania 82%; Latvia 69% (Eurostat 2020b).

6 "Estonia declared it shared these values and was entitled to become a new NATO member" (Riim 2006, 39).

7 Ian Brzezinski, the Deputy Assistant Secretary of Defense for European and NATO Affairs, Dept. of Defense. Tables on the political and military contributions to peacekeeping of the candidates for membership were provided.

8 Petr Polknovnikov, "From Kaliningrad to the Chinese Border: Military Strategic Exercises like ZAPAD – 99 Promise to be Systemic," *Nezavicimoe Voennoe Obozrenie*, 25 (July 2, 1999), 5, as cited in Kofman (2017).

9 "We have decided to establish an enhanced forward presence in Estonia, Latvia, Lithuania and Poland to unambiguously demonstrate ... Allies' solidarity, determination, and ability to act" (NATO Public Diplomacy Division 2018).

10 "Luik said that even though the exercises with short notices held by Estonia are unique in NATO and entail significant challenges, holding such exercises is the only way to ensure a realistic picture of the readiness of the reservist army to mobilize in the event of a crisis" (*Baltic Times* 2019b).

11 For a discussion on the attitude of the Russian-speaking population in Latvia and Estonia, see Rostoks and Vanga (2016) and Veebel and Ploom (2017).

12 Stress is laid in the national security doctrine on building national loyalty and dealing with disinformation emanating from Russia (Ministry of Defense of Latvia 2020).

13 "The three states alone will not be able to address these shortfalls and provide adequate levels of air defense for their territories. They must look to NATO and the Allies for assistance" (Harper et al. 2018, 27).

14 Peterson and Myers (2018, 203): "It may be easy to move around brigades on a large-scale map during a board game, but doing so on terrain dominated by forests and water barriers is quite different. A major 'take-away' from every run of the Hegeman Baltic Campaign Simulation to date is that, even when little NATO reinforcement occurs, two weeks of combat are required to defeat the forces defending the Baltic States."

15 See Burns (2003).

16 This is the subject of a novel by a former NATO Deputy Supreme Allied Commander, Europe: Richard Shirreff, *2017: War with Russia* (Shirreff 2016).

11

Conclusion: moving beyond the 15–20–year anniversaries to stable policies in a time of constant political turmoil

James W. Peterson and Jacek Lubecki

Pierre Nora has been instrumental in articulating how "Realms of Memory" can draw on the "collective heritage" of a state and pull together "the country's shattered identities." It is the task of historians to reconstruct the pieces that led to the experiences of a state, but those who focus on the mental view of that process create images that consist of "rememoration" rather than "reconstruction." As Nora thought about the French experience, he proposed that the very state itself could be an "entirely symbolic reality" (Nora 1996, xviii–xxiv). Realms of memory are also important in the creation of a sustaining sense of national identity. Through them, a person or citizen of the country is in effect holding up a "mirror" that reflects and displays a range of past experiences of those peoples who have been part of the state. Periodic uses of the mirror can bring up treasured memories that have the power to restore "a renewed sense of national self-consciousness." Within the nation, there are inevitably also "symbolic sites" that citizens can visit in efforts to restore both past memories and imagine future activities for the community (Kritzman 1996, ix–xiv). Many times, the public and private connect through these "sites," for there are undoubtedly family members who served in the wars and who may even have lost their lives. At times, such wartime memories can perform as "alloys" that feed into overthrow of an existing regime and construction of its replacement. This happened in dramatic fashion in Russia in 1917, as the Bolsheviks replaced the tsarist regime politically but also attempted to foster new memories of what those earlier centuries meant in terms of repression of the people and also what the new age that was dawning could mean for the memories of future generations (Winter 2010, 312–17).

What about alliances? Can memories of the anniversaries on which states joined them also act as "mirrors" of important past decisions and experiences as well as remind of "symbolic sites" of common missions that have been part of alliance history. Though the anniversaries of NATO and EU membership represent a snapshot of short-range history, they are part of the

Conclusion

important process of "rememoration" of the recent past. Policies and attitudes of American leadership in the Trump administration raise questions in the minds of EU members and NATO partners about what the accurate and true memories of past common projects really are. For three nations, the year 2019 symbolizes the twentieth anniversary of their formal admission into NATO, and it represents the fifteenth anniversary of EU and NATO entry for many others. To what degree do these recent commemorations serve as mirrors of successful pursuit of stability in a time of upheaval and constant political turmoil?

To what extent do these anniversaries commemorate the emergence and growth of more stable policies in tumultuous times? As described in previous chapters, the relationship between stability and turmoil varies among the states of Eastern Europe, for some have achieved equilibrium between these two variables while others struggle to strike a balance. Why is it that the East-Central European states rank highest in security while the Baltic states appear to be still the most challenged? How can we describe those in the middle whose security on some issues is reassuring but on others not?

The Czech Republic, Hungary, and Slovakia are three East-Central European states that have weathered the tensions of the last decade and a half with few severe threats to their national interests on the regional or global stage. Each has contributed in important ways to NATO peacekeeping and peacemaking missions in problematic locations such as Afghanistan and Iraq. Further, each has continued to make domestic economic and political progress in directions that the EU and NATO have outlined for their meaningful and complete inclusion in those Western alliances. All three have been bedeviled by security threats of importance. Slovakia entered NATO five years after the other two, and yet its post-Mečiar governments have contained the basic ingredients of continuity and democracy building. Hungary has reacted through the Orbán government in protective and nationalistic ways to the flow of refugees toward its border. Czechs wrestled with a bid to participate in the American-led missile defense proposal, and protests led to its eventual collapse under the Obama administration. However, none of these controversies led to significant instability for their political systems in their own carefully defined regional security settings.

These three states have also achieved an equilibrium between stability and tension on post-2014 national security issues that relate to Russian ambitions as well. None of the three share a border with Russia, while they all were relatively free of intense anti-Russian attitudes and feelings in pre-communist times. Thus, they possess legacies of a certain tolerance and acceptance of Russian ambitions and drives that may threaten their immediate neighbors. Clearly, the leadership of the Czech Republic has preferred to stay out of the post-Crimea issues that have scorched other states

186 *Defending Eastern Europe*

within Eastern Europe as well as nearby states such as Georgia and Ukraine. Leaders in Slovakia have concentrated on increasing the presence of their state in the region in ways that include trade linkages as far as the Asia-Pacific. Hungarian preoccupation with the flow of refugees from the Middle East into their country after 2015 has generated a stand-alone policy with regard to the pressures from the EU to help locate a certain number of refugees within their state. Perhaps partly as a result, the Orbán government has preserved a dialogue with Russia on selected issues that has not been the case with the other two nations. Thus, each of the three states has achieved their own unique balance between the turmoil that surrounds them and a modicum of security. These factors and variables largely account for the regional and global stability that they have achieved.

For very different reasons, a number of Balkan states have also protected their interests in part through alliance memberships, even though they are closer than the East-Central European states to troubles that have emanated from the nearby Middle East. For very different reasons, Albania and Bulgaria have become less alone and isolated than they were during the Cold War. Bulgaria had a reputation for being the closest ally of the Soviet Union in the Communist bloc, but in recent decades it has balanced that continuing attachment with membership in both NATO and the EU. The Albanian case is very different, for it purposely isolated itself from communist-stoked alliances in the Cold War but did become a valued NATO member during the wars in Iraq and Afghanistan, in part due to its predominantly fellow Muslim population and cultural understandings. However, there have been growing security threats to both states in recent years, as the country of Turkey has linked up with the Turkish minority in Bulgaria in a somewhat challenging and destabilizing way. Albanian leaders have needed to balance partnership in the Western alliance with natural connections with the Albanian communities in Kosovo and North Macedonia, steps that have impacted any relations with Serbia.

Three former Yugoslav Republics have also experienced the same level of equilibrium between surrounding, potential tensions and protection of their own security. Slovenia was a quick entrant to the EU and NATO, while those alliance connections came a bit later for Croatia. However, both have enhanced their own security, in so doing, in parallel ways. Contributions to NATO peacemaking missions have been dependable and at times considerable, given their relatively small populations, and their westward-leaning post-Cold War postures and embrace have freed them from concerns about Russian ambitions to their east and north. The case of Montenegro has been somewhat different, even though its small size provides it with some shared perspectives. The state became an independent one much later than the other two, and the same was true of its NATO entry. In spite of the

Conclusion

security connections through alliance partnerships of all three, their small size makes it much more difficult for them to defend themselves in case of an unexpected attack. Such explosions would be unlikely to center on Russian initiatives but could emerge in connections with the strengthening of internal, ultra-nationalistic movements, unexpected terrorist attacks, economic and trade dislocations, or cyberattacks of several dimensions. Therefore, their sense of security equilibrium is lower overall than is true for the East-Central states.

How prepared in the security sense are the four remaining former Yugoslav Republics, three of which have joined neither NATO nor the EU? Stability in the face of threats and violence includes a very different set of variables for each of them: Bosnia-Herzegovina, Kosovo, North Macedonia, and Serbia. North Macedonia just joined NATO in 2020 and does not yet have a history in terms of formal alliance membership.

For Bosnia-Herzegovina, the political turmoil of the mid-1990s tragic war has echoed throughout the past several decades. The sacrifices of all three ethnic groups create a real obstacle to a permanently stable solution. Further, security has relied mainly on the presence of, first, NATO sponsored units, and, later, on those of the EU. As a result, the state has not obtained admission to either alliance, although they do take part in some peacemaking missions of the former. Future prospects for achieving a healthy equilibrium between threats and political stability depend both on the further passage of time and on preservation of domestic tranquility.

Kosovo's tiny size and overwhelmingly Albanian population have made it vulnerable to outside pressures and incursions. This was particularly true when it was a region in the shrunken Yugoslavia with Serbia and Montenegro from 1991 until 1999, and within Serbia (formally) until its declaration of independence in 2008. Its vulnerability was most on display at the time of the Serbian invasion in 1999, but NATO provided protection through its air strikes until the Serbs pulled back. Since independence, Kosovo has suffered from the ailments of many very small states in the global system. A number of important states such as Russia and Serbia did not grant it formal diplomatic recognition, while the need for the continued presence of NATO forces has guaranteed outside-based security that it probably could not provide for itself.

The equilibrium pursuit of North Macedonia has been complex and multi-faceted. As a former republic in the communist-era Yugoslavia, it opted for independence immediately in 1991. However, the presence of a significant Albanian minority, when coupled with Greek reluctance to recognize the new state, located the nation in a precarious position within the region. Adoption of the lengthy name "Former Yugoslav Republic of Macedonia" communicated an image that it had achieved something less

188 *Defending Eastern Europe*

than statehood. Each of those problematic variables made achievement of genuine security a challenge. Greek resistance to its membership in NATO persisted until the state officially changed its name to North Macedonia in 2019. One result was finally Greek acceptance of the name, while a second outcome was a series of acceptance votes by NATO members that made its alliance membership occur in 2020. In the early years of post-communism, there had been concerns in the region about the eventual emergence of a Greater Albania that would include Kosovo, Albania, and the Albanian communities of Macedonia. Perhaps this possibility encouraged the outbreak of separatist pressures from the Macedonian Albanian minority, but the Ohrid Agreement of 2004 settled that question, for talk of a Greater Albania receded significantly after that.

Serbia has no doubt been the most problematic of the post-Yugoslav, non-alliance members in the Balkan region. Its provocatively aggressive policy, under Slobodan Milošević, toward its immediate neighbors during the entirety of the 1990s transformed the entity into a feared political force that counteracted the desires of other states within the region for increased security. Both in 1995 and in 1999, NATO military strikes aimed at Serbian aggression basically nullified the projects in which Serbia was then engaged. The Dayton Agreement in 1995 pushed back Serbian territorial conquests in Bosnia-Herzegovina and also imposed outside alliance forces as the deterrent to any future Serbian incursions in the new multi-ethnic state. Collective global support to Kosovo after 1999 guaranteed protection against future Serbian initiatives. In the new century, Serbia centered much more on its own development in a democratic framework. It gained PfP status within NATO but pushed the desire for full membership to the backburner after basic global acceptance of the state of Kosovo in 2008.

In conclusion, there are commonalities among the three non-NATO Balkan states and North Macedonia, and a shared history of conflict and cooperation is one of them. However, each has attempted to achieve its own balance between turmoil and stability, since the underlying chords of conflict are dissimilar and quite unique for each of them. Although there are Balkan federations and units to which each belongs, the chances for harmony among all four are as difficult to accomplish as they were during the history of the former Yugoslavia.

In spite of the just-described precarious regional condition of some of the Balkan states, Poland and Romania have each experienced even greater difficulty in establishing a balancing act between conflict and security.

Polish vulnerability exists for two reasons. The first is its geographic location and geopolitical challenges. Situated in the northern part of Europe, it shares with the Baltic states a closeness to Russia that does not characterize states further to the south. Territorial losses after World War II

Conclusion 189

pulled it further from the Soviet Union, but the presence of the now Russian militarized enclave of Kaliningrad between Poland and Lithuania brings it closer to the doorstep of Moscow. Second, the Crimean crisis of 2014 enhanced the vulnerability of northern East Europe to the possibility of future Russian aggressive moves. NATO leaders began to consider location of an actual alliance base in Poland and in fact moved military divisions from the Mediterranean Sea area into Poland and nearby states. Behind these two important factors is a significant history of conflict and tension between Moscow and Warsaw, despite their common Slavic heritage and culture. It has not taken much for the Russian–Western antagonisms after 2014, to re-stoke Russian–Polish animosities. Considerable Polish involvement in the American-designed Iraq War as well as its engagement with the missile shield plan of the Bush administration in 2008 accentuated a picture of a state that was heavily engaged in Western strategic plans that Russians perceived as targeting their national interests too much.

The Romanian sense of considerable threat is rooted in part on its traditional cultural isolation within the Balkans. It does not share Slavic culture with many of the states in all parts of East Europe, but it also does not have a significant Muslim population, as do many other surrounding nations. In part, its vulnerability is rooted in recent efforts to move toward meaningful interaction with the Western alliances to a greater extent than some of the others. NATO membership in 2004 was followed soon thereafter by EU membership three years later. From the vantage point of Washington, Romania and Bulgaria were both bulwarks against the chaos that emanated from the Iraq and Afghan wars of the 2000s. Perhaps as a consequence, American leaders reached out to Romanian leadership to take part in the missile shield program that the Obama administration developed in tandem with NATO after cancellation of the program that the Bush administration had worked out with Czechs and Poles. The Poles continued to participate in the ensuing and changed Obama project, but their chief partners were then the Romanians rather than the Czechs. Also, the eastern part of Moldova is Transnistria, an area separated by a river of the same name, from Moldova proper. For the most part, its culture and population are ethnically Slavic, and there are those who perceive Russian ambitions toward that geographic unit as similar to Moscow's takeover of two parts of Georgia and Crimea in Ukraine. Historically, most of Moldova had been part of Romania, and so these concerns reverberated back to them and contributed to their general sense of unease. Thus, Romania has become a surprisingly vulnerable state and needs to rely heavily on its alliance partners for support and confidence.

The most challenged states in Eastern Europe were Estonia, Latvia, and Lithuania. Although all became, simultaneously, members of both key Western alliances in 2004, the three were clearly the most vulnerable to

190   *Defending Eastern Europe*

Russian interference, especially after 2014. Perhaps part of their vulnerability and sense of challenge is related to the fact that all three were actual republics in the old Soviet Union from the early days of World War II until 1991. As such, post-1991 Russian rulers were quite defensive and even hostile to their movement in a westwards direction. All three became members of both alliances in 2004, and the NATO membership surely touched the nerves of Russian leaders. Another troublesome factor is the small size of their military forces, and this is of course related to the fact that their geographic space and populations are not large. Yet, Estonia, Latvia, and Lithuania have a lengthy border with Russia. This situation made them vulnerable to Russian complaints, military flybys, and even electronic interference and confusion. Relocation by Estonians of a statue that commemorated Soviet capture of Tallinn in World War II, from the center of Tallinn to a cemetery, provoked a Russian reaction. As with Poland, the border shared between Kaliningrad and Lithuania can symbolize the possibilities of Russian military intervention. Thus, it is no surprise that the Russian intervention in Georgia in 2008 and in Ukraine in 2014 reverberated in the Baltic states. Each of the three contained a Russian minority group of consequence, and this would have provided a rationale for Russian intervention. Establishing an equilibrium between such challenges and genuine stability was a continuing concern and one that required assistance from both NATO and the EU.

In conclusion, it is apparent and even obvious that there is quite a variance among the states in meeting the challenge of turmoil with measures that provide at least a modicum of stability and security. Surely, there is a sharp contrast between the mostly secure East-Central European countries and the three challenged Baltic nations. Tucked away in the heart of Europe, Czechs, Slovaks, and Hungarians have carved out a niche of state privacy as well as corresponding security. However, the Baltics are in the corner of the region and share borders with Russia. Therefore, they have needed the help of NATO to establish a zone of at least partial security in their home area. Within the Balkan region to the south, there is a substantial difference between the security zone that protects those that are part of NATO and the greater vulnerability of those that have not received admission to that important security alliance. Bulgaria and Albania on their own have become important members of NATO and have provided support for many of its missions. For those Balkan states that were part of Yugoslavia, some of the differences in their current sense of equilibrium are connected with or even prefigured by sharp differences within that Cold War federation. The northern Yugoslav republics had achieved within that geographic unit a higher level of economic development than had those republics located south of the Sava River. Partially as a result of that historical situation, security is higher for Croatia, Slovenia, and Montenegro than it is for Bosnia-Herzegovina,

Kosovo, North Macedonia, and Serbia. North Macedonia will be a good test case of alliance benefits, for its admission to NATO in 2020 will provide a kind of "symbolic site" that can possibly represent enhanced security.

In the end, 2019 was an anniversary year for many of these states in connection with NATO and EU membership, and as such the year can serve as a "mirror" of substantial gains in national security and defense preparedness. There are 17 states in Eastern Europe, and 12 became NATO members in the anniversary years of 1999, 2004, or 2009; while eight joined the EU in 2004. The military alliance welcomed two others much later, in 2017 and in 2020. The only states that had not become a formal part of NATO were Bosnia-Herzegovina, Kosovo, and Serbia. Given that those three are now very much surrounded or shadowed by NATO, a very real challenge for the future is to provide them with security guarantees that the others enjoy by being alliance members. It is likely that Serbian leaders will prefer connections with the EU more than they will with NATO, but the NATO leaders in Brussels can maintain an openness to their participation in its activities on a volunteer basis and as a continuing PfP member.

Turmoil is a real possibility in any part of Eastern Europe, whether from domestic or from foreign sources. Stable security policies can result from leadership decisions from within each state or from wider regional policies that are funneled through NATO and the EU. Reduction of turmoil is extremely important at a time when unexpected questions have emerged about the continued importance of each organization. Ironically, the unsettled condition of Eastern Europe may be a factor that underpins the strategic importance of maintaining and even strengthening both alliances. If that turns out to be the case, the anniversary dates of their admission to the alliances can become part of a meaningful "realm of memory" in promotion of the defense preparedness of Eastern Europe as a whole.

Bibliography

"2019 Civil Budget Recommendations." 2019. www.nato.int. Accessed December 28, 2019.

"2019 Military Budget Recommendations Executive Summary." 2019. www.nato.int. Accessed December 28, 2019.

Adler, Emanuel, and Barnett, Michael, eds. 1998. *Security Communities*. Cambridge: Cambridge University Press.

"Adriatic Charter." www.mod.gov.al. Accessed January 5, 2019.

Aggestam, Lisbeth. 2004. *A European Foreign Policy? Role Conception and the Politics of Identity in Britain, France, and Germany*. Stockholm: Stockholm University Department of Political Science.

Alauskas, Aurelijus, and Anglickis, Giedrius. 2010. "On Baltic Deployment Experiences: Lithuanian Lessons Learned from International Operations from 1994–2010." *Baltic Defence Review*, 12, no. 2: 134–58.

Alexe, Theodore. 2016. "NATO Faces Problems in Bulgaria." RFE/RL news report. www.rferl.org/a/1080463.html. Accessed January 1, 2020.

Apuzzo, Matt, and Novak, Benjamin. 2019. "Hungary Rolls Out Red Carpet for Obscure Russian Bank, Stoking Spy Fears." *New York Times*, March 18. www.nytimes.com/2019/03/18/world/europe/hungary-russian-bank-spy-orban-putin.html. Accessed June 12, 2020.

Arens, Olavi. 2016. "United States Policy toward Estonia and the Baltic States 1918–1920 and 1989–1991." *Ajalooline Ajakiri, The Estonian Historical Journal*, 3/4: 347–68.

Asmus, Ronald. 2002. *Opening NATO's Door: How the Alliance Remade Itself for a New Era*. Washington, DC: Council on Foreign Policy.

Asmus, Ronald, with Kugler, Richard, and Larrabee, Stephen. 1993. "Building a New NATO." *Foreign Affairs*, 72, no. 4: 28–40.

Autorzy Rzeczpospolitej. 2002a. "Polska-Rosja. po pierwsze pragmatyzm [Poland-Russia. First of All, Pragmatism]." *Rzeczypospolita* (Warszawa), January 15.

Autorzy Rzeczpospolitej. 2002b. "Dobra atmosfera, mało Konkretów [Good Atmosphere, Few Specifics]." *Rzeczypospolita* (Warszawa), January 18.

Baev, Jordan. 2008. "The Warsaw Pact and Southern Tier Conflict." In *NATO and the Warsaw Pact: Intrablock Conflicts*. Kent, OH: The Kent State University Press.

Bibliography

Balogh, Olivér, 2019. "The Importance of the Zrínyi 2026 Defence and Military Development Program." *Vojenské rozhledy*, no. 1. www.vojenskérozhledyc.cz. Accessed January 20, 2020.

"Baltic Air Policing." 2020. Wikipedia. https://en.wikipedia.org'w/index.php?title=Baltic.Air_Policing&oldid=879923875. Accessed August 22, 2020.

Baltic Surveys/Gallup Organization for Republican National Institute. 2018. "Public Opinion Survey: Residents of Moldova May–June 2018." www.iri.org/sites/default/files/2018-7-16_moldova_poll_presentation.pdf. Accessed January 2, 2020.

Baltic Times. 2019a. "Baltic Defense Ministers Agree on New BALTNET Configuration." October 26. www.baltictimes.com/baltic_defense_ministers_agree_on_new_baltnet_configurtion. Accessed August 22, 2020.

Baltic Times. 2019b. "Estonian Minister Changes Made to Conscription Justified." August 22. baltictimes.com/Estonian_minister_changes_made_to_conscript_service_have_proven_justified/#. Accessed August 24, 2020.

Baltic Times. 2020. "Estonia, Latvia, Finland Sign Memorandum on Developing Armored Wheeled Vehicle Platform." December 18. www.baltictimes.com/estonia_latvia_finland_sign_memorandum_on_developing_armored_wheeled_vehicle_platform/. Accessed August 23, 2020.

Banac, Ivo. 1984. *The National Question in Yugoslavia: Origins, History, Politics*. Ithaca: Cornell University Press.

Barany, Zoltan. 1995. "The Military and Security Legacies of Communism." In *The Legacies of Communism in Eastern Europe*, edited by Zoltan Barany and Ivan Volgyes, 101–17. Baltimore: The Johns Hopkins Press.

BBC. 2019. "Nord Stream 2: Germany and Russia Decry US Sanctions." December 21. www.bbc.com/news/world-europe-50879435 . Accessed June 12, 2020.

Berdila, Ioulian. 2005. *Romania's NATO Membership*. Ph.D. Thesis. School of Advanced Military Studies. United States Army Command and General Staff College. Carlisle, PA.

Beschloss, Michael, and Talbott, Strobe. 1993. *At The Highest Levels: The Inside Story of the End of the Cold War*. Boston: Little, Brown, and Company.

Beunderman, Mark. 2006. "Poland Compares German-Russian Pipeline to Nazi-Soviet Pact." EUobserver, May 2. https://euobserver.com/foreign/21486. Accessed June 12, 2020.

Biberaj, Elez. 1990. *Albania: A Socialist Maverick*. Boulder: Westview Press.

Biró, István. 2005. "The National Security Strategy and Transformation of the Hungarian Defense Forces." USAWC Strategy Research Project. handle.dtic.mil/100.2/ADA432740 <http://handle.dtic.mil/100.2/ADA432740. Accessed July 14, 2017.

Bischof, Gunter, Karner, Stefan, and Ruggenthaler, Peter. 2010. "Introduction and Historical Context." In *The Prague Spring and the Warsaw Pact Invasion of Czechoslovakia*, edited by Gunter Bischof and Stefan Karner, Ruggenthaler, 1–22. Lanham: Lexington Books.

Bibliography

Bloomberg News. 2020. "Ще се забавят договорите за модернизация на армията заради коронавирус." www.investor.bg/ikonomika-i-politika/332/a/shte-se-zabaviat-dogovorite-za-modernizaciia-na-armiiata-zaradi-koronavirusa-300524/. Accessed April 3, 2020.

Brezhnev, Lenonid. 1968. "Doktryna Breżniewa – przemówienie Leonida Breżniewa w Warszawie na V zjeździe PZPR, 12 listopada 1968 r." http://stosunki-miedzynarodowe.pl/teksty-zrodlowe/przemowienia/1101-doktryna-brezniewa-przemowienie-leonida-brezniewa-w-warszawie-na-v-zjezdzie-pzpr-12-listopada-1968-r. Accessed April 15, 2017.

BTA. 2019 "Prime Minister Talks with Experts from US Department of State and Department of Energy." www.bta.bg/en/c/DF/id/2119526. Accessed December 10, 2019.

Bulgarian Council of Ministers. 2016. "Report on the Status of the Defense and the Armed Forces 2016 [Доклад за състоянието на отбраната и въоръжените сили през 2016]." Accessed May 19, 2019.

Bulgarian Council of Ministers. 2018. "Report on the Status of the (Bulgarian) Defense and Armed Forces 2018." www.mod.bg/bg/doc/drugi/20190424_Doklad_2018.pdf. Accessed June 5, 2019.

Bulgarian Council of Ministers. 2019. "Report on the Status of the Defense and Armed Forces 2019." www.mod.bg/bg/doc/drugi/20200415_Doklad_otbrana_2019.pdf. Accessed July 3, 2020.

Bulgarian Ministry of Defense. 2019a. "Defense Review." https://websrv.mod.bg/en/doc/cooperation/20190221_Defence_review.pdf. Accessed February 2, 2020.

Bulgarian Ministry of Defense. 2019b. "Report on the Status of Defense and Armed Forces of the Republic Bulgaria was Approved by the Council of Ministers on April 24, 2019 for the National Assembly/Доклад за състоянието на отбраната и Въоръжените сили на Република България, одобрен от Министерския съвет на 24 април 2019 г. за внасяне в Народното събрание." www.mod.bg/bg/doc/drugi/20190424_Doklad_2018.pdf. Accessed November 19, 2019.

Burant, Stephen. 1999. *Poland, Ukraine and the Idea of Strategic Partnership.* Pittsburgh: Center for Russian and East-European Studies, University of Pittsburgh.

Burns, Nicholas. 2003. "NATO Enlargement: Qualifications and Contributions." In US Congress, Senate, *Hearings before the Committee on Foreign Relations United States Senate One Hundred Eighth Congress, First Session March 27 and April 1,3 and 8, 2003,* 51–2. Washington: US Government Printing Office.

Bursztyński, Andrzej. 2009. "Charakterstyka budżetu MON in latach 2001–2008." *Zeszyty Naukowe Akademii Marynarki Wojennej,* 50: 57–86.

Bush, George. 2007. "NATO Stands with the Forces for Freedom." *Hampton Roads International Security Quarterly,* January 15: 5–10.

Bush, George, and Scowcroft, Brent. 1998. *A World Transformed.* New York: Alfred Knopf.

"Butrinti and Oriku Exercise with SNMCM62 Flagship." www.mod.gov.al. Accessed January 4, 2019.

Całka, Marek. 1998. "Polska-Rosja-Ukraina. Perspektywy, szanse i zagroże-nia." In *Polska i Rosja. Strategiczne sprzeczności i możliwości dialogu,* edited by Agnieszka Magdziak-Miszewska, 180–91. Warszawa: Centrum Stosunków Miedzynarodowych. Instytut Spraw Publicznych.

Capital. 1996. "България може да си остане само с диалог за НАТО [Bulgaria Can Be Left Just with the Dialogue about NATO (Membership)]." May 6. www.capital.bg/politika_i_ikonomika/1996/05/06/1026287_bulgariia_moje_da_si_ostane_samo_s_dialog_za_nato/. Accessed October 28, 2019.

Charter of Partnership among the United States of America and the Republic of Estonia, Republic of Latvia, and Republic of Lithuania. 1998, January 16. *Public Papers of the Presidents of the United States, William J. Clinton 1998*, 1. Washington, DC: US Government Printing Office, 2000, 71–74.

Chittick, William O. 2006. *American Foreign Policy: A Framework for Analysis*. Washington, DC: CQ Press.

Chodakiewicz, Jan Marek. 2012. *Intermarium: The Land Between the Black and Baltic Seas*. New Brunswick: Transaction Books.

Cochran, Clarke E., Mayer, Lawrence E., Carr, T.R., and Cayer, N. Joseph. 2003. *American Public Policy: An Introduction*, 7th edition. Belmont: Wadsworth/ Thomson Learning.

Cohen, Lenard J. 1993. *Broken Bonds: The Disintegration of Yugoslavia*. Boulder: Westview Press.

Crampton, R.J. 2005. *A Concise History of Bulgaria*. New York: Cambridge University Press.

Crane, Keith. 1987. "Military Spending in Czechoslovakia, Hungary and Poland." RAND Paper Series, vol. P-73161.

Crisp, James. 2016. "Senior Obama Official: Nord Stream 2 and Brexit may Weaken EU Energy Security." Euractiv.com, March 30. www.euractiv.com/section/energy/interview/senior-obama-official-nord-stream-2-and-brexit-may-weaken-eu-energy-security/. Accessed June 13, 2020.

Csiki, Tamas. 2015. "Lessons Learnt and Unlearnt: Hungary's 15 Years in NATO." In *Newcomers No More? Contemporary NATO and the Future of Enlargement from the Perspective of "Post-Cold War" Members*, edited by Robert Czulda and Marek Madej, 59–72. Warsaw, Prague, and Brussels: NATO Public Diplomacy Division.

Ćwieluch, Juliusz, and Rzeczkowski, Grzegorz. 2017. "Nato Nie Ma Zgody." *Polityka* (Warszawa), March 29–April 4, 10–13. Accessed July 1, 2017.

Davis, Milton Paul. 2008. "An Historical and Political Overview of the Reserve and Guard Forces of the Nordic Countries at the Beginning of the Twenty-First Century." *Baltic Defence Review*, 10: 171–201.

Davis, Milton Paul. 2016. "Overview of the Guard and Reserve Forces of the Baltic Sea Countries at the Beginning of the Twenty-First Century." *Baltic Defence Review*, 16, no. 1: 163–202.

Debeuf, Koert. 2018. "Europe: The Psychological Gap between East and West." Carnegie Europe, November 6. https://carnegieeurope.eu/strategiceurope/77648. Accessed June 14, 2020.

"Declaration by the North Atlantic Treaty Organization and the Islamic Republic of Afghanistan." 2007. September 6. Online Library, North Atlantic Treaty Organization.

"Defence Expenditure of NATO Countries (2012–2019)." 2020. www.nato.int. Accessed December 28, 2019.

Defense Post. 2019. "Lithuania to Purchase 200 Oskosh Joint Light Tactical Vehicles." August 28. www/thedefensepost.com/2019/08/28/lithuania-200-oskosh-joint-light-tactical-vehicles. Accessed August 16, 2020.

Denizova, Vera. 2018. Budget 2019: 5.8 billion more in election year. In *Kapital*, October 22. www.capital.bg/politika_i_ikonomika/bulgaria/2018/10/22/3331296_bjudjet_2019_s_58_mlrd_lv_poveche_v_izborna_godina/. Accessed November 3, 2018.

Deutsch, Karl, Burrell, Sidney A., Kann, Robert A., Lee, Maurice, Lichterman, Martin, Lindgren, Raymond E., Loewenheim, Francis L., and Wageman, Richard W. 1957. *Political Community and the North Atlantic Area: International Organization in the Light of Historical Experience*. Princeton: Princeton University Press.

Deutsche Welle. 2014. "Is Bulgaria Ready Yet to Part with Soviet Weapons? [Узряла ли е България за раздяла със съветското оръжие?]," October 15, 2014. https://bit.ly/2XGHQYT. Accessed May 6, 2019.

Dimitrova, Daniela. 2001. *Bulgarian Quest for NATO Membership*. Master's Thesis. Naval Postgraduate School. Annapolis.

"Directive of Defense for 2017." www.mod.gov.al. Accessed January 3, 2019.

Domber, Gregory. 2014. *Empowering Revolution, America, Poland and the End of the Cold War: The New History of the Cold War*. Chapel Hill: University of North Carolina.

Doyle, Michael. 1986. "Liberalism and World Politics." *American Political Science Review*, 80, no. 4: 1151–69.

Dudek, Antoni. 2003. *Stan Wojenny w Polsce 1981–83*. Warszawa: Instytut Pamieci Narodowej.

Eglitis, Daina Stukuls. 2008. "The Baltic States: Remembering the Past, Building the Future." In *Central and East European Politics: From Communism to Democracy*, edited by Sharon L. Wolchik and Jane L. Curry, 233–52. New York: Rowman & Littlefield.

"Engagement Policy and Evidence of AAF Participation in PK Missions." 2019, January 4. www.mod.gov.al. Accessed January 4, 2019.

"EU Defence Policy Directors Meeting in Bucharest." 2019, January 17 and 18. www.mapn.ro. Accessed January 21, 2019.

Euractiv. 2007. "EU Resists Russia's Attempt to Divide Bloc." May 21. www.euractiv.com/section/med-south/news/eu-resists-russia-s-attempt-to-divide-bloc/. Accessed June 22, 2020.

Euractiv. 2018. "Merkel: No Nord Stream 2 without Guarantee for Ukraine's Gas Transit Role." April 10. www.euractiv.com/section/europe-s-east/news/merkel-no-nord-stream-2-without-guarantee-for-ukraines-gas-transit-role/. Accessed June 20, 2020.

Euractiv. 2019. "Hungary's Orban Defends Russia Cooperation at Putin Visit." October 31. www.euractiv.com/section/politics/news/hungarys-orban-defends-russia-cooperation-at-putin-visit/. Accessed June 27, 2020.

Bibliography

European Commission. n.d. "Third Energy Package." https://ec.europa.eu/energy/en/topics/markets-and-consumers/market-legislation/third-energy-package. Accessed June 20, 2020.

European Council. 2015. "Conclusions – European Council meeting (19 and 20 March 2015)." Brussels, March 20. https://data.consilium.europa.eu/doc/document/ST-11–2015-INIT/en/pdf. Accessed June 12, 2020.

European Union. 1957. "Treaty of Rome, 25 March 1957." http://data.europa.eu/eli/treaty/teec/sign. Accessed June 10, 2020.

Eurostat. 2019. "Statistics Explained: EU Imports of Energy Products – Recent Developments." November. https://ec.europa.eu/eurostat/statistics-explained/index.php/%20EU_imports_%20of_%20energy_products_-_%20recent_developments#Main_suppliers_of_natural_gas_and_petroleum_oils_%20to_the_EU. Accessed June 2, 2020.

Eurostat. 2020a. "PPP/per Capita, Average of EU28 in 2019." https://ec.europa.eu/eurostat/databrowser/view/tec00114/default/table?lang=en. Accessed August 16, 2020.

Eurostat. 2020b. "Real Growth Rate – Volume." https://ec.europa.eu.eurostat/web/national-accounts/data/main-tables. Accessed August 22, 2020.

Fiszer, Michał, and Gruszczyński, Jerzy. 2011. "F-16 Jastrząb pięć lat na polskim niebie." *Lotnictwo*, 11: 38–45.

Flanagan, Stephen J., Osburg, Jan, Binnendijk, Anika, Kepe, Marta, and Dadin, Andrew. 2019. *Deterring Russian Aggression in the Baltic States through Resilience and Resistance*. Santa Monica: RAND Corporation. www.rand.org/pubs/research_reports/RR2779.html. Accessed August 16, 2020.

"Formal Send-off for 9th HRVCDN to Afghanistan (Croatia)." 2018, September 6. www.morh.hr. Accessed September 29, 2018.

Fürst, Rudolf, and Pleschová, Gabriela. 2010. "Czech and Slovak Relations with China: Contenders for China's Favour." *Europe-Asia Studies*, 62, no. 8: 1363–81.

Gagnon, V.P. Jr. 2004. *The Myth of Ethnic War: Serbia and Croatia in the 1990s*. Ithaca and London: Cornell University Press.

Gardner, Timothy, and Humeyra, Pamuk. 2020. "Investors in Russian Pipeline Projects at Risk of U.S. Sanctions, Pompeo Says." www.reuters.com/article/us-usa-pipelines-sanctions/investors-in-russian-pipeline-projects-at-risk-of-u-s-sanctions-pompeo-says-idUSKCN24G26S. Accessed July 16, 2020.

Gates, Robert M. 2007. "Perseverance, Spirit, Unity." *Hampton Roads International Security Quarterly*, April 15: 36–9.

Gazdag, Ferenc. 1994. "The New Security and Defense Policies of Hungary." *European Security*, 3, no. 2: 350.

Gearan, Anne. 2019. "Czech Leader is the Latest to Bask in Trump's Preference for Eastern and Central European Politicians." *Washington Post*, March 7. www.washingtonpost.com/politics/czech-leader-is-the-latest-to-bask-in-tumps-preference-for-eastern--and-central-european-politicians/2019/03/07/03d06826-40ef 11e9-9361-301ffb5bd5e6_story.html. Accessed June 5, 2020.

Bibliography

Germuska, Pal. 2015. *Unified Miliary Industries of the Soviet Block: Hungary and the Division of Labor in Military Production*. Lanham: Lexington Books.

Gilberg, Trond. 1990. *Nationalism and Communism in Romania: The Rise and Fall of Ceausescu's Personal Dictatorship*. Boulder: Westview Press.

Gilbert, Felix. 1961. *To the Farewell Address: Ideas of Early American Foreign Policy*. New York: Harper & Row.

Glenny, Misha. 1995. "Heading off War in the Southern Balkans." *Foreign Affairs*, 47, no. 3: 98.

Głowacki, Bartosz. 2019. "Pro-eurpejscy bratankowie." *Raport. Wojsko-Technika-Obronność*, January, no. 1: 14–20.

Godement, François. 2016. "EU Strength and Weakness Facing China." ECFR Commentary, European Council on Foreign Relations, July 28. www.ecfr.eu/article/commentary_EU_strength_and_weakness_facing_china_7086. Accessed June 8, 2020.

Godement, François, and Vasselier, Abigaël. 2017. *China at the Gates: A New Power Audit of EU-China Relations*. London: European Council on Foreign Relations, December.

Golan, Galia. 1971. *The Czechoslovak Reform Movement*. Cambridge: Cambridge University Press.

Goldgeier, James. 1999. *Not Whether but When: The US Decision to Enlarge NATO*. Washington, DC: Brookings Institution Press.

Goldman, Minton F. 2009. *Rivalry in Eurasia: Russia, the United States, and the War on Terror*. Denver: Praeger Security International.

Górka, Marcin, and Zadworny, Marcin. 2007. "Cztery Szybkie w Wioske." *Gazeta Wyborcza*, July 29. Http://Wyborcza.pl/2029020,84763,5500609. Accessed November 31, 2008.

Gotev, Georgi. 2019. "Russia, Ukraine Agree 'in Principle' New Gas Deal, Signature Expected in Minsk." Euractiv.com, December 20. www.euractiv.com/section/europe-s-east/news/russia-ukraine-agree-in-principle-new-gas-deal-signature-expected-in-minsk/. Accessed December 21, 2019.

Gotev, Georgi, and Brzozowski, Alexandra. 2018. "Three Seas, Two Leaders." Euractiv.com, September 17. www.euractiv.com/section/politics/news/the-brief-three-seas-two-leaders/. Accessed September 18, 2018.

Gotkowska, Justyna. 2019. "US-German Clash Over International Order and Security: The Consequences for NATO's Eastern Flank." Centre for Eastern Studies (OSW), Warsaw, February 22. www.osw.waw.pl/en/publikacje/osw-commentary/2019-02-22/us-german-clash-over-international-order-and-security. Accessed January 20, 2020.

Grashkin, Andrei. 2020. "Russia's Political Influence in Bulgaria." www.fpri.org/article/2020/01/russias-political-influence-in-bulgaria/. Accessed February 10, 2020.

Gray, Colin. 1999. "Strategic Culture as Context: The First Generation of Theory Strikes Back." *International Affairs*, 7, no. 1: 46–69.

Grayson, George. 1999. *Strange Bedfellows: NATO Marches East*. Lanham: University Press of America.

Hadic, Miroslav. 2002. *Yugoslav People's Agony: The Role of Yugoslav People's Army*. Surrey: Ashgate.

Bibliography

Haftel, Yoram C., and Thompson, Alexander. 2006. "The Independence of International Organizations: Concept and Applications." *The Journal of Conflict Resolution*, 50, no. 2: 253–75.

Hammes, T.X. 2019. "The Melians' Revenge: How Small, Frontline, European States Can Employ Emerging Technology to Defend Against Russia." June 27. Washington, DC: Atlantic Council. atlanticcouncil.org/in-depth-research-reports/issue-brief/the-melians-revenge-how-small- frontline-european-states-can-employ-emerging-technology-to-defend-against-russia/. Accessed August 23, 2020.

Hanemann, Thilo, Huotari, Mikko, and Kratz, Agatha. 2019. *Chinese FDI in Europe: 2018 Trends and Impact of New Screening Policies*. A report by Rhodium Group (RHG) and the Mercator Institute for China Studies (MERICS). www.merics.org/en/papers-on-china/chinese-fdi-in-europe-2018. Accessed June 18, 2020.

Harper, Christopher, Lawrence, Tony, and Sakkov, Sven. 2018. "Air Defence of the Baltic States." Tallinn: International Centre for Defense and Security. icds.ee/air-defence-of-the-baltic-states/. Accessed August 23, 2020.

Havel, Vaclav, and Keane, John. 1985. *The Power of Powerless: Citizens Against the State in Central and Eastern Europe*. Abingdon: Routledge.

Heide, D., Hoppe, T., Scheuer, S., and Stratmann, K. 2018. "EU Ambassadors Band Together Against Silk Road." *Handeslblatt*, April 17. www.handelsblatt.com/today/politics/china-first-eu-ambassadors-band-together-against-silk-road/23581860.html?ticket=ST-239468-hZpt0d2f93dxWAYi1Uv4-ap1. Accessed June 11, 2020.

Heinrich, Hans-George. 1986. *Hungary: Politics, Economics, and Society*. Boulder: Lynne Rienner.

Hendrickson, Alan K. 2002. "Distance and Foreign Policy: A Political Geography Approach." *International Political Science Review*, 23, no. 4: 437–66.

Hodges, Ben, Lawrence, Tony, and Wojcik, Ray. 2020. "Until Something Moves: Reinforcing the Baltic Region I Crisis and War." Tallinn: International Centre for Defence and Security. https://icds.ee/en/until-something-moves-reinforcing-the-baltic-region-in-crisis-and-war. Accessed August 22, 2020.

Hook, Steven W. 2014. *U.S. Foreign Policy: The Paradox of World Power*, 4th edition. Washington, DC: Sage/CQ Press.

Hook, Steven W., and Spanier, John. 2004. *American Foreign Policy Since World War II*. Washington, DC: CQ Press.

Hooker, R.D. Jr. 2019. "How to Defend the Baltic States." Washington, DC: The Jamestown Foundation. https://jamestown.org/product/how-to-defend-the-baltic-states/. Accessed August 16, 2020.

Hovi, Gunnar. 2010. "The Afghanistan Mission's Benefit for Estonia." *Baltic Defence Review*, 12, no. 2: 159–65.

Howard, L. 2019. "The Growing Importance of Belarus on NATO's Baltic Flank." In: *NATO at 70 and the Baltic States: Strengthening the Euro-Atlantic Alliance in an Age of Non-Linear Threats*, edited by Mark Voyger, 201–22. Tartu: The Baltic Defence College.

Hungarian Republic Ministry of Defense. 2009. "A Magyar Koztarsasag Nemzeti Katonai Strategiaja." https://honvedelem.hu/images/media/5f58c5742975d884996357.pdf. Accessed January 20, 2020.

Hungarian Republic Ministry of Defense. 2012. "Hungarian National Military Strategy." www.files.ethz.ch/isn/167317/Hungary%202012%20national_military_strategy.pdf. Accessed July 1, 2017.

Hungarian Republic Ministry of Defense. 2017. "The Hungarian Defence Forces Must Be Made a Major Military Force in the Region by 2026." www.kormany.hu/en/ministry-of-defence/news/the-hungarian-defence-forces-must-be-made-a-major-military-force-in-the-region-by-2026. Accessed July 28, 2017.

Hutchings, Robert L. 1997. *American Diplomacy and the End of the Cold War*. Baltimore: The Johns Hopkins University Press.

Hyde-Price, Adrian. 1996. *The International Politics of East Central Europe*. New York: Manchester University Press.

"Informal Meeting of the EU Defence Ministers in Bucharest." 2019, January 30. www.mapn.ro. Accessed January 17, 2019.

IISS (International Institute for Strategic Studies). 2019. *Report 2019*. London: IISS Press.

"International and Regional Organization." www.mod.gov.al. Accessed January 4, 2019.

Isachenkov, Vladimir. 2019. "Russia, Ukraine Finalize Deals for Gas Transit to Europe." AP News, December 30. https://apnews.com/4615057928c343af-b421a24cdd0bedf1. Accessed December 31, 2019.

Itzkowitz, Joshua. 2016. "Deal or No Deal? The End of the Cold War and Offer to Limit NATO Expansion." *International Security*, 40, no. 4: 7–44.

Ivanova, Denisa. 2016. "Всеки четвърти българин в чужбина е с висше образование, сочи ново изследване." https://dariknews.bg/novini/bylgariia/vseki-chetvyrti-bylgarin-v-chuzhbina-e-s-visshe-obrazovanie-sochi-novo-izsledvane-1607506. Accessed September 10, 2019.

Jakstaite, Gerda. 2019. "The US Foreign Policy towards the Baltic States: The Implications of Ukraine Crisis." *Journal of Baltic Security*, 5, no. 1: 27–39.

Jeszenszky, Geza. 1996. "Hungary's Bilateral Treaties with the Neighbours." *Ethnos-Nation. Eine europäische Zeitschrift*, 1–2. www.hungarianhistory.com/lib/jeszenszky/jesz5.pdf. Accessed August 7, 2017.

Jones, Christopher. 1981. *Soviet Influence in Eastern Europe: Political Autonomy and the Warsaw Pact*. Westport: Praeger.

Jowitt, Kenneth. 2013. *The New World Disorder: The Leninist Extinction*. Berkeley: University of California Press.

Kajetanowicz, Jerzy. 2013. *Wojsko Polskie w systemie bezpieczeństwa państwa 1945–2010*. Czestochowa: Wydawnictwo im. Stanislawa Podobinkskiego Akademii im. Jana Dlugosza.

Kalb, Marvin. 2015. *Imperial Gamble: Putin, Ukraine, and the New Cold War*. Washington, DC: Brookings Institution Press.

Kamińska, Joanna. 2013. "Poland: The New Agenda Setter." In *The New Member States and the European Union*, edited by Michael Baun and Dan Marek, 22–36. Abingdon: Routledge.

Kasekamp, Andres. 2010. *A History of the Baltic States*. New York: Palgrave.

Bibliography

Kasekamp, Andres. 2013. "Estonia: Eager to Set an Example in Europe." *The New Member States and the European Union: Foreign Policy and Europeanization*, edited by Michael Baun and Dan Marek, 99–111. Abingdon: Routledge.

Kasekamp, Andres. 2018. "Are the Baltic States Next? Estonia, Latvia, and Lithuania." In *Strategic Challenges in the Baltic Sea Region: Russia, Deterrence, and Reassurance*, edited by Ann-Sophie Dahl, 61–72. Washington, DC: Georgetown University Press.

Kelley, Robert E. 2007. "Security Theory in the New Regionalism." *International Studies Review*, 9, no. 2: 197–229.

Kirschbaum, Stanislav J. 1995. *A History of Slovakia: The Struggle for Survival*, 2nd edition. Hampshire: Palgrave Macmillan.

Kofman, Michael. 2017. "Zapad 2017 – Russia Military Analysis." https://russian-militaryanalysis.wordpress.com/tag/zapad-2017. Accessed August 23, 2020.

Kofman, Michael. 2019. "Russian Defense Spending is Much Larger, and More Sustainable than it Seems." May 3. www.defensenews.com/opinion/commentary/2019/05/03/russian-defense-spending-is-much-larger-and-more-sustainable-than-it-seems/. Accessed August 23, 2020.

Konrád, György. 1984. *Antipolitics*. San Diego: Harcourt.

Kopínski, Dominik. 2012. "Visegrad Countries' Development Aid to Africa: Beyond the Rhetoric." *Perspectives on European Politics and Society*, 13, no. 1: 33–49.

"Kosovo's President Promoted KSF Minority Members." 2017, November 13. www.mksf-ks.org. Accessed September 30, 2018.

"Kosovo Security Force Conducted Medical Visits to the Communities." 2017, October 4. www.mksf-ks.org. Accessed September 30, 2018.

Koziej, Stanislaw, and Brzozowski, Adam. 2015. "Strategie bezpieczeństwa narodowego RP 1990–2014. Refleksja na ćwierćwiecze." In *Strategia bezpieczeństwa narodowego Rzeczypospolitej Polskiej. Pierwsze 25 lat*, edited by Robert Kupiecki, 17–54. Warszawa: Wojskowe Centrum Edukacji Obywatelskiej im. plk. dypl. Mariana Porwita.

Kraft, Michael E. and Furlong, Scott R. 2013. *Public Policy: Politics, Analysis, and Alternatives*. Washington, DC: Sage/CQ Press.

Kramer, Mark. 2010. "The Prague Spring and the Soviet Invasion in Historical Perspective." In *The Prague Spring and the Warsaw Pact Invasion of Czechoslovakia in 1968*, edited by Günter Bischof, Stefan Karner, and Peter Ruggenthaler, 35–58. New York: Rowman & Littlefield.

Krastev, Ivan. 2018. "Eastern Europe's Illiberal Revolution: The Long Road to Democratic Decline." *Foreign Affairs*, May/June: 49–56.

Kritzman, Lawrence D. 1996. "Forward: In Remembrance of Things French." In *Realms of Memory: Rethinking the French Past. Volume I: Conflicts and Divisions*, under the direction of Pierre Nora, translated by Arthur Goldhammer, ix–xiv. New York: Columbia University Press.

Kříž, Zdeněk, and Chovančík, Martin. 2013. "Czech and Slovak Defense Policies Since 1999: The Impact of Europeanization." *Problems of Post-Communism*, 60, no. 3: 49–62.

202 Bibliography

Krysteva, Yoana. 2019. "Над 2 млн. пенсионери с по-високи пенсии от юли [Over 2 mln. Retirees with Higher Pensions from July]." *Daric News*, June 24. https://dariknews.bg/novini/bylgariia/nad-2-mln.-pensioneri-s-po-visoki-pensii-ot-iuli-2172988. Accessed September 8, 2019.

Kubiak, Krzysztof. 2019. "Pod sztandarem Skanderberga. Sily zbrojne Albanii." In *Raport. Wojsko-Technika-Obronność*, August, 42–4.

Kucharczy, Jacek, and Meseznikov, Grigorij. 2016, February 26. "Reakcje krajów Grupy Wyszehradzkiej na konflikt rosyjsko-ukrainski." https://pl.boell.org/pl/2016/02/26/reakcjekrajowgrupywyszehradzkiejnakonfliktrosyjsko ukrainski. Accessed June 22, 2020.

Kufčák, Jacub. 2014. "The V4 Countries and the Impact of the Austerity Cuts on their Defence Spending and Armed Forces." *Obrana a Strategie*, 60, no. 2: 35–48.

Kulisha, Nicholas. 2007. "An Afghanistan War-Crimes Case Tests Poland's Commitment to Foreign Missions." *New York Times*, November 29.

Kuźniar, Roman. 2008. *Droga do wolności. Polityka zagranicza III Rzeczypospolitej.* Warszawa: Wydawnictwo Naukowe "Scholar."

Kwaśniewski, Aleksander. 2003. "Wystąpienie Prezydenta RPAleksandra Kwaśniewskiego podczas uroczystoci pożegnania żołnierzy sił głównych PKW udających się do Iraku" (Address by President Kwaśniwski to Troops Departing to Iraq). *Gazeta Wyborcza*, July 31. www2.gazeta.pl. Accessed February 24, 2004.

Laaneots, Ants. 2017. "Eesti riigikaitse sünd, 1991–2017." *Riigikogu toimetised*, 36: 1–29.

Laar, Mart. 2014. "Estonia: The Most Radical Reforms." In *The Great Rebirth: Lessons from the Victory of Capitalism over Communism*, edited by Anders Åslund and Simeon Djankov, 73–87. Washington, DC: Peterson Institute for International Economics.

Lange, Heinrich, Combes, Bill, Jermalavičius, Tomas, and Lawrence, Tony. 2019. "To the Seas Again: Maritime Defence and Deterrence in the Baltic Region." Tallinn: International Centre for Defence and Security. icds.ee/en/to-the seas-again-maritime-defence-and-deterrence-in-the-baltic-region/. Accessed August 16, 2020.

Larrabee, Stephen. 2003. "The Baltic States and NATO Membership." Testimony presented to the United States Senate Committee on Foreign Relations on April 3, 2003, Rand, https://www.rand.org/pubs/testimonies/CT204.html. Accessed January 19, 2020.

Lebor, Adam. 2006. *"Complicity with Evil": The United Nations in the Age of Modern Genocide.* New Haven: Yale University Press.

Lees, Lorraine. 2010. *Keeping Tito Afloat: The United States, Yugoslavia, and the Cold War, 1945–1960.* University Park: Penn State Press.

Leff, Carol Skalnik. 1997. *The Czech and Slovak Republics: Nation Versus State.* Boulder: Westview Press.

Le Jeune, Christine. 2010. *New NATO Member States: The Benefits and Drawbacks of Enlargement,* in *The Land Warfare Papers*, September 2010, 77. www.ausa.org/sites/default/files/benefits-drawbacks-nato-enlargement.pdf. Accessed November 6, 2019.

Lewis, William. 1982. *Warsaw Pact: Arms, Doctrine and Strategy.* Cambridge: Institute for Foreign Policy Analysis.

Likowski, Michal. 2017. "Kontrowersyjna Obrona Terytorialna." *Raport Wojsko Technika Obronnosc*, March: 40–8.

Lindley-French, Julian. 2004. "The Revolution in Security Affairs: Hard and Soft Security Dynamics in the 21st Century." *European Security*, 13, nos. 1–2: 1–15.

Lis, Tomasz. 1999. *Wielki Final. Kulisy Wstepowania Polski Do NATO.* Kraków: Wydawnictwo "Znak."

Łoskot-Strachota, Agata. 2019. "The Gas Directive Revision: EU Law Poses Problems for Nord Stream 2." *OSW Analyses*, Warsaw, February 21. www.osw.waw.pl/en/publikacje/analyses/2019-02-21/gas-directive-revision-eu-law-poses-problems-nord-stream-2. Accessed June 9, 2020.

Łoskot-Strachota, Agata, Bajczuk, Rafał, and Kardaś, Szymon. 2018. "Nord Stream 2 Divides the West." *OSW Commentary*, no. 273, Warsaw, June 18.

Łoskot-Strachota, Kardaś, Szymon, Szymański, Piotr, and Matusak, Sławomir. 2019. "Denmark Gives Go-Ahead for Nord Stream 2." *OSW Analyses*, Warsaw, October 31. www.osw.waw.pl/en/publikacje/analyses/2019-10-31/denmark-gives-go-ahead-nord-stream-2. Accessed June 8, 2020.

Lubecki, Jacek. 2005. "Poland in Iraq: The Politics of the Decision." *The Polish Review*, 50, no. 1: 69–92.

Luik, Jüri. 2019. *Postimees.* May 9. https://leht.postimees.ee/7063306/kaitseminister-juri-luik-kaitsekulutusi-ei-tohi-vahendada. Accessed September 22, 2020.

Macrotrends. 2020a. "Slovenian Military Budget." www.macrotrends.net/countries/SVN/slovenia/military-spending-defense-budget. Accessed September 13, 2020.

Macrotrends. 2020b. "Macedonian Military Spending." www.macrotrends.net/countries/MKD/north-macedonia/military-spending-defense-budget. Accessed September 13, 2020.

Magdziak-Miszewska, Agnieszka. 1998. "Zapis dyskusji." In *Polska i Rosja. Strategiczne sprzeczności i możliwości dialogu*, edited by Agnieszka Magdziak-Miszewska, 233–91. Warszawa: Centrum Stosunków Miedzynarodowych. Instytut Spraw Publicznych.

Magstadt, Thomas M. 2004. *An Empire if You Can Keep It: Power and Principle in American Foreign Policy.* Washington, DC: CQ Press.

Magyarics, T. 2013. "Hungary in NATO: The Case of Half Empty Glass." In *NATO's European Allies: Military Capabilities and Political Will*, edited by Janne Haaland Mattlary and Magnus Petersson, 232–61. Palgrave Macmillan.

Mahncke, Dieter. 2004. "Transatlantic Security: Joint Venture at Risk?" In *Redefining Transatlantic Security Relations: The Challenge of Change*, by Dieter Mahncke, Wyn Rees, and Wayne C. Thompson. New York: Manchester University Press.

Maisel, Adam and DuVal, Will. 2017. "Do Bulgaria's Historical Russian Ties Spell Trouble for NATO and the Black Sea Region?" Modern War Institute. www.atlanticcouncil.org/blogs/natosource/do-bulgaria-s-historical-russian-ties-spell-trouble-for-nato-and-the-black-sea-region/. Accessed May 4, 2017.

Maison, George. 2018. "Bulgaria as a Russian Trojan Horse in the EU and NATO." https://medium.com/@GeorgeMaison/bulgaria-as-a-russian-trojan-horse-in-the-eu-and-nato-e010455beff9. Accessed July 8, 2019.

Matei, Florina Cristiana. 2013. "The Impact of NATO Membership on Military Effectiveness: Hungary." In *Routledge Handbook of Civil-Military Relations*, edited by Thomas Bruneau and Cristiana Florina Matei, 219–32. London and New York: Routledge.

Malvout, Blandine. 2017. "Nord Stream 2 Splits the EU." *Eyes on Europe*, November 28. www.eyes-on-europe.eu/nord-stream-2-the-eus-divide/. Accessed July 12, 2019.

Mastny, Vojtech, and Byrne, Malcolm. 2005. *A Cardboard Castle? An Inside History of the Warsaw Pact, 1955–1991*. Budapest: Central European University Press.

Matlock, Jack F. Jr. 1995. *Autopsy of an Empire*. New York: Random House.

Mattelaer, Alexander. 2017, May 5. "Sharing the Burden of Keeping Europe Whole, Free, and at Peace." www.nato.int. Accessed December 19, 2019.

Medjunarodna Politika. 1970. *Yugoslav Concept of General People's Defense*. Belgrade: Medjunarodna Politika.

Michta, Andrew. 1990. *Red Eagle: The Army in Polish in Polish Politics, 1944–1988*. Stanford: Hoover Institute Press.

Michta, Andrew. 2006. *The Limits of Alliance: The United States, NATO, and the EU in North and Central Europe*. New York: Rowman & Littlefield.

Military Technology. 2003, April 1. Two Interviews, 86–92.

"Minister Vulin: The EU to Support Brave Efforts of President Vucic (Serbia)." 2018, September 26. www.mod.gov.rs. Accessed September 30, 2018.

"Minister Vulin: EU to Take a Clear Position on Migration (Serbia)." 2018, September 26. www.mod.gov.rs. Accessed September 30, 2018.

Ministry of Defense of Albania. 2011. "Opening Page of Ministry Website." March 19. www.md.gov.al. Accessed June 2, 2020.

Ministry of Defense of Bosnia-Herzegovina. 2011. "First Rotation of AFBiH Infantry Unit in Afghanistan." March 20. www.gov.ba. Accessed September 4, 2019.

Ministry of Defense of Bulgaria. 2017. "Peace Support Operations." February 18. www.md.government.bg. Accessed June 12, 2020.

Ministry of Defense of Croatia. 2011. "Opening Page of Ministry Website." March 20. www.arhiva.morh.hr. Accessed March 12, 2019.

Ministry of Defense of the Czech Republic. 2007a. "SOG." August 29. www.army.cz. Accessed June 20, 2014.

Ministry of Defense of the Czech Republic. 2007b. "Completion of the Rotation in the Mission ISAF-PRT." August 13. www.army.cz. Accessed June 21, 2014.

Ministry of Defense of the Czech Republic. 2010. "ISAF-Provincial Reconstruction Team in Logar." February 19. www.army.cz. Accessed June 20, 2014.

Ministry of Defense of the Czech Republic. 2016. "History of the Czech Military Participation in Missions Abroad 1990–2016." December 22. www.army.cz. Accessed June 21, 2014.

Ministry of Defense of Latvia. 2020. "Comprehensive National Defence in Latvia." www.mod.gov.lv/en/dokumenti. Accessed August 24, 2020.

Ministry of Defense of Macedonia. 2011. "Participation in ISAF Mission in Afghanistan." April 5. www.morm.gov.mk. Accessed June 21, 2014.

Ministry of Defense of Montenegro. 2011. "Contingent of Montenegrin Army is with ISAF in Afghanistan." April 8. www.odbrana.gov.me. Accessed June 24, 2014.

Ministry of Defense of Poland. 2017. "Koncepcja Obronna Rzeczypospolitej Polskiej." June 13. www.gov.pl/web/obrona-narodowa/koncepcja-obronna-kraju. Accessed June 23, 2018.

Ministry of Defense of the Republic of Lithuania. 2010. "Lithuania's Participation in NATO-Led Operations." February 17. www.urm.lt. Accessed July 20, 2020.

Ministry of Defense of the Republic of Lithuania. 2017. "Lithuanian Defense Policy: White Paper." kam.lt/en/defence_policy_1053/important_documents/the_white_paper_on_lithuanian_defence-policy.html. Accessed August 23, 2020.

Ministry of Defense of the Republic of Lithuania. 2018. "Lithuanian Defence System: Facts and Trends." kam.lt/en/defence_policy_1055/important_documents/Lithuanian_defence-system_facts-trends.html. Accessed August 23, 2020.

Ministry of Defense of Serbia. 2011. "White Paper on Defence of the Republic of Serbia." April 13. www.mod.gov.rs. Accessed July 2, 2014.

Ministry of Defense of the Slovak Republic. 2016. "Foreign Operations." December 28. www.med.gov.sk. Accessed June 20, 2014.

Ministry of Foreign Affairs of Bulgaria. 2010. "The Participation of the Republic of Bulgaria in NATO." February 18. www.mfa.bg. Accessed June 12, 2014.

Ministry of Foreign Affairs of Estonia. 2010. "Estonia's Contribution to Rebuilding Afghanistan." February 17. www.vm.ee. Accessed July 27, 2014.

Ministry of Foreign Affairs of Hungary. 2010a. "Hungary's Role in Afghanistan (ISAF, PRT)." February 19. www.mfa.gov.hu. Accessed July 20, 2014.

Ministry of Foreign Affairs of Hungary. 2010b. "Hungary's Role in the Stabilization of Iraq." February 19. www.mfa.gov.hu. Accessed July 12, 2014.

Ministry of Foreign Affairs of Kosovo. 2011. "The Programme and Core Objectives of the Ministry of Foreign Affairs." April 4. www.mfa-ksnet. Accessed June 14, 2014.

Ministry of Foreign Affairs of Latvia. 2010. "Foreign Minister Maris Riekstins Welcomes Government Decision to Support Latvia's Increased Engagement in Afghanistan." February 16. www.am.gov.lv. Accessed June 2, 2014.

Ministry of Foreign Affairs of Latvia. 2014. "Baltic Defence Co-operation" Main Joint Projects." December 2. mfa.gov.lv/en/security-policy/co-operation-with-nato-member-states-and-candidate-countries/baltic-defence-co-operation-main-joint-projects#. Accessed April 12, 2020.

Ministry of Foreign Affairs of Lithuania. 2010. "Lithuania's Participation in NATO-Led Operations." February 17. www.urm.lt. Accessed August 1, 2014.

Ministry of Foreign Affairs of Romania. 2010. "Romania, an Active Ally within an Active and Solid Alliance." www.mae.ro. Accessed June 12, 2014.

Ministry of Foreign Affairs of Slovakia. 2010. "Slovakia's Engagement for Peace in the World." February 17. www.foreign.gov.sk. Accessed July 12, 2014.

Mitchell, Wes, and Havranek, Jan. 2013. "Atlanticism in Retreat." *Atlantic Times*, November/December: 41–9.

Bibliography

Mizokami, Kyle. 2016. "Revealed: How the Warsaw Pact Planned to Win World War Three in Europe." *National Interest*, July 2. http://nationalinterest.org/feature/revealed-how-the-warsaw-pact-planned-win-world-war-three-16822. Accessed April 17, 2017.

Moldova (Republic of). 2006. "Constitution of 1994 with Amendments through 2006". www.constituteproject.org/constitution/Moldova_2006.pdf. Accessed January 2, 2020.

MTI. 2014, June 18. "Sovereign Hungary Needs Strong Armed Forces, Says Defence Minister." www.politics.hu/20140618/sovereign-hungary-needs-strong-armed-forces-says-defence-minister/. Accessed July 1, 2017.

mzv.cz. 2018a. "Foreign Security Policy Coordination Committee (FSPCC)." March 14. www.mzv.cz. Accessed June 2, 2020.

mzv.cz. 2018b. "Security Policy." March 14. www.mzv.cz. Accessed June 4, 2020.

mzv.cz. 2018c. "Czech Republic and NATO." March 14. www.mzv.cz. Accessed June 4, 2020.

mzv.cz. 2018d. "Czech Republic and the EU Common and Security Policy." March 14. www.mzv.cz. Accessed June 3, 2020.

mzv.cz. 2018e. "Programme for the Czech Presidency of the Visegrad Group 2015–2016: V4 Trust." March 3. http://mzv.cz. Accessed June 12, 2020.

mzv.cz. 2018f. "Programme for the Czech Presidency of the Visegrad Group 2015–2016: V4 Trust." March 3. http://mzv.cz. Accessed June 12, 2020.

mzv.sk. 2018a. "Slovak Foreign and European Policy Agenda in 2015." March 14. www.mzv.sk. Accessed June 13, 2020.

mzv.sk. 2018b. "EUCSDP." March 14. www.mzv.sk. Accessed June 12, 2020.

Nagy, Boldizsár. 1997. "Hungary-Romania: Treaty on Understanding, Cooperation and Good Neighborliness." In J-stor, *International Legal Matters* 36(2). www.jstor.org/stable/20698661?seq=1#page_scan_tab_contents. Accessed August 7, 2017.

"The National Report 2013 Albania." www.mod.gov.al. Accessed January 3, 2019.

NATO. 1949. "Washington Treaty, 4 April 1949." www.nato.int/cps/ic/natohq/official_texts_17120.htm/. Accessed August 16, 2020.

NATO. 1994. "Partnership for Peace: Invitation Document, 10 January 1994." www.nato.int/cps/en/natolive/official_texts_24468.htm. Accessed August 16, 2020.

NATO. 1997. "Founding Act on Mutual Relations, Cooperation and Security between NATO and the Russian Federation, 27 May 1997." www.nato.int/cps/ic/natohq/official_texts_25468.htm/. Accessed August 16, 2020.

NATO. 1999. "Membership Action Plan." April 24, 2–5. www.nato.int/cps/ic/natohq/official_texts_27444.htm? Accessed August 16, 2020.

NATO. 2014. "Wales Summit Declaration." September 5. www.nato.int/cps/ic/natohq/official_texts_112964.htm. Accessed March 16, 2020.

NATO Public Diplomacy Division. 2017. "Defence Expenditure of NATO Countries (2009–2016)." www.nato.int/nato_static_fl2014/assets/pdf/pdf_2017_03/20170313_170313-pr2017-045.pdf. Accessed May 2, 2017.

NATO Public Diplomacy Division. 2017 and 2019. "NATO's Enhanced Forward Presence: Fact Sheet." May 2017 and February 2019. www.nato.int/_static_fl2014/assests/pdf/pdf-2017_05/1705-factsheet-efp.pdf. Accessed August 16, 2020.

Bibliography 207

NATO Public Diplomacy Division. 2018. "Brussels Summit Declaration." July 11, 5–6. https://nato.int/cps/en/natohq/official_texts_156624.htm. Accessed August 16, 2020.

NATO Public Diplomacy Division. 2019. "NATO-Russia Relations: The Facts." nato.int/cps/en/natohq/topics_111767.htmlc/803. Accessed August 16, 2020.

NATO Public Diplomacy Division. 2020. "Defence Expenditure of NATO Countries (2013–2019)." *The Secretary General's Annual Report 2019*, 118. www.nato.int/cps/en/natohq/opinions_74406.htm. Accessed March 22, 2020.

Naumescu, Valentin. 2017. "Stability, Ambiguity and Change in the Discourses of NATO Allies in the Black Sea Region: The Cases of Romania, Bulgaria and Turkey." *Croatian International Relations Review – CIRR XXIII*, 80: 187–209.

Navratil, Jaromir, ed. 2006. *The Prague Spring 1968: A National Security Archive Document Reader*. Budapest: Central European University Press.

Nelson, Daniel. 1986. *Alliance Behavior in the Warsaw Pact*. Boulder and London: Westview Press.

Niebuhr, Robert. 2004. "Death of the Yugoslav People's Army and the Wars of Succession." *Polemos*, 7: 91–107.

Nikolov, Boyko. 2020. "The Armored Vehicle Project for Bulgarian Army Might be Restarted." March 19. https://bulgarianmilitary.com/2020/03/19/the-armored-vehicle-project-for-bulgarian-army-might-be-restarted. Accessed April 19, 2020.

Nora, Pierre. 1996. "Preface to the English Language Edition." In *Realms of Memory: Rethinking the French Past. Volume I: Conflicts and Divisions*, under the direction of Pierre Nora, translated by Arthur Goldhammer, xv–xxv. New York: Columbia University Press.

Obama, Barack. 2014. "Remarks by President Obama to the People of Estonia." September 3. https://obamawhitehouse.archives.gov/the-press-office/2014/09/03/remarks-president-obama-people-estonia. Accessed August 23, 2020.

OJEU. 2007. "Treaty of Lisbon," *Official Journal of the European Union*, C306, December 17, 1–271.

Okov, Slav. 2019. "Bulgaria Eyes F-16s as NATO's Eastern States Ramp Up Spending." www.bloomberg.com/news/articles/2019-01-09/bulgaria-eyes-f-16s-as-nato-s-eastern-members-ramp-up-spending. Accessed January 4, 2020.

"Olta Xhačka." 2019. www.mod.gov.al. Accessed January 6, 2019.

Omitruk, Tomasz. 2015. "Realizacja planu modernizacji technicznej sił zbrojnych RP [The Implementation of the Polish Armed Forces Technological Modernizaton Plan]." Special issue of *Nowa Technika Wojskowa*, 1230–655.

Onuf, Nicholas. 1989. *The World of Our Making*. Chapel Hill: University of North Carolina Press.

Onyszkiewicz, Janusz. 1999. *Ze Szcztów Do NATO. Z Ministrem Obrony Narodowej Januszem Onyszkiewiczem rozmawiają Witold Bereś i Krzysztof Burnetko*. Warszawa: Dom Wydawnicz Bellona.

Opriş, Petre. 2004. "Doctrina militară a României, asemănătoare cu cea a Iugoslaviei [Romanian Military Doctrine Based on the Yugoslavian One]." https://jurnalul.antena3.ro/scinteia/special/doctrina-militara-a-romaniei-asemanatoare-cu-cea-a-iugoslaviei-519821.html. Accessed July 10, 2019.

208 *Bibliography*

Orbán, Victor. 2014. "Full Text of Viktor Orbán's speech at Baile Tusnad (Tusnádfürdo) of 26 July 2014." http://budapestbeacon.com/public-policy/full-text-of-viktor-orbans-speech-at-baile-tusnad-tusnadfurdo-of-26-july-2014/10592. Accessed July 27, 2017.

Orbán, Victor. 2017, July 24. "Will Europe Belong to Europeans." https://Visegradpost.com/en/2017/07/24/full-speech-of-v-orban-will-europe-belong-to-europeans/. Accessed July 26, 2017.

Ordzhonikidze, Sergei A. 2009. "New Security Challenges: Soft and Hard," Address by UN Under-Secretary-General, Director-General of the UN Office at Geneva, Conference on "Belgium in the UN Security Council 2007–2008 – An Assessment," Brussels, April 3. https://reliefweb.int/report/occupied-palestinian-territory/new-security-challenges-soft-and-hard-address-mr-sergei. Accessed February 22, 2014.

Ost, David. 1991. *Solidarity and the Politics of Anti-Politics*. Philadelphia: Temple University Press.

Ozoliņa, Liene. 2019. "Embracing Austerity? An Ethnographic Perspective on the Latvian Public's Acceptance of Austerity Politics." *Journal of Baltic Studies*, 50, no. 4: 515–31.

Paczkowski, Andrzej, and Byrne, Malcolm. 2008. *From Solidarity to Martial Law: The Polish Crisis of 1980–1981: A Documentary History*. Budapest: Central European University Press.

Paljak, Piret. 2013. "Participation in International Military Operations." In *Apprenticeship, Partnership, Membership: Twenty Years of Defence Development in the Baltic States*, edited by Tony Lawrence and Tomas Jermalavičius, 234–9. Tallinn: International Centre for Defence Studies.

Papp, Daniel S., Johnson, Loch K., and Endicott, John E. 2005. *American Foreign Policy: History, Politics, and Policy*. New York: Pearson/Longman.

Pataccini, Leonardo, Kattel, Rainer, and Raudla, Ringa. 2019. "Introduction: Europeanization and Financial Crisis in the Baltic Sea Region: Implication, Perceptions, and Conclusions Ten Year after the Collapse." *Journal of Baltic Studies*, 50, no. 4: 403–8.

Paterson, Thomas G., Clifford, Garry, Maddock, Shane J., Kisatsky, Deborah, and Hagan, Kenneth J. 2005. *American Foreign Relations, Volume 2: A History Since 1895*, 6th edition. Boston: Houghton Mifflin Company.

"Path to Partnership for Peace (Bosnia-Herzegovina)." 2016, April 27. www.gov.ba. Accessed September 30, 2018.

Paunovski, Georgi. 2019a. "Херо Мустафа: България може да развие потенциала си с независими медии и върховенство на закона." *Dnevnik*. www.dnevnik.bg/bulgaria/2019/11/24/3996577_hero_mustafa_bulgariia_moje_da_razvie_potenciala_si_s/?ref=id&_ga=2.74769426.1246570711.1574698129-377939814.1513029584#comment-55. Accessed November 26, 2019.

Paunovski, Georgi. 2019b. "Правителството отпусна още 16 млн. лева, за да летят МиГ-29, докато дойдат F-16 [The Government Released Another 16 Million Leva to Let MIG-29 Fly until the F-16 Arrive." *Dnevnik*. www.dnevnik.bg/bulgaria/2019/12/04/4000985_pravitelstovoto_otpusna_16_mln_leva_za_da_letiat/. Accessed December 6, 2019.

Bibliography

Pécsvarady, Szabolcs. 2010. "Special Operations Forces of Hungary: Is a Transformation Necessary?" Master's Thesis. Army Command and General Staff College Fort Leavenworth. www.dtic.mil/docs/citations/ADA536818. Accessed July 12, 2017.

Perović, Jeronim. 2007. "The Tito-Stalin Split: A Reassessment in Light of New Evidence." *Journal of Cold War Studies*, 9, no. 2: 32–63. https://muse.jhu.edu/. Accessed July 9, 2019.

Peters, B. Guy. 2016. *American Public Policy: Promise and Performance*, 10th edition. Washington, DC: Sage/CQ Press.

Peterson, James W. 2011a. *European Security East and West: The Significance of the Missile Shield Proposal*. The Carl Beck Papers in Russian & East European Studies, Number 2101.

Peterson, James W. 2011b. *NATO and Terrorism: Organizational Expansion and Mission Transformation*. New York: Continuum.

Peterson, James W. 2013. *Building a Framework of Security for Southeast Europe and the Black Sea Region: A Challenge Facing NATO*. Lewiston: The Edwin Mellen Press.

Peterson, James, and Lubecki, Jacek. 2019. *Defense Policies of East-Central European Countries since 1989: Creating Stability in Times of Uncertainty*. Manchester: Manchester University Press.

Peterson, Philip A., and Myers, Nicholas. 2018. *Baltic Net Assessment* , 2nd edition. Tartu: Estonian Defence College.

Petrescu, Dragos. 2014. *Entangled Revolutions: The Breakdown of Communist Regimes in East-Central Europe*. Bucharest: Editura Enciclopedica.

Peverhous, Jon C. 2002. "With a Little Help from My Friends? Regional Organizations and the Consolidation of Democracy." *American Journal of Political Science* 46, no. 3: 611–26.

Pindják, Peter. 2014. "Engagement of the Slovak Armed Forces in Future Crisis Management Operations." *INCAS Bulletin*, 6, no. 3: 81–8.

Plakans, Andrejs. 2011. *A Concise History of the Baltic States*. Cambridge: Cambridge University Press.

Plokhi, Serhii. 2014. *The Last Empire: The Final Days of the Soviet Union*. New York: Basic Books.

Pridham, Geoffrey. 2018. "Latvia's Eastern Region: International Tensions and Political System Loyalty." *Journal of Baltic Studies*, 49, no. 1: 3–20.

Public Papers of the Presidents of the United States, William J. Clinton 1998, 1. 2000. Washington, DC: US Government Printing Office.

Putin, Vladimir. 2002. *NATO-Russia Council/Rome Summit 2002*. Brussels: NATO Office of Information and Press. https://nato.int/docu/comm/2002/0205-rome/rome-eng.pdf. Accessed August 16, 2020.

Putin, Vladimir. 2020. "The Real Lessons of the 75th Anniversary of World War II." *National Interest*, June 18. https://nationalinterest.org/feature/vladimir-putin-real-lessons-75th-anniversary-world-war-ii-162982. Accessed August 24, 2020.

Pye, Lucian W. 1966. *Aspects of Political Development*. Boston: Little, Brown and Company.

Racz, András. 2012. "As Afghanistan Exits Loom, Let's Not Forget Hungary's Contribution." www.paprikapolitik.com/2012/02/as-afghanistan-exits-loom-let-s-not-forget-hungary-s-contribution. Accessed July 11, 2014.

Racz, András, and Erzsebet, Rozsa. 2012. "The Democratic Soldier in Hungary." In *Democratic Civil-Military Relations: Soldiering in 21st Century Europe*, edited by Sabine Mannitz, 146–66. London and New York.

Radio Free Europe/Radio Liberty. 1997. "Slovakia: Ties to Moscow Strengthen; Relations with Brussels Strained." News report, May 22. www.rferl.org/a/1084799.html. Accessed December 31, 2019.

Ramet, Sabrina P. 1992. *Nationalism and Federalism in Yugoslavia*. Bloomington: Indiana University Press.

Ramet, Sabrina P. 1996. *Balkan Babel: The Disintegration of Yugoslavia from the Death of Tito to Ethnic War*. Boulder and Oxford: Westview Press.

Ratesh, Nestor. 1991. *Romania: The Entangled Revolution*. New York: Praeger.

"Regional Meeting of Defense Ministers in Grace (Bosnia-Herzegovina)." 2018, September 27. www.mod.gov.ba. Accessed September 30, 2018.

"Relations with Bosnia and Herzegovina." 2018, October 1. www.nato.int. Accessed October 1, 2018.

"Relations with the former Yugoslav Republic of Macedonia." 2018, July 11. www.nato.int. Accessed October 1, 2018.

"Relations with NATO." 2019. www.mod.gov.al. Accessed January 4, 2019.

"Relations with Serbia." 2017, December 1. www.nato.int. Accessed October 1, 2018.

Remington, Robin Alison. 1984. "Yugoslavia." In *Communism in Eastern Europe*, 2nd edition, edited by Teresa Rakowska-Harmstone, 238–82. Bloomington: Indiana University Press.

Republic of Hungary. 2004. "National Security Strategy of the Republic of Hungary." www.files.ethz.ch/isn/157029/Hungary_English-2004.pdf. Accessed July 13, 2017.

Republic of Hungary. 2012. "National Security Strategy of the Republic of Hungary." www.eda.europa.eu/docs/default-source/documents/hungary-national-security-strategy-2012.pdf. Accessed July 13, 2017.

"Responsibility for Demining Workshops in the Municipalities of Bosanska Krupa and Brod (Bosnia-Herzegovina)." 2018, September 27. www.mod.gov.ba. Accessed September 30, 2018.

Rettman, Andrew. 2007. "Barroso Promises to Push Putin on Lithuania Oil." EUobserver, March 8. https://euobserver.com/foreign/23654. Accessed June 12, 2020.

Rettman, Andrew. 2016. "Eastern EU Leaders to Warn Juncker on Nord Stream II." EUobserver, March 17. https://euobserver.com/foreign/132726. Accessed June 12, 2020

Rettman, Andrew. 2018. "EU Documents Lay Bare Russian Energy Abuse." EUobserver, April 12. https://euobserver.com/foreign/141584. Accessed June 12, 2020.

Bibliography

Reuters. 2007. "Russia Won't Re-open Oil Pipeline, Lithuania Says." October 11. https://uk.reuters.com/article/lithuania-russia-oil/russia-wont-re-open-oil-pipeline-lithuania-says-idUKL1159854520071011. Accessed June 13, 2020.

Reuters. 2017. "Gabriel warnt Europäer vor Spaltung durch China." August 30. https://de.reuters.com/article/deutschland-eu-china-idDEKCN1BA1XU. Accessed June 14, 2020.

Riim, Toomas. 2006. "Estonia and NATO: A Constructivist View on a National Interest and Alliance Behaviour." *Baltic Defence Review*, 8: 34–52.

Ritter, László. 2005. "War on Tito's Yugoslavia? The Hungarian Army in Early Cold War Soviet Strategy." February 2005, Parallel History Project on Cooperative Security (PHP). www.php.isn.ethz.ch/lory1.ethz.ch/collections/coll_tito/documents/introduction_ritter.pdf. Accessed July 9, 2019.

Ross Johnson, A. 1977. "Soviet-East European Military Relations." RAND Paper Series, vol. 374. www.dtic.mil/get-tr-doc/pdf?AD=ADA511838. Accessed March 26, 2017.

Rossi, Frederico. 2002. "The Elite Coup: Transition to Democracy in Bulgaria." Cosmos Paper. https://cadmus.eui.eu/bitstream/handle/1814/26183/2012WP10COSMOS. pdf?sequence=1&isAllowed=y. Accessed January 1, 2020.

Rostoks, Tom, and Vanga, Nora. 2016. "Latvia's Security Defence Post-2014." *Journal of Baltic Security*, 2, no. 2: 71–108.

Rupp, Richard. 2002. "Lithuania's Campaign for NATO Membership." *Lituanus*, 48, no. 2: 2–10.

Rzeczpospolita Polska. 1992. *Założenia polityki bezpieczeństwa* and *Polityka bezpieczeństwa i strategia obronna Rzeczypospolitej Polskiej*. Polkoziej.pl/wp-content/uploads/2015/07/Strategia_RP_z_92_r.doc. Accessed May 5, 2017.

Rzeczpospolita Polska. 2014. "Strategia Bezpieczeństwa Narodowego Rzeczypospolitej Polskiej." http://koziej.pl/wp-content/uploads/2015/09/Strategia-BN-pol.pdf. Accessed April 2, 2017.

Rzeczpospolita Polska. 2020, May 12. "The National Security Strategy of the Republic of Poland." www.bbn.gov.pl/ftp/dokumenty/National_Security_Strategy_of_the_Republic_of_Poland_2020.pdf. Accessed September 14, 2020.

Sanecka-Tyczynska, Joanna. 2011. "Modele bezpieczeństwa zewnętrznego państwa w myśli politycznej Prawa i Sprawiedliwości." *Zeszyty Naukowe WSOWL*, 161, no. 3: 218–31.

Sapronas, Robertas. 1999. "BALTBAT and Development of Baltic Defence Forces." *Baltic Defence Review*, 2: 55–70.

Sayle, Timothy Andrews. 2019. *Enduring Alliance: A History of NATO and the Postwar Global Order*. Ithaca: Cornell University Press.

Scaparrotti, Curtis M., and Bell, Colleen B., co-chairs. 2020. "Moving Out: A Comprehensive Assessment of European Military Mobility." Washington, DC: Atlantic Council. www.atlanticcouncil.org/in-depth-research-reports/report/moving-out-a-comprehensive-assessment-of-european-military-mobility/. Accessed August 23, 2020.

Scott, Mark. 2019. "Pipe-Laying Company Suspends Nord Stream 2 Work Over US Sanctions." Politico.eu, December 21. www.politico.eu/article/nord-stream-2-russia-sanctions-us-donald-trump/. Accessed June 4, 2020.

Seaman, John, Huotari, Mikko, and Otero-Iglesias, Miguel, eds. 2017. "Chinese Investment in Europe: A Country-Level Approach. A Report by the European Think-tank Network on China (ETNC)." https://www.ifri.org/en/publications/publications-ifri/ouvrages-ifri/chinese-investment-europe-country-level-approach. Accessed June 22, 2018.

"SEDM, Its Role, Dynamics, Engagement and Extension in South East Europe." 2019. www.mod.gov.al. Accessed January 5, 2019.

"SEEBRIG." 2019. www.mod.gov.al. Accessed January 5, 2019.

Shekovtsov, Anton. 2014. "Calculated Marriage: Kremlin and the European Ultra-Rights [Брак по расчёту: Кремль и европейские ультраправые]." www.opendemocracy.net/ru/brak-po-raschetu/. Accessed August 5, 2019.

Sherr, James. 2000. "Nato's New Members: A Model for Ukraine? The Example of Hungary." www.files.ethz.ch/isn/97634/00_Sep_3.pdf. Accessed July 14, 2017.

Shirreff, Richard. 2016. *2017: War with Russia*. London: Coronet.

Shlapak, David A. 2017. "Deterring Russian Aggression in the Baltic States." Testimony presented before the House Armed Services Committee, Subcommittee on Tactical Air and Land Forces on March 1, 2017. Santa Monica: RAND Corporation. rand.org/pubs/testimonies/CT467z1.html. Accessed August 23, 2020.

Shlapak, David A., and Johnson, Michael W. 2016. "Reinforcing Deterrence on NATO's Eastern Flank: Wargaming the Defense of the Baltics." Santa Monica: RAND Corporation. rand.org/pubs/research_reports/RR1253.html. Accessed August 23, 2020.

Simon, Jeffrey. 1998. "Bulgaria and NATO: 7 Lost Years." Strategic Forum 138–142, May 1998. http://connections-qj.org/system/files/01.19_Monitor_Simon.pdf. Accessed November 6, 2019.

Simon, Jeffrey. 2002. *Hungary and NATO: Problems in Civil-Military Relations*. Lanham: Rowman & Littlefield.

Simon, Jeffrey. 2003. *NATO and the Czech and Slovak Republics: A Comparative Study in Civil-Military Relations*. New York: Rowman & Littlefield.

Simon, Jeffrey. 2004. *Poland and NATO: A Study in Civil-Military Relations*. Lanham, Boulder, and New York: Rowman & Littlefield.

Simon, Steven. 2008. "The Price of the Surge: How U.S. Strategy is Hastening Iraq's Demise." *Foreign Affairs*, 87, no. 3: 57–76.

Smith, Keith C. 2008. "EU Soft Security: Myth or Reality? Russian Economic Pressure on EU's Central European Members." Washington, DC, Center for Strategic and International Studies (CSIS), February 11–12. https://csis-prod.s3.amazonaws.com/s3fs-public/legacy_files/files/media/csis/pubs/080407_soft_security.pdf. Accessed February 21, 2019.

Snow, Donald M., and Brown, Eugene. 2000. *United States Foreign Policy: Politics Beyond the Water's Edge*, 2nd edition. New York: Bedford/St. Martin's.

Snyder, Jack. 2000. *From Voting to Violence: Democratization and Nationalist Conflict*. New York: W.W. Norton.

Sperling, James. 2001. "The United States: Strategic Vision or Tactical Posturing." In *Building a Bigger Europe: EU and NATO Enlargement in Comparative*

Perspective, edited by Martin Smith and Graham Timtmins, 115–35. London and New York: Routledge.

Sprenger, Sebastian. 2020. "Hungary Plunks Down $1 Billion for New Air Defenses." Defensenews.com, August 13. www.defensenews.com/global/europe/2020/08/13/hungary-plunks-down-1-billion-for-new-air-defenses/. Accessed September 13, 2020.

Staff. 2016a. "Orbán has Launched the Training of His Border Chasseurs." *Visegrad Post – English*, September 18. https://visegradpost.com/en/2016/09/18/orban-has-launched-the-training-of-his-border-chasseurs/. Accessed July 26, 2017.

Staff. 2016b. "Orbán Plans to Double the Hungarian Army and Raise Patriotism among Children." *Visegrad Post – English*, October 19. https://visegradpost.com/en/2016/10/19/orban-plans-to-double-the-hungarian-army-and-rise-patriotism-among-children/. Accessed July 25, 2017.

Staff. 2017. "Hungary to Increase Military Spending in 2018." *The Budapest Beacon.* http://budapestbeacon.com/news-in-brief/hungary-increase-military-spending-2018/46796. Accessed July 25, 2017.

Stelzenmüller, Constanze. 2019. *Hostile Alley: The Trump Challenge and Europe's Inadequate Response.* Washington, DC: Brookings Institution.

Stoessinger, John G. 1985. *Crusaders and Pragmatists: Movers of American Foreign Policy*, 2nd edition. New York: W.W. Norton & Company.

"Strategic Defense Review of Croatia 2013." www.morh.hr. Accessed September 29, 2018.

"Strategic Defense Review 2018 of the Republic of Macedonia." 2018, September 30. www.morm.gov.mk. Accessed September 30, 2018 and October 1, 2018.

"Strategic Defense Review of Montenegro 2013." www.med.gov.me. Accessed September 29, 2018.

"Strategic Defense Review of Slovenia 2016." www.mo.gov.si. Accessed September 27, 2018.

Strzelczyk, Joanna. 2005. *Ucieczka Ze Wschody (Escape from the East).* Warszawa: Oficyna Wydawnicza "RYTM."

Sutowski, Michal. 2016. "Komorowski Kontra Macierewicz. Wojna doktryn obronnych PO i PiS." https://oko.press/komorowski-kontra-macierewicz-wojna-doktryn-obronnych/. Accessed July 23, 2017.

Sytas, Andrius. 2016. "EU Leaders Sign Letter Objecting to Nord Stream-2 Gas." Reuters, March 16. https://uk.reuters.com/article/uk-eu-energy-nordstream-idUKKCN0WI1YV. Accessed February 13, 2019.

Szayna, Thomas. 2020. *NATO Enlargement 2000–2015.* Santa Monica: Rand.

Szenesz, Zoltan. 2007. "Peacekeeping in the Hungarian Armed Forces." *AARMS: Academic and Applied Research in Military Science*, 6, no. 1: 121–33.

Szicherle, Patrik, Mesežnikov, Grigorij, Syrovátka, Jonáš, Merc, Jakub, and Krekó, Péter. 2019. *Doors Wide Shut: Russian, Chinese and Turkish Authoritarian Influence in the Czech Republic, Hungary and Slovakia.* Political Capital/Social Development Institute, Budapest, December.

Szymański, Piotr. 2016. "The Multi-Speed Baltic States: Reinforcing the Defence Capabilities of Lithuania, Latvia, and Estonia." Centre for Eastern Studies

(OSW), Warsaw, 68 (August). www.osw.waw.pl/en/publicacje/osw-studies/2017-08-16/multi-speed-baltic-states-reinforcing-defence-capabilities. Accessed August 16, 2020.

Szymański, Piotr. 2018. "With Russia Right Across the Border: Finland's Security Policy." Centre of Eastern Studies (OSW) Warsaw. www.osw.waw.pl/en/publikacje/osw-studies/2018-05-30/russia-right-across-border. Accessed August 16, 2020.

Szymański, Piotr. 2019. "The Northern Tandem: The Swedish-Finnish Defence Cooperation." Centre for Eastern Studies (OSW), Commentary 298, March 20. www.osw.waw.pl/en/publikacje/osw-commentary/2019-03-20/northern-tandem-swedish-finnish-defence-cooperation. Accessed August 16, 2020.

Szymański, Piotr. 2020. "New Ideas for Total Defence: Comprehensive Security in Finland and Estonia." Centre for Eastern Studies (OSW), Warsaw, March 31. www.osw.waw.pl/sites/default/files/OSW-Report_New-ideas-for-total-defence_net_0.pdf. Accessed August 16, 2020.

Talas, Peter and Csiki, Tamas. 2013. "Hungary." In *Strategic Cultures in Europe: Security and Defense Policies Across the Continent*, edited by Heiko Biehl, Bastian Giegerich and Alexandra Jonas, 165–80. Springer-Verlag.

Talbott, Strobe. 2002. *The Russia Hand: A Memoir of Presidential Diplomacy.* New York: Random House.

Taylor, Paul. 2018. *"Fort Trump" or Bust? Poland and the Future of European Defence.* Friends of Europe, Brussels, December.

Than, Krisztina, and Szakacs, Gergely. 2017, January 12. "Hungary to Boost Defence Spending to 2 Percent of GDP – Minister." www.reuters.com/article/uk-hungary-defence-minister-idUKKBN14W2D1. Accessed July 2017.

TOC. 2020. "Bulgaria Begins Talks with Lürssen Shipyard for Two New Warships." July 16. https://bulgarianmilitary.com/2020/06/16/bulgaria-begins-talks-with-lurssen-shipyard-for-two-new-warships/. Accessed July 19, 2020

Trainor, Bernard E. 1988. "East German Military: Warsaw Pact's Finest." *New York Times*, November 8. Archived from the original on August 1, 2018. www.nytimes.com/1988/11/08/world/east-german-military-warsaw-pact-s-finest.html. Accessed 30 January 2019.

"Transfer of Authority between the Polish Contingents at Craiova." 2019. www.mapn.ro. Accessed January 17, 2019.

Treisman, Daniel. 2018. "Crimea: Anatomy of a Decision." In *The New Autocracy: Information, Politics, and Policy*, 277–97. Washington, DC: Brookings Institution Press.

Trenin, Vladimir. 2019. "Changing Identity: In Search of a Role in the 21st Century." Carnegie Moscow Center, July 18. https://carnegie.ru/commentary/79521. Accessed August 23, 2020.

Tzvetkov, Georgi. 2014. "Defense Policy and Reforms in Bulgaria since the End of the Cold War: A Critical Analysis." *Connections*, 13, no. 2: 74. https://pdfs.semanticscholar.org/1f8e/888e79a88c0dfaea23ff9bfc90dfb2d1dc8a.pdf?_ga=2.232443423.1663846583.1614714268-242914935.1614714268. Accessed July 18, 2019.

Bibliography

Urbelis, Vaidotas. 2003. "Defence Policies of the Baltic States: From the Concept of Neutrality to NATO Membership." NATO-EAPC Individual Fellowship Report. www.nato.int/acad/fellow/01-03/vaidotas.pdf. Accessed January 2, 2020.

US Congress, Senate. 2003. *Hearings before the Committee on Foreign Relations United States Senate One Hundred Eighth Congress, First Session March 27 and April 1,3 and 8, 2003.* Washington, DC: US Government Printing Office, 2003.

Valášek Tomáš. 2017. "China and Central Europe: Don't Believe the Hype." Carnegie Europe, November 28. https://carnegieeurope.eu/strategiceurope/74844. Accessed June 2, 2020.

Veebel, Vilja, and Ploom, Illimar. 2017. "Estonian Perception of Security: Not Only about Russia and the Refugees." *Journal of Baltic Security*, 2, no. 2: 35–70.

Vegh, Zsusanne. 2015. "Hungary's 'Eastern Opening' Policy Towards Russia: Ties That Bind?" *International Issues and Slovak Foreign Policy Affairs*, 24, no. 1–2: 47–65.

Velinger, Jan. 2006. "Czechs Hand Training Over to Iraqis at Police Academy." Czech Radio 7, Radio Prague. November 8. www.radio.cz. Accessed June 2, 2010.

Verona, Sergiu. 1989. "The Withdrawal of Soviet Troops from Romania in 1958. Analysis of the Decision." Final Report to the National Council of Soviet and Eastern European Research, 1989, https://www.ucis.pitt.edu/nceeer/1989–803–01-Verona.pdf. Accessed July 13, 2019.

Vilpišauskas, Ramūnas. 2013. "Lithuanian Foreign Policy since EU Accession: Torn Between History and Interdependence." In *The New Member States and the European Union: Foreign Policy and Europeanization*, edited by Michael Baun and Dan Marek, 127–41. Abingdon: Routledge.

Visegrad Insight. 2018. "Central European Futures: Five Scenarios for 2025," special edition.

Vseviov, Jonatan. 2018. "Challenges of Real National Defence." *Diplomaatia*, November 16. https://icds.ee/en/challenges-of-real-national-defence/. Accessed August 22, 2020.

Wagner, Peter and Marton, Peter. 2014. "Hungarian Military and the War on Terror." *The Polish Quarterly of International Affairs,* 2: 107–20.

"The Wales Declaration on the Transatlantic Bond." 2014, September 5. www.nato.int. Accessed December 28, 2019.

Wallat, Josefine. 2001/2. "Czechoslovak/Czech Foreign and Security Policy 1989–1999." *Perspective*, 17: 14–29.

Waller, Douglas, and McAllister, J.F.O. 1997. "How Clinton Decided on NATO Expansion." *Time*, 150, no. 2: 58.

Warsaw Treaty. 1955. "Treaty of Friendship, Co-operation and Mutual Assistance." Signed at Warsaw, on May 14, 1955, in United Nations Treaty Collection. https://treaties.un.org/doc/Publication/UNTS/Volume%20219/volume-219-I-2962-Other.pdf. Accessed March 26, 2017.

Wemer, David A. 2018. "State Department Official Sounds Warning on Russian, Chinese Influence in Central and Eastern Europe." *New Atlanticist*, October 19. www.atlanticcouncil.org/blogs/new-atlanticist/state-department-official-sounds-warning-on-russian-chinese-influence-in-central-and-eastern-europe/. Accessed June 24, 2020.

Wendt, Alexander. 1999. *Social Theory of International Politics*. Cambridge: Cambridge University Press.

White, Stephen. 2011. *Understanding Russian Politics*. New York: Cambridge University Press.

"White Paper on Defence Bucharest 2017." www.mapn.ro. Accessed January 16, 2019.

Whitney, Craig R. 1991. "War in the Gulf: Europe." *New York Times*, January 25. www.nytimes.com/1991/01/25/world/war-in-the-gulf-europe-gulf-fighting-shatters-europeans-fragile-unity.html?pagewanted=1. Accessed December 15, 2018.

Wilkes, William. 2018. "U.S. Warns Sanctions Possible If Nord Stream 2 Pipe Proceeds." Bloomberg, May 17. www.bloomberg.com/news/articles/2018-05-17/u-s-warns-sanctions-possible-if-nord-stream-2-pipe-proceeds. Accessed June 12, 2020.

Windsor, Phillip, and Roberts, Adam. 1969. *Czechoslovakia 1968: Reform, Repression and Resistance*. London: Chatto & Windus.

Winter, Jay. 2010. "Sites of Memory." In *Memory: Histories, Theories, Debates*, edited by Susannah Radstone and Bill Schwarz, 321–4. New York: Fordham University.

"The Wishes of KSF Minister Rrustem Berisha on the 10th Anniversary of Kosovo's Independence." 2018, June 14. www.mksf-ks.org. Accessed September 30, 2018.

Young, Thomas-Durell. 2017. *Anatomy of Post-Communist Defense Institutions: The Mirage of Military Modernity*. London: Bloomsbury.

Young, Thomas-Durell. 2019. "NATO's Selective Sea Blindness: Assessing the Alliance's New Navies." *Naval College Review*, 72, no. 3: 1–27.

Yu, Yixiang. 2019. "From 16+1 to 17+1: The EU's Challenge from the Rebranded China-CEEC Initiative." American Institute for Contemporary German Studies, April 26. www.aicgs.org/2019/04/from-161-to-171-the-eus-challenge-from-the-rebranded-china-ceec-initiative/. Accessed June 12, 2020.

Zaborowski, Marcin. 2019. "Between the Eastern Flank and Mitteleuropa: Security and Defence Policies in Central Europe." *Visegrad Insight*, October 9. https://visegradinsight.eu/between-the-eastern-flank-and-mitteleuropa/. Accessed July 18, 2020.

Index

admission to NATO 5, 84, 94, 137, 191
Adriatic Charter 109, 138
adversaries 4, 5, 52, 168
Afghanistan 1, 3, 4, 11, 13, 14, 29, 40,
46, 49, 54–64, 87, 91, 92, 95,
101, 102, 107, 108–10, 116, 123,
126, 129, 134, 135, 136–8, 141,
142, 147, 148, 150, 151, 154,
155, 169, 170, 176, 186
Afghanistan and Iraq 12, 55, 57, 106,
130, 151, 161, 185
Albania 3, 5, 6, 13, 15, 21, 27, 31, 34,
37, 42, 45, 46, 47, 49, 51, 55,
57, 63, 69, 106–10, 128, 129,
130, 154, 161, 170, 179, 186,
188, 190
Albanian military 108, 110
Albanian populations 138, 187
Albanians 46, 48, 55, 108, 110, 132,
141, 186
alliance activities 12, 53, 103
alliance framework 132, 145
alliance membership 53, 106, 109,
110, 132, 142, 145, 146,
186, 188
alliance missions 58, 91, 110, 134, 167
alliance partners 1, 3, 54, 56, 62, 108,
110, 137, 142, 150, 189
alliance planners 12, 52, 55, 62, 138
alliance politics theory 129, 131, 133,
144, 145
alliances 12, 14, 52, 53, 61, 64, 95,
103, 106, 132–4, 143, 145, 146,
152, 160, 163, 191

alliance theory 2, 7, 9, 10, 12, 16, 18,
20, 48, 52, 130, 133
allies 4, 5, 23, 27, 31, 94, 146, 148,
152, 183, 186
American forces 59, 170, 178
anniversaries 2, 6, 140, 184, 185
anti-communist revolutions 7, 34, 54
anti-tank weaponry 174, 175, 178
APCs (armored personal carrier)
31, 149
armored vehicles 99, 173, 177, 178
Austria 32, 49, 74, 79, 112, 117
autonomy 8, 21, 44, 90
Azerbaijan 120, 161

Balkan region 143, 144, 154, 188, 190
Balkan states 13, 15, 60, 106, 186, 188
Balkan wars 2, 54, 55, 87, 110,
131, 160
Ballistic Missile Defence Agreement
(BMDA) 153
Baltic air policing 171, 193
Baltic airspace 172, 173, 176, 178
Baltic countries 3, 37, 40, 148, 152,
165, 166, 171, 172, 178, 179
Baltic militaries 170, 178
Baltics 13, 17, 18, 42, 46, 47, 51, 79,
146, 158, 165, 166, 173, 175,
177, 178, 179, 180, 181, 190
Baltic Sea 73, 176, 180
Baltic states 4, 8, 17, 18, 59, 64, 68, 71,
76, 79, 154, 165–215
base 56, 85, 128, 136, 151, 166,
167, 172

battlegroups 62, 88, 96, 100, 152
Beijing 77, 78, 93, 129
Belarus 69, 71, 73, 88, 126, 172, 180, 181
Belt and Road Initiative 77
bilateral relationships 90, 162, 163
Black Sea 73, 79, 94, 119, 121, 126, 128, 150–2, 162
Black Sea Forum for Dialogue and Cooperation 150, 152
Borisov 119, 121, 122, 125
Bosnia 10, 36, 37, 48, 55, 57, 91, 134, 137, 139, 142, 143, 144, 161, 169, 170
Bosnia-Herzegovina 5, 6, 10, 14, 15, 48, 55, 57, 64, 94, 107, 108, 109, 131, 132, 133, 138, 139, 142, 151, 169, 172, 187, 188, 190, 191
Bosniaks 5, 15, 48, 49
Brezhnev 26
Brussels 74, 118, 139, 191
Bucharest 116, 146, 153
Bulgaria 3, 6, 7, 8, 13–15, 21, 27, 28, 30, 33, 35, 37, 40, 42, 43, 47, 51, 52, 54, 59–64, 72, 76, 106, 111–30, 154, 161–2, 168, 186, 189, 190
Bulgarian Army 115, 116, 117
Bulgarian Council of Ministers 124
Bulgarian membership 43, 118
Bulgarian military 113, 115, 117, 121, 123
Bulgarian military participation in NATO-EU operations 115
Bulgarian Ministry 122, 126, 129, 130, 194
Bulgarian politics 43, 111
Bulgarians 42, 43, 111–13, 118, 120, 121, 124–9, 194

capabilities 52, 59, 62, 64, 85, 91, 98, 100, 142, 167, 168
capacity 57, 65, 66, 67, 68, 73, 75, 81, 103, 156

Ceaușescu, Nicolae 28, 30
Central Europe 24, 96
Central Europeans 19, 80, 83, 86, 88, 94
changes, climate 66, 67, 68, 81, 159
China 3, 66, 68, 76–81, 88, 93
Chinese investment 77, 78
citizens 67, 68, 90, 122, 175, 184
civil war 8, 9, 10, 15, 17, 20, 31, 49, 165
Clinton, Bill 41, 42, 51, 169
Cold War 6, 20, 21, 27, 28, 29, 31, 52, 53, 129, 160, 165, 186
command structures 92, 108
  new 158
Commission 73, 74, 75
Common Security and Defense Policy
  see CSDP
communism 7, 9, 20, 23, 24, 28, 29, 31, 34, 35, 146, 149
communists 6, 7, 20, 21, 23, 89
communist bloc 28, 160, 186
communist countries 22, 29, 30
  former, 37, 168
communist era 16, 71, 129, 154
communist party 21, 29, 31, 45, 106
communist past 20, 35, 40, 129, 143
communist period 6, 106, 146
communist rule 6, 20
communities 90, 139, 140, 162, 182, 184
  international 142, 144, 165
conflict 15, 17, 21, 31, 35, 36, 90, 111, 113, 129, 131, 138, 139, 188, 189
conflict resolution 39
contributions 1, 11, 13, 59, 60, 87, 93, 135, 137, 151, 154, 161, 170, 186
cooperation 46, 50, 51, 114–17, 120, 122, 123, 150, 152, 168, 172, 173, 182
coordination 24, 25, 94, 122, 178
countries
  candidate 40, 137, 169

Index

poorest 27, 42, 45
post-communist 38, 40, 47, 50, 104
Crimea 3, 12, 14, 18, 61, 83, 84, 85,
   95, 96, 101, 103, 129, 134, 146,
   150, 152, 189
Crimean crisis 16, 85, 102, 103, 135,
   141, 150, 189
crisis 1, 2, 22, 23, 28, 29, 85, 87,
   88, 93, 94, 96, 100,
   103, 104
Croatia 1, 3, 5, 6, 13, 14, 15, 36, 48,
   49, 55, 56, 63, 96, 109, 116,
   131–43, 148, 151, 161, 169, 179,
   186, 190
Croats 5, 15, 48
CSDP (Common Security and Defense
   Policy) 44, 65, 86, 95, 102,
   103, 110
cultures 15, 19, 56, 92, 93, 131,
   145, 189
Cyprus 14
Czech leaders 87
Czech leadership 95, 96
Czechoslovakians 22, 26, 28, 32, 39
Czechoslovakia 6, 7, 8, 22, 23, 24,
   25, 26, 27, 29–33, 35, 39, 40,
   47, 154
Czechoslovak military 32
Czech Republic 3, 4, 5, 8, 9, 11, 12,
   40, 47, 56, 58, 63, 64, 72, 73,
   76, 80, 83, 85, 86, 87, 89, 102,
   148, 153, 161, 167, 168, 171,
   179, 185
Czechs 11, 12, 18, 26, 39, 54, 56, 60,
   83, 84, 85, 86, 87, 88, 89, 93,
   94, 96, 98, 100, 102, 112, 185,
   189, 190

defense
   civil 173, 174, 175
   collective 62, 79, 92, 108, 167, 177
defense budgets 1, 62, 64, 101, 149,
   158, 170, 171
defense capabilities 83, 95, 103, 122
defense expenditures 1, 63, 182

defense policies 4, 11, 18, 20, 39, 41,
   47, 52, 90, 92, 97, 108, 136,
   147, 149, 155, 156, 160, 176
defense preparedness 9, 141, 142, 191
defense reforms 44, 46, 88, 108
defense sector 8, 100, 141, 142,
   150, 153
defense spending 52, 63, 94, 99, 134,
   135, 144, 169
demilitarization 6, 23, 30, 89
democracy 8, 39, 42, 43, 80, 102, 159,
   160, 167
democratic values 143, 169
Denmark 32, 75, 148, 169, 179, 180
dependence, 7, 71, 72, 75, 95, 102,
   120, 136
deployments 1, 10, 36, 45, 46, 51, 87,
   88, 92, 100, 149, 170, 172
development 11, 23, 26, 27, 47, 48, 53,
   79, 84, 91, 95, 120, 122
   democratic 10, 13, 132, 139,
   144, 147
dialogue 101, 102, 143, 150, 152,
   168, 186
disintegration 157, 165, 179
distances
   gravitational 131, 133, 145,
   146, 160
   typological 131, 133, 145, 146, 160

East-Central Europe 20, 30, 31, 37, 42,
   167, 171, 179
East-Central Europeans 4, 11, 32, 37,
   38, 40, 41, 42, 47, 185, 190
East-Central European NATO members
   83, 85, 87, 89, 91, 93, 95, 97,
   99, 101, 103, 105
Eastern Europe 2, 10, 22, 38, 61, 63,
   65, 66, 73, 75, 76, 77, 79, 80,
   81, 114, 148, 153, 169, 185,
   186, 189, 191
Eastern European (EE) 9, 10, 25, 63,
   66, 68, 69, 71, 76, 84
Eastern European states 2, 6, 20, 21,
   23, 25, 27, 29, 31, 33, 64, 77

220 *Index*

Eastern Ukraine 84, 122, 129
East Europeans 4, 11, 12, 15, 52,
  150, 154
East Germany 22, 24, 30, 31, 35, 37
elections 2, 43, 45, 51, 76, 90, 97, 114,
  119, 122, 127, 160, 166
  parliamentary 39, 40, 43, 46,
  97, 156
ESDP (European Security and Defense
  Policy) 86, 95
establishment 15, 22, 31, 61, 91, 101,
  132, 146, 166
Estonia 1, 5, 11, 17, 46, 52, 53, 59, 63,
  64, 72, 73, 84, 101, 109, 148,
  150, 161, 165–90
Estonians 59, 176–9, 182, 190
ethnic groups 5, 9, 15, 54, 142, 187
Ethnic Russians 46, 70
ethnic tensions 143, 144
Euractiv 70, 75, 76
Europe 8, 9, 36, 38, 39, 45, 46, 50, 76,
  77, 78, 80, 159, 172
  post-communist 37, 38, 164
European Commission 72, 110, 118
European Council 72
European energy security 74
Europeanization 86, 93
European security 66, 81, 86, 95
European Security and Defense Policy
  see ESDP
European States 78, 80, 166, 182, 199
European Union 18, 80, 167
European Union Common Security and
  Defense Policy *see* CSDP

F-16 149
F-35 fighter bombers 158
federations 8, 14, 53, 59, 132,
  133, 145
FMF (Foreign Military Financing) 127
forces
  all-volunteer 87, 92
  conscript-based 24, 149
  territorial 22, 157
  total 175, 177

foreign policy 3, 27, 63, 101, 107, 150,
  160, 181
Foreign Security Policy Coordination
  Committee (FSPCC) 94
former Soviet republics 10, 17,
  102, 168
former Soviet Union 50, 142, 160
former Yugoslav states 133, 135, 137,
  139, 141, 143
FSPCC (Foreign Security Policy
  Coordination Committee), 94

gas 74, 75, 120
Gazprom 73, 74
Georgia 1, 42, 69, 88, 94, 95, 100, 102,
  108, 128, 129, 137, 148, 150,
  161, 186, 189, 190
German unification 37, 165
Germany, 4, 32, 37, 41, 73, 74, 77,
  78, 84, 112, 126, 171, 176,
  179, 180
Gheorghiu-Dej 27
Greater Albania 188
Greece 3, 6, 14, 28, 56, 77, 82, 112,
  113, 116, 142, 157
growth of illiberal nationalism 66, 76,
  79, 80, 81

Herzegovina 115, 116, 123, 129, 139
HOMAR 156
Hungarians 8, 23, 38, 39, 83, 85,
  86, 89, 90, 92, 97, 99, 102,
  104, 190
Hungarian Defense Forces 91
Hungarian military 32, 92
Hungarian National Military
  Strategy 98
Hungarian Republic Ministry of
  Defense 89, 90, 92, 98, 99, 105
Hungary 3, 4, 5, 6, 9, 12, 22, 23, 24,
  25, 26, 30–3, 35, 39, 41, 47, 51,
  54, 58, 60, 63, 64, 72–83, 86, 89,
  90, 91, 92, 97, 98, 99, 100–4,
  116, 120, 128, 148, 151, 152,
  161, 167, 168, 171, 179–85

Index

illiberalism, domestic 4
illiberal nationalism 66, 76, 79, 80, 81
illiberal tendencies 80
independence 22, 104, 106, 139, 143, 147, 151, 165, 166, 167, 168, 172, 187
insecurity 73, 90
instability 8, 31, 46, 47, 95, 132, 134, 142, 146, 150
institutions 2, 21, 25, 35, 50, 68, 80, 129, 152
  liberal 7, 15, 36, 160
International Security Assistance Force *see* ISAF
intervention 18, 68, 69, 132
Iraq 1, 3, 12, 13, 19, 40, 46, 49, 54, 55–61, 91, 92, 101, 102, 106–8, 130, 137, 138, 142, 147, 148, 151, 154, 161, 169, 170, 185
Iraq and Afghanistan 4, 13, 14, 54, 56, 148, 154, 155, 186
Iraq War 11, 61
ISAF (International Security Assistance Force) 58, 59, 116, 137, 138, 139
Italy 46, 49, 77, 107, 112, 121, 125, 148, 179

joining NATO 34, 40, 113, 151, 159, 160, 169

Kabul Airport 58, 59, 108, 109, 151
KFOR (Kosovo Force) 129, 139
Kiev 72, 74, 75, 84, 101
Kosovo 3, 6, 10, 14, 15, 36, 48, 55, 56, 57, 64, 69, 86, 87, 91, 95, 103, 107, 108, 116, 129–51, 164, 169, 170, 186–8, 191
Kosovo Albanians 14, 15, 36
Kosovo Security Force *see* KSF
Kosovo's leaders 139, 140
Kraijna 36, 48
KSF (Kosovo Security Force) 140

land forces 124, 125, 135, 150, 174
Latvia 5, 17, 46, 53, 59, 60, 63, 72, 73, 84, 96, 101, 109, 150, 152, 161, 165–83, 189–91
leaders, communist 21, 22, 26
leadership, authoritarian 15, 56, 143
legacies, 3, 6, 7, 16, 37, 48, 71, 106, 129, 135, 185
liberal democracy 33, 97, 145, 146
liberal internationalism 89, 90
liberalism, 2, 3, 5, 7, 30, 89, 90, 97
Lithuania 5, 17, 18, 46, 47, 51, 53, 59, 60, 61, 63, 70–3, 84, 101, 109, 161–90
Lithuanians 70, 175, 180
London 116, 170

Macedonia 6, 15, 36, 46, 48, 49, 55–7, 94, 109, 137, 138, 142, 161, 188
  former Yugoslav Republic of 116, 138, 187
MAP *see* Membership Action Plan
member countries 30, 128
Membership Action Plan (MAP) 46, 116, 139, 167
membership in NATO 39, 41, 44, 50, 51, 54, 84, 88, 91, 92, 106, 108, 111, 129, 133, 134, 136, 188
member states 25, 27, 61, 62, 65, 68, 70, 71, 75, 76, 78, 80, 81, 95
Middle East 46, 76, 186
migration 66, 141
  increased 76
  legal 118
migration patterns 123
militarism 30, 35, 48
military alliance 11, 61, 140, 141, 160, 191
military budget 24, 32, 105, 136, 163
military capabilities 11, 18, 55, 63, 141
military contributions 12, 14, 60, 183
military doctrine 28, 31, 115, 154, 155
military education 135, 152, 173
military equipment 25, 32, 56, 124
military exercises, joint 50, 128

222   *Index*

military forces 10, 16, 61, 64, 110, 151, 159, 175, 190
military operations 61, 65, 86, 87, 93
military personnel 18, 31, 58, 59, 60, 63, 93, 123, 124, 136, 151
military spending 3, 24, 30, 31, 32, 62, 89, 92, 97
Ministry of Defense of Bulgaria 60, 120
Ministry of Foreign Affairs of Hungary 58, 60
missions 1, 13, 14, 58, 59, 61, 87, 91, 92, 93, 95, 100, 101, 102, 107, 109, 116, 123, 137, 138, 148, 152, 162, 169, 170, 172, 190
modernization 92, 95, 101, 117, 119, 120, 122, 126, 128, 156
Moldova 3, 6, 15–17, 35, 42, 44–7, 69, 95, 100, 102, 116, 128, 145, 150, 159, 161, 164, 189
Montenegro 5, 6, 13, 15, 48, 49, 55, 56, 57, 63, 69, 93, 109, 116, 128, 131, 133, 136, 141, 143, 164, 170, 179, 186, 187, 190
Moscow 6, 7, 16, 18, 30, 54, 59, 66, 69, 70, 72, 73, 74, 75, 76, 78, 81, 82, 84, 129, 143, 147, 160, 165, 189
MPFSEE (Multinational Peacekeeping Force of Eastern Europe) 109

national defense 98, 113, 117, 134, 157, 158
nationalism 14, 34, 35, 90
National Military Strategy 90, 91, 92, 150
national security 88, 91, 94, 114, 116, 118, 129, 133, 155, 191
National Security Strategy 90, 91, 146, 147, 152, 155, 158, 162, 163, 175
NATO
  activities 102, 103, 169
  admission 138, 141
  countries 10, 63, 169, 173, 175

  enlargement 168
  EU 47, 90
  expansion 37, 41, 42, 48, 50, 84, 168, 181
  forces 57, 108, 116, 172, 176, 181, 182, 187
  goals 102, 134
  Headquarters 113, 114
  interests 86, 103
  interventions 15, 55
  members 13, 18, 37, 109, 111, 133, 136, 151, 173, 180, 183, 188, 191
    new 5, 56, 58, 59, 60, 61, 94
  membership 12, 39, 40, 42, 46, 47, 51, 57, 108–17, 168, 189, 190
  military exercises 108, 134
  missions 56, 58, 87, 123, 141, 142, 171
  operations 11, 59, 61, 108, 110, 121, 147
  planners 62, 176
  program 50, 113
  projects 58, 135
  Public Diplomacy Division 135, 136, 144, 157, 172, 173, 179, 183
  Response force (NRF) 88, 93, 107, 152
  Security Investment Program (NSIP) 126, 152
  troops 84, 179, 181
  Wales Summit 64, 151
natural gas 71, 72, 147
NCOs 108, 138
neighborhood 6, 9–11, 53, 65, 83, 106, 130, 142
neighbors 8, 90, 101, 140, 142, 185, 188
new members 2, 11, 13, 41, 53, 54, 59, 66, 69, 94, 151
new member states 1, 66, 69, 70, 71, 77, 145
non-EU states 82, 182
non-military 66, 67, 147
Nord Stream 66, 71, 73

Nord Stream and Turkish Stream 73
Northern Europe 18, 182
North Macedonia 3, 5, 6, 11, 13, 15, 55, 57, 69, 109, 131–8, 141–3, 186, 187, 188, 191
NRF (NATO Response force) 88, 93, 107, 152
NSIP (NATO Security Investment Program) 126, 152

Obama, Barack 153, 170
officers 35, 45, 108, 124, 137, 138, 166, 173
operations
  international 172, 192
  peacekeeping 36, 88, 110, 135, 169, 174
optimism 168, 169
Orbán, Victor 86, 89, 96–9, 100, 104
Orbán and FIDESZ's rhetorical shift 97
Orbán's ideological 98
Orbán's rhetoric 97
order 30, 34, 46, 99, 112
OSCE (Organization for Security and Cooperation in Europe) 36, 50, 100, 101, 109

partners 11, 53, 78, 108, 110, 133, 136, 141, 151, 167, 182
Partnership for Peace see PfP
peace 3, 9, 36, 90, 153, 158
peacekeeping 2, 87, 91, 142, 183
peacekeeping forces 57, 109, 132, 135, 137, 169
peacekeeping missions 108, 172, 176
PfP (Partnership for Peace) 5, 41, 42, 45, 46, 50, 52, 53, 133, 139, 140, 167
PfP member 54, 56, 57
pipelines 66, 71, 73, 74, 75, 95, 102, 120
PiS 148, 157, 163
Poland 1, 3, 5, 6, 12, 15–18, 23–51, 58, 60–4, 68–85, 94, 101, 121, 126, 145–90

Poland and Romania 15, 16, 99, 146, 153, 160, 188
Poland's security 11, 147, 149, 162
Poles 11, 32, 189
policies 4, 5, 85, 86, 95, 97, 103, 154, 155, 156, 185, 186
Polish 22, 23, 29, 31, 32–40, 146–57, 163
Polish Crisis 28, 29
Polish defense policies 149, 154, 155, 157
Polish membership in NATO 39, 147
Polish Solidarity 6, 7
political culture 12, 29, 132, 146, 160
political systems 7, 9, 43, 97, 143, 185
population 55, 56, 61, 64, 123, 127, 137, 140, 142, 161, 164, 189, 190
post-communism 34, 188
post-communist transformation 12, 35, 38, 89
post-Yugoslav states 10, 15, 131
power 14, 15, 21, 40, 41, 43, 44, 76, 79, 80, 81, 142, 143, 147, 148
  external 66, 68, 78
Prague NATO Summit 87, 109
Prague Spring 25, 54, 193
Prague Summit 168
preparedness 10, 13, 86, 88, 96, 150, 151
procurement contracts 99, 158
procurement spending 163
professional force, small 149, 173, 176
professionalism 23, 24, 140
professionalization 93, 156
pro-NATO 40, 48
pro-Russian 3, 40, 45
protection, environmental 96, 159
PRT (Provincial Reconstruction Team) 59, 134, 170
public opinion 4, 11, 23, 29, 30, 42, 43, 44, 47, 68, 163

RAND Corporation 177
refugees 1, 3, 4, 18, 36, 185, 186
Republic of Hungary 41, 90, 91, 92, 104

224 *Index*

Republic of Macedonia 137, 138
Republic of Poland 155, 162
resistance 28, 29, 47, 111, 113
  armed 35
Revolutions 29, 35, 37, 39, 41, 43, 45,
  47, 49, 51
Romania 1, 3, 5, 6, 13, 15, 16, 17, 27,
  28, 30–4, 40–54, 61, 63, 64, 68,
  72–80, 90, 99, 106, 116, 119,
  122, 128, 145–79, 188, 189
Romanians 27, 28, 43, 44, 154,
  160, 189
roundtables 96, 101
Russia 3, 4, 8, 12, 14, 16, 17, 18,
  31, 38, 42, 43, 44, 45, 47, 51,
  52, 61, 64, 66–78, 80–6, 95,
  96, 97, 99, 101, 102, 111,
  112, 115, 119–48, 155–9, 166,
  168–84, 185–90
Russians 12, 14, 17, 18, 44, 45, 51, 62,
  63, 64, 66, 70, 83, 84, 85, 103,
  111, 121, 157, 161, 163, 168,
  177, 179, 181, 182, 189
  aggression 16, 177, 179
  ambitions 4, 185, 186, 189
  attack 177, 179
  behavior 83, 84, 103
  Empire 84, 111
  energy 71–5, 120
  forces 177, 178, 180
  influence 111, 120, 159
  intervention 62, 190
  leaders 70, 96, 190
  military 171, 178, 179
  pressure 66, 69, 71, 72, 75, 76
  reaction 17, 190
  takeover 83, 84, 95, 101, 134,
  150, 152
  threat 16, 52, 146, 156, 181
Russia-NATO Founding Act 18
Russian-speaking populations 179

sanctions 74, 90, 96, 102, 119, 120
sea 108, 122
sea spaces 24

secession 48, 84
security 6, 17, 57, 66, 68, 109, 142,
  148, 153, 159, 162, 168, 181,
  185, 186, 188, 190
  collective 25, 65, 182
  hard 65, 66, 67, 69, 80, 81
  regional 142, 151, 156
security benefits, soft 68, 69, 81
security communities 67, 68, 81
security dilemma 67, 81, 89, 90
security guarantees 37, 39, 168, 191
  hard 38, 69
security policy 4, 6, 34, 39, 50, 79,
  89, 153
security protection, soft 67, 68, 69
security provider 65, 67, 69, 71, 73, 75,
  76, 77, 79, 81
security strategy 94, 95, 98
security threats 65, 66, 67, 68, 81, 83,
  95, 185
SEDM (Southeastern European Defense
  Ministerial) 109, 152, 154
Serbian 35, 36, 132, 188
Serbs 5, 14, 36, 48, 55, 141, 151, 187
shatter-belt 130, 131, 133, 143, 145
Slovakia 3, 5, 8, 11, 12, 40, 47, 53,
  56, 59, 60, 64, 72–90, 93–103,
  148, 161, 167, 168, 179,
  185, 18
Slovak Republic 59, 63, 64, 93, 104
Slovaks 11, 12, 26, 40, 54, 59, 83, 84,
  86, 93, 101, 102, 103, 190
Slovenia 5, 11, 13, 14, 15, 35, 40–64,
  72, 96, 116, 128–35, 141–3,
  161–79, 186, 190
soft security 65–9
  provider of 65–81
soldiers 31–3, 59, 60, 100, 101, 104,
  112, 124, 135, 136, 151, 152,
  153, 170, 172
  professional 174, 175
solidarity 1, 6, 29, 66, 69, 70, 71,
  72, 75, 81
Southeastern European Defense
  Ministerial *see* SEDM

Index

South-Eastern Europe Brigade (SEEBRIG) 108, 109
Southeast Europe 14, 55, 57, 101, 107, 152, 162
Southern Europe 16, 76, 77, 104
sovereignty 4, 34, 38, 94, 156, 168
Soviet bloc 22, 23, 25, 29
Soviet controls 7, 10, 16, 22, 23, 25, 26, 27, 32, 52
Soviet empire 21, 22, 31, 34, 35
Soviet invasion of Czechoslovakia 22, 27
Soviet occupation 21, 165
Soviets 7, 17, 20, 21, 22, 23, 24, 25, 26, 27, 28, 30, 32, 33, 44, 48, 112, 166, 175, 182
Soviet Union 6, 8, 16, 17, 20, 21, 23–44, 46, 53, 73, 76, 84, 106, 143, 146, 166, 179, 182, 186, 189, 190
stability 9, 10, 19, 25, 26, 31, 55, 57, 68, 89, 94, 106, 133, 141, 143, 144, 153, 181, 185, 187, 188, 190
political 13, 67, 80, 187
Stable Balkan NATO/EU members 106, 107–29
status, candidate 6, 132, 145, 167
Strategic Defense Review 137, 138, 155
strategy 8, 78, 90, 94, 97, 114, 115, 134, 155, 156, 158, 163
Suwalki corridor 178, 180
Sweden 71, 121, 125, 175
Szymański 21, 22, 165, 173, 174, 175

territorial defense 100, 149, 156, 174, 176
terrorism 4, 5, 54, 67, 87, 99, 147
threats 4, 5, 33, 64, 66, 67, 68, 74, 76, 81, 96, 147, 156, 157, 187
Tito 21, 22, 26, 133
Total People's Defense 22
tradition 6, 8, 16, 19, 28, 78, 84

transformation 32, 95, 101, 117, 135, 193
transition 31, 33, 34, 35, 38, 69, 88, 119, 127, 139, 143
Transnistria 3, 8, 13, 16, 17, 35, 42–5, 179, 189
Transnistrians 44
Transnistrian separatists 45, 159
Trump, Donald 1, 2, 18, 62, 75, 78, 120, 150
Turkey 6, 10, 28, 51, 68, 73, 81, 112, 113, 116, 119
Turkish Stream 73, 75

Ukraine 18, 42, 62, 69, 71, 72, 73, 74, 75, 83, 84, 85, 88, 90, 94, 95, 96, 100, 101, 102, 103, 122, 128, 137, 147, 150, 154, 161, 170–9, 186, 189, 190
Ukrainians 17, 84, 98, 103
uncertainties 11, 19, 52, 65, 67, 78, 85, 95
United Kingdom 18, 53, 128, 129, 170, 179, 180, 182
United States 5, 18, 22, 32, 33, 36, 37, 38, 40, 41, 42, 44, 48, 49, 53, 54, 55, 58, 66, 76, 78, 79, 81, 86, 92, 103, 104, 107, 109, 112, 119–33, 148, 150, 157–68, 170–82
US Air Force 112, 168, 178
US ambassador 169, 182
US decisions 4, 41
US military 126, 168
US troops 39, 175

vacuum 9, 103, 131, 143, 145
Very High Readiness Joint Task Force 96, 172
violence 10, 51, 187
Visegrád 11, 86
Visegrád countries 42, 148
vision 85, 93, 95, 115, 155, 169, 173
Vucic, President 141

Wałęsa 39, 42
Wałęsa's pleading 41
Wales Declaration 61
Wales Summit 18, 94, 122, 172
wars, conventional 156, 180
Warsaw 25, 50, 70, 71, 80, 189
Warsaw Pact 3, 7, 8, 23, 25, 27
Warsaw Pact invasion of
    Czechoslovakia 7
Warsaw Treaty Organization
    see WTO
wars of Yugoslavian succession 8, 22,
    28, 34, 36, 37, 38, 47, 48, 49
Washington 78, 79
weapons 18, 60, 87, 113, 173, 174
    nuclear 32, 171
weapons systems 23, 24, 173
Western alliances 15, 18, 19, 107, 108,
    110, 136, 138, 139, 148, 151,
    185, 186, 189
Western defense organizations 52, 57
Western Europe 38, 73, 171
Western Europeans 8, 36, 49, 68, 79
Western European Union
    (WEU) 93
Western institutions 40, 47, 53
Western military alliance 13, 17, 56,
    58, 93, 94, 96, 107, 134

WEU (Western European Union) 93
women 108, 110, 118, 140, 143,
    153, 163
World War I 14, 28, 111, 165
World War II 1, 21, 22, 28, 33, 36, 44,
    46, 165, 188, 190
WTO (Warsaw Treaty Organization)
    6, 7, 24, 25, 27, 28, 33, 37,
    38, 39, 50
WTO members 6, 33, 35

Yugoslavia 6, 7, 8, 10, 13, 14, 20,
    21, 27, 28, 31, 34, 49, 54, 56,
    91, 116, 131, 132, 133, 143,
    154, 190
    communist 14, 15, 21, 22, 27, 48
Yugoslavians 8
Yugoslavian conflicts 36, 37
Yugoslavian military culture 49
Yugoslavian succession 8, 22, 28, 37,
    38, 47, 48, 49
Yugoslav People's Army 22
Yugoslav space 132, 133
    former 14, 55

Zapad 171, 180, 183
zone, buffer 131, 133, 145
Zrínyi 98, 99

EU authorised representative for GPSR:
Easy Access System Europe, Mustamäe tee 50,
10621 Tallinn, Estonia
gpsr.requests@easproject.com

www.ingramcontent.com/pod-product-compliance
Lightning Source LLC
LaVergne TN
LVHW011226090925
820435LV00036B/161